The Fall and Rise of
DONCASTER ROVERS

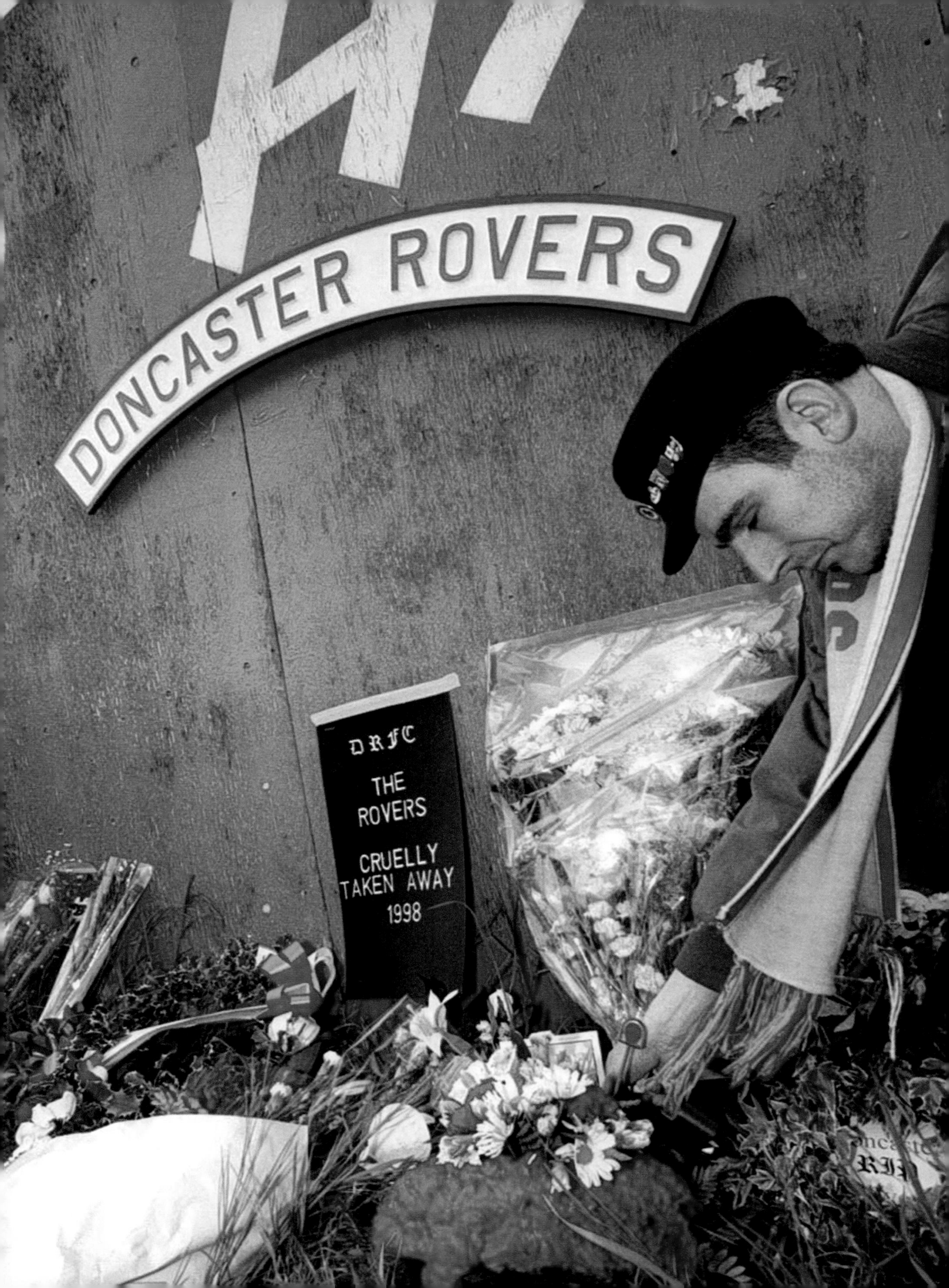
DONCASTER ROVERS
DRFC
THE ROVERS
CRUELLY TAKEN AWAY
1998

The Fall and Rise of
DONCASTER ROVERS

Tony Bluff & Steve Uttley

breedon **books**
PUBLISHING

First published in Great Britain in 2008 by
The Breedon Books Publishing Company Limited
Breedon House, 3 The Parker Centre, Derby, DE21 4SZ.

ISBN 978-1-85983-648-4

Printed and bound by Scotprint, Haddington, Scotland.

Contents

Introduction

Doncaster Rovers were formed in 1879 and played friendly games until 1888, when they played and lost at home to Rotherham Town, their first game in the FA Cup. Two years later they were founder members of the Midland Alliance, finishing in second place. The following year they joined the Midland Counties League, winning the Championship in 1897 and 1899. Election to the Football League Division Two came in 1901 but they were voted out after their second season. One season in the Midland League sufficed and they were accepted back into the League in 1904. But a disastrous season, in which they only obtained 8 points from 34 Division Two games, saw them pushed back to the Midland League.

Having shut down during World War One, the club re-formed in 1920 and joined the Football League Division Three North in 1923. After winning promotion to the Second Division in 1935, they had two seasons there before returning to the Third Division North. The first season after World War Two, 1946–47, was an exceptional season for the club. Promotion to Division Two was won at a canter, with a record number of points and numerous League records were set. Although they only had one season in Division Two, they came back in 1950 under the managership of Peter Doherty. Their stay lasted until 1958 when they fell, in successive seasons, from Division Two to Division Four. Promotions were won in 1966, 1969, 1981 and 1984 as they yo-yoed between the Third and Fourth Divisions. In 1992–93 the club struggled to survive, both financially and on the pitch. The previous season Aldershot had dropped out of the League and at the beginning of the 1992–93 season Maidstone United had gone bankrupt. Who would be the next to go? The Rovers were certainly in the frame but was that a knight in shining armour on the horizon?

The Takeover
by Dinard Trading Ltd & Ken Richardson

The calendar year of 1993 began for Doncaster Rovers with a shareholders' meeting to ratify a share issue to increase the share capital of the club from £300,000 to £450,000 by creating 300,000 new shares at 50p each. This had been spectacularly defeated by a large majority in October 1992 but this time it was approved unanimously when it was made known that the Inland Revenue had issued a winding-up petition for an outstanding debt of £70,000. Within days it was announced that the new share issue had been completely taken up and no more were on offer. A payment of £30,000 was made to the Revenue, who agreed to accept the balance in March 1993.

On 10 March James Burke, the Rovers chairman, announced that the club had been taken over by an Isle of Man-based company, Dinard Trading Ltd, who had acquired 52 per cent of the shares to give them a controlling interest. Their representative, described as a 'consultant', was Mr Ken Richardson, a wealthy businessman and horse racing aficionado from East Yorkshire, who had overseen the building of Bridlington Town into a successful club. In his three years at the helm there five managers had come and gone – some were fired and others resigned, citing interference in the management of the team. However, he had provided an interest-free loan to build a new stand and to refurbish the clubhouse. His horse racing days had ended in 1984 when he was convicted of being involved in the Flockton Grey betting swindle of 29 March 1982. He and two colleagues were found guilty of conspiracy to defraud

by substituting a 'ringer' for a horse called Flockton Grey in the Knighton Auction Stakes, a five-furlong race for two-year-olds, at Leicester. The horse won by 20 lengths and the off-course betting soon aroused suspicion. An investigation by the Jockey Club led to their results being passed to the police, who subsequently decided that the horse was actually a three-year-old called Good Hand. In June 1984 Ken Richardson was fined £20,000, given a nine-month suspended prison sentence and ordered to pay the costs of the prosecution. Two colleagues, Colin Mathison and Peter Boddy, were also convicted of conspiracy. The Jockey Club, the horse racing authority of the time, later warned Mr Richardson off all racecourses for 25 years. In December 1991 he petitioned the Home Secretary for the case to be referred to the Court of Appeal. Six months later he was told that his case had been unsuccessful and would not go to the Court of Appeal.

Mr Burke was quoted in the local evening paper, the *Doncaster Star*, as saying that it was 'the start of a bright new era for the club'. He also believed that the takeover was in the best interests of the club. Mr Paul Dumbleton, a solicitor representing Dinard, said that money would be available to improve the team and the facilities and that

Ken Richardson.

Help Save The Rovers!!

Telephone: Geoff Bull on 0302 875530

*WE ARE PLANNING A WEEKLY COLLECTION OF UNWANTED PAPERS, ALUMINIUM CANS, POP BOTTLES YOU CAN'T BE BOTHERED TO TAKE BACK (OR ANYTHING ELSE YOU CAN THINK OF), TO RAISE FUNDS FOR **YOUR** LOCAL FOOTBALL TEAM.*

We would appreciate your help

✱ Rovers Survival Squad ✱

Mr Richardson had been encouraged by the positive attitude displayed by Doncaster Council towards the football club. He went on to add that they 'were very keen to talk to the local authority about the long-term future of Doncaster Rovers because we want to give the town a football club and a soccer stadium which it can feel proud of.' The company did not intend to take a seat on the Board immediately but Mr Richardson would be actively involved in all aspects of the club, particularly in team-building and the signing of players. Mr Dumbleton concluded by stating that the manager, Steve Beaglehole, had the full backing of the new owners.

On 31 March the Rovers were in the High Court again because the balance owing to the Inland Revenue had not been paid but an adjournment was granted for a further month when the Revenue agreed to the extension, provided that a £10,000 payment was made in the next seven days and the remainder within a further 28 days after that.

On 1 April, at a special meeting to confirm the appointment of a new director, Tommy Nuttall, who was elected unopposed to the Board, the shareholders demanded to know why the tax bill had not been paid off. After all, that was the reason why the share issue had been voted through in January. It should have brought in £150,000 and paid off the tax bill with money to spare. However, it emerged that only £38,000 in cash had been raised and a Board meeting had voted in favour of the directors being able to convert their loans into shares, a practice that did not put any extra money into the club's coffers. It was also revealed that the new owners had asked to buy shares but had been refused. However, Dinard Trading Ltd had later acquired a majority holding of 453,558 shares from existing shareholders. As for the money owing to the taxman, Dinard had been expected to pay off the debt but they were still going through the club's books in order to be fully aware of the financial position before putting money into the club.

On the field of play the team finished the season in 16th place, out of 22 clubs, in the Third Division, with manager Steve Beaglehole struggling to find players of quality because of the financial constraints. The Inland Revenue was eventually paid in May and at the end of that month Dinard announced that, after a thorough investigation of the Rovers' accounts, they were ready to commit themselves to the takeover of the club. With the accounts showing debts of over £360,000, this news appeared to suggest that the club was on the brink of a new era.

1993-94

On the evening of Tuesday 8 June a shareholders' meeting took place to appoint two new directors of Dinard's choosing and to remove Mike Collett, a director since 1986 and chairman from 1989 to 1991, after he had been invited to resign by Dinard but had refused to do so. He was one of the directors who had converted a £15,000 loan into shares and also purchased shares worth £10,000 in cash. He had also acted in the interests of the club by cancelling a cheque for £10,000 from the Rovers for money owed to him in return for shares. He had expressed some disquiet about some things relating to the takeover but his questions had not been answered. The meeting duly elected Ray Kennan, chief executive of Dinard Trading Ltd and Kenneth Haran as directors but a motion to remove Mike Collett was withdrawn after he tendered his resignation. Later, the meeting took a dramatic turn when Richardson made critical comments about the abilities of John Bird, the chief coach, who had been brought in by Steve Beaglehole at a time when the club could not afford to pay him. He had thus worked for next-to-nothing for several months. Both Steve Beaglehole and John Bird were at the meeting and countered the accusations, with Bird calling for a meeting to sort it out, a suggestion which received loud applause. The two of them then walked out of the meeting, which caused ructions in the audience. Richardson offered to resign if the shareholders were not behind him. He said he had been appointed by Dinard to bring players to the club and had 10 players lined up to join, all of whom were good enough to play in a higher Division than the one the Rovers were in. Acting chairman Ken Chappell called for a vote of confidence in Richardson, which was duly passed but shareholders expressed strong support for Steve Beaglehole and said that Richardson's comments had been, at best, undiplomatic. However, as one shareholder so succinctly put it, 'we don't care if Attila the Hun is in charge as long as Rovers are successful.' One wonders how that shareholder felt some five years later!

Both Beaglehole and Bird, speaking the day after, said that they felt they were not wanted and that their jobs were under threat. The manager also expressed his reservations about the fact that he would seemingly have no say in which

Team picture 1993–94.

players would be signed by the club. He went on to say that he would not walk away, he would stick it out but he did not want to be a puppet manager. John Bird, the chief coach, said he had felt insulted at being criticised in public and was obviously not wanted by the club but he had a two-year contract and would carry on doing his best until the matter was sorted out. Steve Beaglehole then went away on holiday, only to come back to find that Kennan had criticised him for attending the shareholders meeting 'because he wasn't a shareholder' and for 'showing bad manners'. Beaglehole's response was to state that he had been invited to the meeting, which had always been the club's policy and, as far as he knew, Richardson was not a shareholder either. Also, if defending a member of his staff, who was being criticised in public, was bad manners then he pleaded guilty. Steve Beaglehole was present at the AGM of the supporters' club, on Thursday 24 June, by invitation but there was no representative of the new owners, Richardson having sent his apologies at being unable to attend. Beaglehole said that, at this stage, there were only five players signed on contracts after the clearout at the end of the previous season and he revealed to the supporters that he had no responsibility for the signing of players, a state of affairs that had not been discussed with him and he called for the new owners to 'back him or sack him'. The fans also voiced their disapproval at the lack of action regarding the signing of players and also the complete lack of communication from the club. Following a four-hour Board meeting on Wednesday 30 June, the new owners gave Steve Beaglehole a vote of confidence to end the speculation among the fans regarding his position and standing at the club.

A week later, the first player to be signed under the new regime was revealed to be Tony Cunningham, coming on a free transfer from neighbours Rotherham United. A further 11 players were added to the squad throughout July, including Kevin Hulme from Bury for a tribunal-fixed fee of £42,500 and Russ Wilcox, from Hull City, for a tribunal-fixed fee of £60,000. The month ended with the resignation of James Burke as chairman for health reasons following heart surgery, although he remained on the Board. The newcomer to the Board, Ray Kennan, took over the position of chairman.

On Wednesday 4 August an open meeting for supporters was held at the Park Hotel. It had been originally called as a special meeting for shareholders to hear of the club's plans to raise £250,000 through a new share issue. However, the notice to shareholders was declared invalid on a technicality, so it went ahead as an open meeting. The new chairman of the club, Ray Kennan, stated at the meeting that he had received a letter indicating that John Ryan and Mike Collett,

Goalmouth action against Bury at Belle Vue.

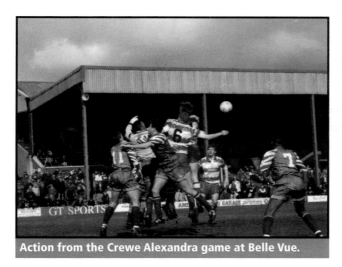
Action from the Crewe Alexandra game at Belle Vue.

with a combined shareholding of 43 per cent, would vote against a new share issue so as not to water down their shares. This would block the share issue, which needed 75 per cent of shareholders to vote it through. John Ryan was away on holiday and so was unable to attend the meeting.

Meanwhile, on the pitch, Steve Beaglehole had gradually moulded his new squad into a team after a series of friendly games and a few matches in the new pre-season competition, the Yorkshire Electricity Cup, in which they were defeated in the group stage on goal difference by Bradford City. The League season opened at Chester City on 14 August and the Rovers were able to start, somewhat fortuitously, with a goal from David Moss that ensured a win. Two days later, at Belle Vue, they suffered a single-goal reverse in the Coca-Cola League Cup first-leg game against Second Division Blackpool. As the week went on Eddie Gormley, already on loan to League of Ireland side Drogheda United, having refused a new contract with the Rovers because of his wish to return to his home country, joined the Irish club on a permanent basis. Tony Cullen, on non-contract terms with the club, was also released. A goalless draw at home to Carlisle United in the League was followed on the Tuesday with a 3–3 draw at Bloomfield Road in the League Cup second leg. The Rovers had run up a three-goal lead just past the half-hour but were pegged back in the second half, which gave Blackpool the victory on aggregate following their single-goal win at Belle Vue. The following day it was announced that Stuart Hicks had made his loan move to Huddersfield Town permanent, with the Rovers due a five-figure fee and three more players – Steve Prindiville, Mark Hine and Craig Bennett – had been put on the transfer list at their own request after failing to win a place in the first-team line up.

On Thursday 26 August an extraordinary meeting of shareholders was called to vote on a new share issue worth £250,000. Any fears that large shareholders, John Ryan and Mike Collett, who owned 43 per cent of current shares between them, would vote against the motion were allayed when both attended the meeting and voted for the issue,

giving a unanimous outcome to the meeting. Dinard would take new shares worth £127,500 to keep their majority holding. Other shareholders would also have the chance to buy shares before they went public and any shares left would be purchased by the owners.

The following Saturday the Rovers went to Walsall and won three points with a 2–1 victory that put them in fourth place in the League table after three games. Three days later, on the last day of

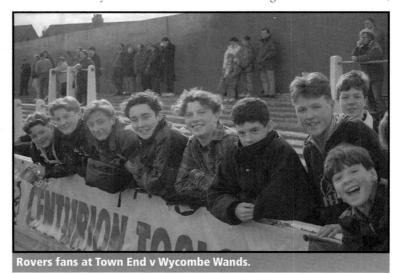
Rovers fans at Town End v Wycombe Wands.

August, the Rovers went to Gillingham and came away with a goalless draw that dropped them to sixth place (a win would have put them on top), with a record of two wins and two draws in their first four games. They had only played one game at home, with 2,500 spectators attending but the club hoped to increase attendances by introducing concessionary pricing for unemployed people in time for the next home game against Wigan Athletic, which produced a 3–1 win in front of just over 3,000 fans.

The Rovers lost their unbeaten record on Saturday 11 September, on the plastic artificial pitch at Preston. Although the players found the pitch difficult to play on, the manager, Steve Beaglehole, did not use that as an excuse. The Rovers went behind in the first minute and finished up losing 3–1, with the Preston manager, John Beck, rating them as one of the best sides in the Division. The month ended with the Rovers signing Steve Harper, a right-winger, for a £25,000 fee from Burnley. He had been on loan up to this point. Included in the deal was Ian Measham, a right-back.

The next two League games and an Autoglass Trophy game were lost and the club started October by selling their biggest asset, Mike Jeffrey, to Newcastle United in exchange for £60,000 and David Roche moving to Belle Vue. On the same day Paul Whitmarsh, a young West Ham United forward, was brought in on loan. Roche started and scored in his first match, at home to Rochdale in the League on the second of that month and set the team on the road to a win after a run of four losses. On the Monday Charles Dunn, a local businessman who had been chairman of Bridlington Town, was appointed to the Board of Directors of the Rovers and also took over as the managing director. Thursday 7 October dawned with the news that John Bird had left his position as coach by 'mutual consent' after assisting Steve Beaglehole for two years. Then, in the evening, an extraordinary meeting of shareholders was held at the Park Hotel, just six weeks after the last meeting had authorised the sale of shares to take the share capital of the club to £700,000. This meeting had been called to authorise the issue of a further 500,000 shares at 50p each, which would take the share capital to a total of £950,000. The directors also wanted authorisation to oversee the issue and allot shares or permit the conversion of securities into shares. However, this attempt to raise the share capital fell through because of a mix-up over proxy votes.

Meanwhile, the wheeling and dealing in players continued. Lee Turnbull was brought back to the club from Chesterfield, with David Moss and £10,000 going the other way. Jamie Hewitt also went to Chesterfield on a month's loan and Sean Dunphy was brought in on loan from Lincoln City. In this period of 10 days the Rovers played three games – two League and one Autoglass – at Belle Vue and lost them all. With Richardson handling the player situation, the comings and goings on almost a daily basis had to make the manager's job difficult at the very least.

Lee Turnbull.

Tuesday 19 October brought the resignation of James Burke and John Ryan from the Board of Directors. Burke had been a director for 12 years and chairman for two, while Ryan had been on the Board for four years. The following day an announcement from the club stated that Julie Richardson, Ken's daughter and his niece, Lisa Mabbett, had been appointed to the Board as directors. Towards the end of the month the club obtained a shirt sponsorship deal worth £30,000 with a firm new to the town, European Car Rental, which would run until the end of the season.

However, an advert in the *Daily Telegraph* on Monday 25 October offered for sale approximately 14.2 acres in a prime position opposite Doncaster Racecourse, which was being used by Doncaster Rovers Football Club. The advertiser sought a developer for the site and replies should go to the chairman of Doncaster Rovers FC. Doncaster Council, quite understandably, were furious when this was brought to their attention. After all, the land belonged to the council and was only leased to the football club. Thus was the seed sown for what followed in the relationship between Mr Richardson and Doncaster Council.

On 13 December, at the headquarters of the Football Association, an investigating committee met to discuss Doncaster Rovers, Bridlington Town and Ken Richardson and the financial transactions between the two clubs. This, one assumes, is why the FA later rebuffed all the Rovers supporters that accused the

Penalty against Bury at Belle Vue.

FA of doing nothing. The results of their deliberations were never made public.

On the field of play, three League wins at the back end of October put the club back in the top half of the table as more players came and went. Unfortunately, to the end of the year they only won one of six League games and drew at Shrewsbury in the FA Cup, losing the replay at Belle Vue. This all culminated on New Year's Eve with Steve Beaglehole being relieved of his duties as manager. Tony Cunningham, the most senior player, was handed the reins as caretaker manager. Steve Beaglehole was offered the post of director of youth coaching, which he accepted a week later. Cunningham's period at the helm covered four League games – three lost, one drawn – and a win over Lincoln City on 22 January – the evening that a new manager was appointed. The new man was Ian Atkins, a former Shrewsbury Town, Sunderland, Everton and Ipswich Town player, who had management experience as player-manager at Colchester United and as assistant manager at Birmingham City. He seemingly made an immediate impact because his first three games were all drawn.

On 12 February at Torquay the team lost the game but an incident occurred that put the game of football into perspective. Challenging for a high ball in the 24th minute, Ian Measham fell to the floor and did not move. Eventually taken to hospital with his head and neck immobilised, he was found to have suffered a fracture and displacement of his neck vertebrae, which obviously put his career at risk and could so easily have been more serious.

The club made the front page of the local evening newspaper on Thursday 27 January. The previous evening, at a public meeting at the Lonsdale Hotel, managing director Charles Dunn had complained about Doncaster Council's position regarding the club's efforts to build a new stadium at the Dome Leisure Park. In October 1993 an advert had appeared in a national newspaper for commercial bids on the Belle Vue site, which was owned by the council but the Rovers club had a lease of 70 years left on the site. The club claimed they had received bids that were four times higher than the figure of £1.6 million given by Keepmoat, a company in which the council held a stake of 50 per cent. The Rovers claimed that the significance of the figures was that the club would only receive a grant of £500,000 on the £1.6

Paul Whitmarsh gets in a shot at goal against Shrewsbury Town in an FA Cup replay at Belle Vue.

million figure but would qualify for a grant of £2 million on a valuation figure of £8 million. Dunn stated that he had whittled the bids down to a handful for the consideration of the council but was told that only Keepmoat would be involved. Richardson, consultant to the club, claimed that, since the club had such a long lease on such a prime site, he felt that they should be entitled to around 30 per cent of any monies raised by the sale of the site. He had suggested to the council that both parties should invest around £2.5 million in the proposed new stadium, which the club would rent. He went on to tell the meeting that such a deal would have left both parties with about £1.5 million and pledged that a percentage of the money received by the club would go on strengthening the team. Richardson then called on all supporters and shareholders to put pressure on their local councillors in a bid to get the scheme moving forward. He told the meeting that he was not interested, as some people were saying, in making any money out of the club and added that the stance of the council would make Dinard re-examine their position. He continued by saying that he personally had bought £80,000 worth of shares and given the club an unsecured loan of £93,000. He asked why he should put more money into the club when two other major shareholders, with a total of 34 per cent of shares, were refusing to put money in.

On the field the Rovers had dropped to 18th, out of 22 clubs in the Division, by the end of March but they were nine points clear of the bottom club, who would be relegated and with three wins and two draws from their last seven games they lifted themselves up the table to finish in 15th place. But things were happening in the boardroom, with the announcement on Tuesday 12 April that Ken Haran would become vice-chairman and Charles Dunn would become chief executive alongside his job as managing director. This was followed a month later by the resignations of Ray Kennan as chairman and Tim Sedgwick as financial director.

With the end of the season came changes in the club's managerial personnel. Steve Thompson, brought in by Tony Cunningham as a coach in January, left the club after the last League game and the fans were disturbed to hear at the end of June that Ian Atkins had been dismissed because he refused to move his home from Solihull to Doncaster. The club's explanation was that they required players and management to live locally so that they could participate in community affairs.

A happy dressing-room after playing against Shrewsbury in the second half.

A manager was immediately appointed at the beginning of July in the form of Sammy Chung, a former manager of Wolverhampton Wanderers, who pledged to move from Wolverhampton to Doncaster. Of course, players came and went but a major signing was former Manchester City, Crystal Palace and England Under-23 goalkeeper Perry Suckling, from Watford. However, two players, Stewart Talbot from Moor Green and Darren Roberts from Wolverhampton Wanderers, signed on before the dismissal of Atkins, asked for and received the cancellation of their contracts. All told, eight players were added to the squad before the League season began: Perry Suckling; Warren Hackett from Leyton Orient; Ryan Kirby from Arsenal; James Meara from Watford; Darren Finlay from Queen's Park Rangers; O'Neill Donaldson from Shrewsbury Town; Gudmundor Torfason from St Johnstone and Gary Brabin, signed from Conference club Runcorn for £40,000.

An article in the *Yorkshire Post* on 10 June had detailed Doncaster Council's plans to build a new stadium, which would seat 12,000 and cost around £5 million, on former industrial land close to the Dome Leisure Complex. The plan was welcomed by both the Rovers and the Dragons, the Rugby League club and could be built for the start of the 1995–96 season but it all depended on the owners of the Rovers agreeing a price with the council for the remaining 70 years of the lease. A special shareholders meeting at the Lonsdale Hotel was called by the club on Monday 4 July to discuss the council's offer of a new shared stadium. Ken Richardson, Dinard's representative, told the meeting that the council had put a figure of £50,000 as the cost of the long-term lease on Belle Vue but he was not sure if the District Valuer was aware of all the facts in determining this figure. At a meeting with the council in October 1993 the club had been told that the land was worth £1.6 million and when the club had tried to find out the true value by advertising the land for sale, offers between £6.5 million and £8 million were received. Richardson added that a precedent had suggested that the Rovers leasehold was worth 30 per cent of the development value of the land and based on a development figure of £7 million the club would be entitled to £2.1 million from the sale of the site. The shareholders rejected the council's offer of £50,000 as derisory and an insult to the club and called for another meeting with council representatives and MPs under an independent chairman. Meanwhile, the directors of the club were looking at three other sites so that they could develop a ground of their own with the help of Football Trust grants. The following day the new manager, Sammy Chung, appointed George Smith, a former FA and Queen's Park Rangers coach, as his assistant. They both welcomed the players to the first day of training on the Wednesday and joined the Rovers squad at the training camp at the Doncaster College complex at High Melton, where they were to spend the week training.

Graeme Jones.

The manager had cancelled the pre-season games arranged by Ian Atkins against Aston Villa and Norwich City, deeming them too tough for what would be a team of completely new players. The Rovers' first pre-season friendly was played at Stainforth against Hatfield Main on the evening of Tuesday 19 July, which they won by a single goal scored by Ryan Kirby. The following evening, at Thorne Colliery, Chung played a completely different team, including a number of trialists and newly-acquired centre-half Steve Gallen, signed on a free transfer from Queen's Park Rangers. Goals from Mark Yates, Leroy Chambers and Sean Parrish gave the Rovers a comprehensive 3–0 win. Former Hull City midfielder Lee Warren impressed the management and was signed on the following day, bringing the total

Sammy Chung signing up another young footballer.

number of new signings to nine. Meanwhile, a transfer tribunal ruled that the Rovers should pay Telford United a fee of £20,000 plus 20 per cent of any future transfer fee for full-back Sean Parrish. This figure was twice the figure offered by the Rovers but half the figure that Telford wanted. On Saturday 23 July the Rovers lost by three clear goals in a Yorkshire Electricity Cup game at home to Hull City but the general consensus was that the scoreline flattered the Tigers, with Chung saying that he was not too bothered about the defeat at this stage. The following Tuesday the Rovers visited the Walks ground, the home of King's Lynn, where trialists O'Neill Donaldson, Leroy Chambers and 'keeper Dean Williams all played in a hard-earned 2–1 win. The following night another line-up, which included former Tranmere Rovers midfield player Dave Martindale, played against Boston at their Tattershall Road ground, the Rovers winning 3–0 with two goals from Graeme Jones and another by Jamie Lawrence. The following day the club were brought before an FA Commission in Birmingham to answer for their poor disciplinary record during the previous season, when their tally of 265 points was one of the worst in the League. They were given a suspended fine of £6,000, which was to be activated at the end of the season if their disciplinary record did not improve. Chung, not responsible for things during the previous season, had already imposed a new disciplinary code at the club that would see that figure drop. For the match at Runcorn on Saturday 30 July, Icelandic international and former St Mirren and St Johnstone striker Gudmundor Torfason played alongside Donaldson and, despite the goalless scoreline, impressed Sammy Chung so much that he was signed later in the week. Another team of first-teamers played a 'reserve' match at Brodsworth Welfare, with goals from Graeme Jones and Mark Yates sealing the win.

On the evening of 2 August a Yorkshire Electricity Cup match against Halifax Town at the Shay ended goalless, leaving Sammy Chung very disappointed in his team's performance. At the same time Kevin Hulme handed in a written transfer request and would not be considered for first-team action while on the transfer list. Two days later the signings of Gunnar Torfason and Dave Martindale were completed. The final pre-season game, a Yorkshire Electricity match against Barnsley at Belle Vue, was played on Saturday 4 August, with the club asking for the supporters' forbearance as parts of the terraces on the Popular and Main Stand sides were closed off, while development work costing around £80,000 was completed. The match ended in a 1–1 draw, leaving Sammy Chung pleasantly surprised by his team's performance against a team two divisions above them. Now that the pre-season games had been completed, Chung had seen the talent at his disposal and the next stage was to prepare for the start of the League season on 13 August at Hereford. Part of that preparation was to call in new League referee, Roger Furnandiz, to explain the changes that FIFA had introduced for the new season in the interpretation of the offside laws and the clampdown on dissent and time-wasting. Those changes were: attackers to be given the benefit of the doubt regarding offside, with players in offside positions but deemed by the referee to not be interfering with play and therefore not penalised for offside; the tackle from behind was to be a red-card offence; strict guidelines on dissent and time-wasting; players would no longer be allowed to receive treatment on the pitch for injury.

On Wednesday 10 August Ken Richardson was excused from appearing at Bow Street Magistrates Court, London to answer a charge of theft of shares from a business in a private prosecution brought by Yorkshire businessman Jeffrey Port. He was accused, with three others, Ralph Seligman, a Bahamas-based lawyer, George Auger, a London insolvency practitioner and Fallig Finanz AG, based in Lichtenstein, of stealing the whole of the issued share capital in Tradam Trading Company (Bahamas) Ltd and also charged with stealing one half of the issued share capital of Whittakers Investments Ltd to the beneficial entitlement of the Ronson Trademark and the royalties there from belonging to Anthony Port, Martin Port and Amanda Jager. The hearing was adjourned to a date to be fixed.

At Belle Vue Mark Yates left the club for Conference Champions Kidderminster Harriers and Dave Martindale asked to be released from his contract, having decided he had made a mistake in joining the club. Two days later, on the Friday, Kevin Hulme was transferred back to Bury for the same fee paid for him by the Rovers, £42,500 and goalkeeper Andy Beasley, likely to be displaced by Perry Suckling, moved on a free transfer to Chesterfield. Chung, having lost his backup 'keeper, immediately signed up Dean Williams, who had been on trial at the club.

When the first League tables were published after three games the Rovers were on top, with three wins coming away against Hereford United where Darren Finlay was mysteriously sent off eight minutes from time, at home to Northampton Town and away at Colchester United without conceding a goal, although interspersed with these games were two legs of the first round of the Coca Cola League Cup in which they lost the home game 4–2 and drew away to Wrexham. On the evening of 24 August the Rovers held a 'meet the players night' at the Lonsdale Hotel followed the next evening by an invitation from Sammy Chung to supporters to attend a special question and answer session at

Rovers against Scunthorpe United at Glanford Park.

Russ Wilcox leads out the Rovers against Scunthorpe United at home.

the Park Hotel. Three goalless draws followed against Fulham, the Rovers having Jamie Lawrence sent off after 26 minutes and Darlington, both at Belle Vue and Barnet away before they suffered their first defeat at high-flying Bury, by two clear goals, thus conceding their first League goals of the season. Earlier in the day of the Bury defeat on Tuesday 13 September had come the shock news that George Smith, the assistant manager and chief coach, had left the club by 'mutual agreement', with Sammy Chung saying there had been no rift between them. Former Tottenham Hotspur player Jimmy Neighbour accompanied Chung on the Rovers bench at Bury and then assisted with the coaching duties in the days to follow. After playing well on a trial basis thus far, both Dean Williams and O'Neill Donaldson signed full contracts for the club. The Rovers continued their good form with a win at home over Hereford United by three clear goals, thus breaking the goal drought that had lasted for the previous four games but the Friday night match drew a crowd of only 1,938. The following Wednesday the club appointed a new general manager, Bruce McLellan, who would also take over the role of chief scout. He had served West Ham United as assistant chief scout for the past 18 years. However, he could not take up his appointment at Doncaster until 19 October,

after working a month's notice. The last Saturday in September brought Preston North End to Doncaster but the long-ball game of John Beck was overcome by stout defence and two goals in the second half from Steve Harper and Gary Brabin. Preston did score in the 89th minute, the first goal that the Rovers had conceded at home in five matches. The following Tuesday the Rovers met Second Division Hull City at Boothferry Park in the Auto Windscreens Shield before a crowd, or rather an attendance, of 890, 150 of whom had travelled from Doncaster. Goals from Lee Thew and Graeme Jones gave the Rovers a 2–0 win. As the end of the month approached, Jimmy Neighbour was officially appointed as first-team coach.

On the last day of September a public meeting was held at the Park Hotel, with Ken Richardson and Charles Dunn in attendance. Richardson announced that he would leave the club at the end of the season unless he received more support from fans coming through the turnstiles (match attendances averaged around 2,000 at this stage) and supporting the club's fundraising activities. He stated that the club's fortnightly wage bill had risen to about £30,000 and added that about £500,000 would be required to see the club through to the end of the season. It was also revealed that nearly all the new players had been brought to the club by Richardson with just two, O'Neill Donaldson and Dean Williams, brought in by the manager, Sammy Chung. Richardson concluded by saying he would carry on and strengthen the team at considerable cost until the end of the season when he would review the situation.

The Rovers lost at Rochdale by two clear goals on the first day of October after having Gary Brabin sent off after 35 minutes. David Roche, for Rovers, had a penalty saved after 72 minutes by Neil Dunford, who was making his League debut but two minutes later the referee awarded a goal to the home team, despite angry protests from the

Rovers players, when he deemed the ball had crossed the goalline from a header by Paul Williams. Jason Peake scored a second nine minutes from time to leave the Rovers in fifth place in the League. A week later, however, they hit the winning trail and put five goals past bottom club Wigan Athletic, although they let three in at the other end. It took 35 minutes and a penalty, converted by Roche, to set the Rovers on the way but goals from Brabin and Harper either side of one from Leonard for Wigan gave them a 3–1 interval lead. Shortly after half-time Leonard put away a penalty to give Wigan some hope but further goals from Brabin and Harper emphasised the ascendancy of the Rovers before an injury-time goal by Benjamin completed the scoring. This high-scoring match was, unfortunately, attended by the smallest crowd in the whole of the League.

Early in October Martin Carter left the club after only a few weeks as commercial director and Robert Kantecki resigned as a non-executive director. For the match at Scarborough on Saturday 15 October, the Rovers included Andy Turner, a Republic of Ireland Under-21 international signed on loan from Tottenham Hotspur earlier in the week. Also included in the team was Gary Brabin, who had won an appeal to the FA on the previous day which quashed his three-match ban for the sending-off at Rochdale. However, lowly Scarborough went in at half-time two goals ahead and were looking good for a much-needed three points but in the 87th minute the Rovers were awarded a penalty, which Roche converted for what seemed a consolation goal. However, they were awarded another penalty in injury time as the home team defended desperately. Roche stepped up again to score an equaliser from the spot and win a point. Later, the Scarborough police reported Warren Hackett to the referee for allegedly taunting the Scarborough fans by running towards them and goading them, saying that even if the FA failed to act they would consider taking action against the player. Five people, four of whom were from Doncaster, were arrested during the game for invading the pitch and other public order offences. On Monday the Rovers played Lincoln City at Belle Vue in the Auto Windscreens Trophy, with a single goal scored by Andy Turner after 37 minutes giving them the win to top the group stage and go through to a home tie in the knockout stage. Despite a reduction in the prices for the game only 1,480 attended. The following Saturday, a 1–0 win at Mansfield Town, with yet another penalty slotted in by Graeme Jones, lifted the Rovers up to third place in the League table. This particular season had only the top two clubs automatically promoted and the next four clubs taking part in the Play-offs, as the Premier League and Football League reorganised the number of clubs in each division. The month of October ended with a resounding three-goal defeat of Torquay

Marvin Bryan on the ball at home to Scunthorpe United.

Goalmouth action at Belle Vue against Bury.

United at Belle Vue. Goalless at the break despite dominating the game, Hackett opened the scoring after 50 minutes but it took two goals in the last four minutes from Jones and Lawrence to give the scoreline the emphatic look that the Rovers' play deserved.

The Tuesday evening edition of the *Doncaster Star* for 1 November contained an article stating that John Ryan and Mike Collett had decided to sell their substantial shareholding in the club, which amounted to half a million shares worth about £250,000, which they hoped would be purchased by a local businessman. Mr Ryan went on to say that he could not work with Mr Richardson and although he had put £50,000 extra into the club at the start of the 1993–94 season he was constantly being badgered to donate further amounts. He also revealed that shareholders had been circulated with a notice of a special meeting to consider increasing the share capital of the club but said that he and Mike Collett would block the resolution until they had disposed of their shares. He pointed out that any person or company who acquired 75 per cent of the shares would have unrestricted powers, which would not be in the club's best interests. This meeting went ahead at the Park Hotel on Wednesday 16 November but the motion was defeated by the proxy vote of Messrs Ryan and Collett. It also transpired that the Inland Revenue had issued a winding-up notice against the club for an unpaid bill of £36,000, with a deadline date of 6 December. Mr Richardson assured the meeting that it would be paid.

In the meantime, the month of November had brought some good results on the pitch. Guy Fawkes' Night produced fireworks at Exeter as the Rovers overwhelmed the home team 5–1 after leading at half-time by four clear goals. Parrish, with two goals, Turner and Harper scored in the first half and, despite the loss of Roche, sent off after 47 minutes, a late goal by Jones completed the rout. The following Saturday brought the Second Division leaders Huddersfield Town to Belle Vue in the first round of the FA Cup before a crowd of 6,626, the biggest attendance for nearly 10 years. The Town responded by scoring twice in the first 12 minutes and putting the Rovers on the back foot immediately. The task proved impossible after Roche was sent off in the 31st minute, his second successive dismissal and the Rovers eventually went down by four goals to one. The next game was at home to bottom club Hartlepool United and the Rovers included a new signing, Jon Schofield from Lincoln City, in the team that gained a comfortable three goals to nil win, the goals coming from Brabin, Harper and Meara. A tenth clean sheet in the 16 League games played pleased the manager, who sent his troops, including another signing, Mickey Norbury from Preston North End, to Carlisle on the last Saturday in November to do battle against leaders Carlisle United. They achieved a 1–1 draw, courtesy of a goal from Jamie Lawrence and a late goal from Dean Walling for the Cumbrians in a hard-fought encounter worthy of the billing as a top-of-the-table game. Meanwhile, David Roche was sitting out a three-match suspension for his sending-off at Exeter and was then hit with a four-match ban for the Huddersfield dismissal. This meant he was unavailable until the New Year. For this he was severely disciplined by the club. Injuries suffered at

Carlisle caused the Rovers to make changes for the AWS (Auto Windscreens) Trophy game against Bury at Belle Vue on the following Monday. An early goal from Pugh after six minutes meant the Rovers were playing catch up for the rest of the game. The Shakers defence, known for their meanness when it came to letting goals in, defended tenaciously until the 54th minute when Jones was fouled in the penalty area. He took the penalty kick but his lack of power allowed Kelly to save comfortably. Thus the Rovers exited another Cup competition, leaving them free to concentrate on the League.

The end of November brought bad news for the club when a winding-up petition was brought against them by the Inland Revenue for an unpaid bill of £36,000. Although Mr Richardson had promised that it would be paid, if it was not paid by 7 December it would mean a High Court hearing in London. But the issue of the winding-up order once again ignited the conflict between the owners of the club and its major shareholders. Mr Richardson told the *Yorkshire Post* on 28 November that John Ryan owned 25 per cent of the club but refused to pay his share of the tax bill. He went on to say that he could not get on with Ryan, who he thought should sell his shares or put some money into the club and he could not see how he (Richardson) could stay. It made him angry because he had put a lot of his own money into the club to make it successful. In reply Mr Ryan said he had resigned from the Board a year ago and was now trying to get rid of his shares. He went on to say that he did not have any contact with the club as Ken Richardson ran it lock, stock and barrel. He thought that for Mr Richardson to blame him was scandalous as he seemed to think that he could run up what debts he liked and then blame him (Ryan) when they were not paid. The following day a statement issued by the club's Board of Directors accused Mr Ryan of acting in a vindictive manner and blamed him for blocking the proposed increase in share capital. The club went on to state that there were people wanting to purchase the shares, the money from which would enable the club to clear its debts. They also revealed three telephone numbers for Mr Ryan in Manchester. The Board also announced plans for a £250,000 share issue at a meeting of shareholders on 21 December, in order to fight the winding-up petition.

On Thursday 1 December John Ryan, who held 24.7 per cent of the existing shares, issued a statement saying he believed he was acting in the best interests of the club and, having been stung by recent comments from Ken Richardson, he would attend the shareholders' meeting to answer the accusations. He went on to say that he felt it was unhealthy for Dinard to increase their shareholding in the club but he was prepared to sell his own shares, with a value of about £175,000, to anyone who had no connection with Dinard and would then put the money into the club as an act of good faith. The statement concluded with Mr Ryan stating that he was seriously worried about the long-term future of the club that he had supported since he was seven years old.

Meanwhile, Mr Richardson was allegedly furious when he learned of the result of the tribunal that had decided the fee for Mickey Norbury. The Rovers were ordered to pay Preston North End £10,000 down, with two further increments of £10,000 depending on the number of appearances plus 30 per cent of any profit if he was transferred from the club. As the Rovers had made an unconditional bid they had to go through with the deal. The Rovers had a blank weekend at the start of December, which was an FA Cup second round date. However, with no action on the pitch, there seemed to be plenty going on off it. On Wednesday 7 December 1994 an application to wind up the Doncaster Rovers club from the Inland Revenue, who claimed to be owed nearly £236,000, was adjourned in the High Court until 18 January 1995. The club had put up as their defence that they had misunderstood the petition, believing it to be for £40,000 when it was actually over £100,000. They also claimed that a third-party shareholder would provide £250,000 following a meeting on 21 December which would confirm the share capital and pay off the current and any future debts.

Meanwhile, on the football side of things, Marvin Bryan had been brought in on loan from Queen's Park Rangers and turned out against Northampton Town, next to the bottom of the table, at the Cobblers' new ground at Sixfields. A goalless draw kept the Rovers in third position but the next match, played on a Friday night at Belle Vue, was lost to Colchester United by the odd goal in three and was the U's first win at Belle Vue since March 1967. With the other results going for them the following day, the Rovers hung on to third place.

In the week before Christmas there was plenty of activity going on behind the scenes. It was announced by the club that Bruce McLellan, recruited two months earlier as general manager and chief scout and Jimmy Neighbour, the former Spurs player, appointed assistant manager and chief coach in September, had both left the club. To assist Sammy Chung, John McClelland, the former Leeds United and Rangers player, was brought in to help with the coaching. While this was going on a letter had been sent out from the club to all shareholders warning that if the motion to increase the share capital was not passed then players would be sold and the club would be playing in the Doncaster Senior League the following season. The shareholders' meeting duly took place on 21 December and, after a stormy debate, the motion was defeated. John Ryan, with 25 per cent of the shares, blocked the issue because of the fear that the lease on the ground, valuable because of its longevity with over 60 years still to run, would be sold for development.

The Christmas games, at Chesterfield on Boxing Day and at home to Scunthorpe United the following day, produced just one point from a 1–1 draw with Scunthorpe, Bryan being the scorer. The Chesterfield game was lost by two clear goals in pouring rain, resulting in the Rovers dropping down to fifth in the League. It was also reported at this time that the club had been banned from conducting any more transfers and that the Professional Footballers Association were paying the players' wages. Sammy Chung was quoted as saying that the off-the-field activities were not doing the team any favours but he was not using that as an excuse for the poor display at Chesterfield. Neither was he using as an excuse the fact that he had an injury crisis, with six regulars out with injuries and a further two out following the Chesterfield game which meant the youth-team captain, Scott Maxfield, played against Scunthorpe. Even so, O'Neill Donaldson was allowed to go on loan to Mansfield Town and scored twice on his debut for them in a 7–1 win over Hereford United on Boxing Day. The year of 1994 ended with a trip to the Bescot Stadium on New Year's Eve to play third-placed Walsall. The controversial sending-off of Gary Brabin after 36 minutes did not help the Rovers' fortunes as they eventually went down to a 79th-minute goal.

The new year of 1995 started with the postponement of the Gillingham game at Belle Vue on Monday 2 January because of heavy frost but on 5 January came the news that the fans did not want to hear. They knew that a player had to be sold to help pay off the debts but it came as a shock when it was learned that Jamie Lawrence had been sold to Leicester City, a Premier League club, for £175,000 plus various increments to a total of £300,000 and a sell-on clause. Lawrence had cost the Rovers £20,000 from Sunderland and had become such a crowd favourite with his skill on the ball that the expectation level always rose when he was in possession. That same day Ken Richardson appeared at Bow Street Magistrates Court in London for a two-day hearing 'in camera' of a private prosecution brought by a Yorkshire businessman, Jeffrey Port, against Richardson, George Auger, an insolvency partner at the London offices of Stoy Hayward, Ralph Seligman, a lawyer based in Nassau in the Bahamas and a Liechtenstein based company, Fallig Finanz, for alleged theft. The summons alleged that the three men had stolen shares in a company belonging to Mr Port's three children. However, the Stipendiary Magistrate, Peter Badge, stated that the court had not been appraised of a previous prosecution at Leeds Magistrates Court in 1989. As the proceedings were the same and had been discontinued at Leeds he would not go on with this case. He dismissed the summonses, ruling that Mr Port had abused the judicial process by failing to disclose the previous case when they were issued in May 1994.

Over the first weekend in January, an FA Cup third round date, the Rovers had no game but a war of words broke out over O'Neill Donaldson between Andy King, the Mansfield Town manager and Sammy Chung. Donaldson had scored six goals in four games for the Nottinghamshire club while on loan and had attracted interest from other clubs. Chung duly informed Donaldson of this interest and as a matter of courtesy also told King. King came out with a statement that he would not be held to ransom over Donaldson and claimed that a fee of £15,000 had been agreed between the clubs if the loan deal were made permanent and it would be wrong of Doncaster to take advantage because the player had done well at Mansfield. The clubs were due to meet on the following Tuesday, 10 January, in a re-arranged League game and Donaldson was named in the Mansfield Town squad but was recalled by the Rovers on the Monday evening to meet Premier League club Sheffield Wednesday, with the transfer being completed for a fee of £50,000. No doubt Mansfield and manager King got some satisfaction out of the game the following evening when they came to Belle Vue and took away all three points with a two-goal win. This was the seventh League game without a win and only three points had been gained from draws and just three goals scored. The situation prompted letters to the local evening newspaper from disgruntled fans, bringing into the open the rumours going round that as well as not signing the players, the manager did not even pick the team and it had not gone unnoticed that at Chesterfield and against Colchester it had been Richardson giving the team talk on the field with Chung on the sidelines. The general call was for Richardson to stop threatening that the club would drop to the Doncaster Senior League, stop blaming John Ryan for the lack of progress and let the manager do the job that he was being paid to do. The following Saturday, at Lincoln, the Rovers dropped down to ninth place as a result of losing by a single goal to lowly Lincoln City.

On Wednesday 18 January the club issued a statement regarding their financial situation and stated that the club would undoubtedly finish the season in the Third Division and would not be wound up or liquidated. However, further comments were made that if the situation did not improve then there was a good chance of the club resigning from the Football League at the end of the season. The statement went on to say that everything depended on the club moving to a new stadium where they would attract bigger gates and better sponsorship and advertising. It read that 'delicate negotiations had been going on for some time and if they came to fruition then the situation could alter the destiny of the club. Belle Vue Stadium stood on a very valuable site, which could be developed, with the club being

compensated and relocated in a new stadium giving Doncaster Rovers a secure future.' The following day, the winding-up order against the Rovers was lifted at the High Court in London. The court was told that the debts leading to the winding-up petition had been paid.

Further good news came with the appointment of John McClelland as first-team coach after a month on trial. However, when Saturday came for the home match against Exeter City the weather intervened. A lunchtime pitch inspection pronounced the game on but heavy rain then forced the referee to postpone the match just an hour before the kick-off. This inactivity on the pitch led to the Rovers dropping to their lowest position of the season, 11th. The last Saturday of the month meant a trip to Torquay, who were level on points with the Rovers in the middle of the table but had scored more goals. The Rovers adjusted their League position to eighth by winning with a single goal from Warren Hackett 20 minutes from time. A further

Steve Harper.

Steve Harper congratulating Sean Parrish on scoring at Exeter.

single-goal victory over Exeter City on the following Tuesday at Belle Vue, the goal scored by Brabin after Exeter goalkeeper Peter Fox had dropped a cross, catapulted the Rovers up to fourth place at the end of January.

The first Saturday in February brought a visit to Belle Vue from leaders Carlisle United, 16 points clear of the field and on a run of 17 games unbeaten. The Rovers' second highest attendance of the season, 3,587, saw their favourites hold the Cumbrians to a hard-fought goalless draw. The following Tuesday and a rearranged League game against third-from-bottom Gillingham at Belle Vue only attracted half the crowd from Saturday, even though a win for the Rovers would move them into second place. However, the Rovers badly missed that chance by going down 2–1 to the men from Kent. Before the match, Mr Richardson had again raised the spectre of the club going out of the League and said they had applied for entry to the Doncaster Senior League for season 1995–96 because of the poor support that the club was getting. To compound the financial situation at the club, on Saturday 11 February the team travelled all the way to Hartlepool, where an early-morning pitch inspection had passed the pitch as fit for play, only to be told two hours before kick-off, after the team had had a pre-match meal, that further torrential rain had rendered it totally unplayable.

In the *Doncaster Star*, a campaign under the banner of 'SAVE OUR ROVERS' was being run. The problem of the fans staying away was mooted as lack of communication with the public so that none of the fans knew what was going on at the club; nobody knew who Dinard Trading Ltd were and what connection Mr Richardson had with them; fans looked on Mr Richardson as an asset stripper with his sole interest being the amount of money he could make by selling the lease on Belle Vue back to Doncaster Council. The general consensus was that admission prices had been set too high at the beginning of the season and the recent run of three home games in a week had not helped, with a lot of supporters finding it difficult to afford the money to attend all the games. Other comments suggested that, although the club had been in difficulties a number of times over recent years, it was now in a worse position than ever before, with no-one ever suggesting before that the club should drop out of the League. Instead of winding the club down the current owners should be actively searching for new owners with the necessary finance and the interests of the club at heart.

Another home game followed on 18 February, with Lincoln City the visitors and the Rovers racking up a 3–0 win, with goals from Wilcox, Finlay and Harper. Darren Finlay was the leading scorer for the reserve team but it was his first goal for the first team in only his fifth start. Then, three days later, he played for Northern Ireland B against Scotland B, thus becoming the second Rovers player to win international honours that season after Steve Gallen, yet to play a first-team game for the Rovers, had played for the Republic of Ireland's Under-21 team against Latvia earlier in the season. On Saturday 25 February a fifth successive home game, against lowly Rochdale, drew a similar crowd to the Lincoln game, just over 2,200. An unchanged Rovers team, still missing five regular players, went down to a single-goal defeat and dropped to fifth position in the League.

On Thursday 2 March an open meeting of supporters was attended by Sammy Chung, who explained to the packed audience that the club would be continuing in the Football League but would probably not run a reserve or youth team next season. While this was part good news and part bad news, the supporters knew that the affable manager was limited as to how much he could say. Saturday came with a visit to Preston North End, who were a few places below the Rovers in the table. The Rovers had four of their regulars back: Gary Brabin, Sean Parrish, Graeme Jones and Warren Hackett. Preston included new signing Simon Davey, who had cost them £75,000 from Carlisle United, David Moyes and a player called David Beckham on the substitutes' bench. Beckham, a promising young player, was on loan from Manchester United. The Rovers led at half-time through a goal by Jones 10 minutes earlier but at the start of the second half David Beckham was introduced to the fray. Two minutes in and a move initiated by Beckham was finished by Davey to equalise the score. Ten minutes later and Preston went in front when Beckham's inswinging corner, aided by the blustery wind, defeated the efforts of Perry Suckling in the Rovers goal and went into the top corner of the net. The Rovers fought hard and on 76 minutes Wilcox scored the equaliser to keep them in a Play-off place, sixth. News then filtered through during that week that Mrs Julie Ormrod, a director of the club since December and daughter of the managing director, Charles Dunn, had died suddenly at her home in Ripponden. On Thursday 9 March, despite the fact that a reserve team might not be run the next season, the Rovers had applied for and were elected to the Pontins Central League for 1995–96. Two days later a crowd of 1,900 plus attended a 1–1 draw at Belle Vue against Barnet, with the Rovers dropping another place in the table and Sammy Chung bemoaning the fact that the team's poor home form was losing them ground in the promotion chase. The following Wednesday, Steve Beaglehole and Jim Golze, the coaches in charge of the reserves and youth teams, received letters signed by Ken Haran, the club vice-chairman, informing them that their services would not be required after 1 May and that they would be made redundant because there would be no positions for them without a reserve or youth team. However, on that same day came the news that Ian Measham, who had been out for just over a year with a broken neck, could resume his playing career. The team travelled to Fulham on 18 March and enhanced their consistent away record by going away with a win by two clear goals scored by Graeme Jones in the first half and Sean Parrish in the second. Three days later they lost by the odd goal in three to Hartlepool United in a rearranged League fixture at Hartlepool, which saw David Roche have a penalty saved and Gary Brabin sent off after two bookings.

The next day, Wednesday 22 March, there came a shock announcement in the form of a statement that read 'Due to circumstances regarding the Belle Vue ground the directors have no alternative but to put all the players up for sale. Staged payments will be accepted.' Nobody at Belle Vue was available to elaborate on the statement or explain what it was all about. The next day was transfer deadline day, which saw Chris Swailes move to Ipswich Town for £225,000 and David Roche go to Southend United for £50,000.

However, undaunted by the sale of two important players, the following Saturday at Darlington the Rovers regained their away form by scoring twice in the second half, with a Wilcox penalty after Andy Crosby, a former Rovers player, had been sent off for a foul on Parrish and a goal from Graeme Jones without reply, which enabled them to hang on to seventh place in the table.

The possibility of promotion via the Play-offs was tempered, however, by the emergence of the fact that the application to join the Doncaster Senior League had not been withdrawn and was still on the table, with Senior League officials thinking it would be for a reserve or youth side. The supporters of the club were concerned at this news, thinking that it was in all possibility going to be the first team, as stated in the letter to shareholders in December. It had been stated then that the issue of shares worth £250,000 would secure the financial future of the club but players had been sold for amounts totalling nearly twice that and the club was still in trouble. With rumours flying round the town that the club would drop out of the Football League at the end of the season, Doncaster Council reiterated on the following Monday that they were still committed to the offer of building a new multi-million pound sports stadium for the Rovers and other sporting clubs in the town to share, within a mile radius of Belle Vue, at no cost to the clubs, provided that agreement could be reached on the amount of compensation for the Rovers for the release of the long-term lease on Belle Vue. On Tuesday 28 March, in a meeting with the Rovers representatives Ken Richardson, Chic Hicken, Alan Criddle and George Jessop, none of whom were directors or even employees of the club, most of the people present left with the idea that the basis for an agreement had been reached. The council, however, remained adamant that any compensation figure regarding the lease would have to be endorsed by the District Valuer. If agreement could be reached at this stage the new stadium could be operating for 1996–97. Richardson then reported to the Board on the following day and issued their reply, which was that agreement had to be reached by the weekend of 1 April otherwise the club would withdraw from the Football League at the end of the season. What amounted to an ultimatum was unacceptable to the council, who were not moved by the threat of withdrawal from the League, with the council leader, Cllr Peter Walsh, explaining that such decisions were a matter for the directors of Doncaster Rovers and not Doncaster Council, who had explained at the meeting earlier in the week that a formal decision had to be ratified by a properly constituted committee that could not be convened at such short notice. Thus was achieved a stalemate, with the supporters of the club believing that it was the end for their club.

Saturday 1 April 1995 dawned with the news that the Rovers had taken back their threat to withdraw from the Football League and announced before the game against promotion rivals Bury, at Belle Vue, that they hoped to move into a new stadium in 12 months time following the expected agreement being reached with Doncaster Council. Although the club's supporters were very worried about the threat of leaving the Football League, that august body confirmed that 5pm on 1 April was the deadline date for withdrawal and the Rovers had failed to do this. In fact, under Football League rules, clubs wanting to withdraw and play in another League had to give initial notification by 31 December and written confirmation by 1 April. As the club had only notified the League in February of their intention to withdraw they had failed to meet any of the deadlines if they withdrew before the start of the next season they would be subject to fines and other penalties unless they were wound up or went out of business. So what was the point of issuing such a threat because the club would not settle for paying any fines and other penalties? Did it mean that the club would be put out of business? A dangerous game of brinkmanship seems to have been played here.

However, there was a different game to play that afternoon against Bury and a win was essential for their promotion prospects. The FA secretary, Graham Kelly, was present in the directors' box to witness the Rovers 'keeper, Dean Williams, save a penalty from David Pugh after 17 minutes. Seventeen minutes later, Russ Wilcox made no mistake from the spot after Harper had been brought down, the Rovers going in at half-time with that one-goal lead. It was not to be enough, however, because Bury's £65,000 signing from Cardiff City on deadline day, Phil Stant, scored twice in the second half to consolidate the Shakers' Play-off place and leave the Rovers, still in seventh place, one below the Play-off places.

On the Monday came news that David Roche, who had only left the club 10 days earlier, had been arrested on Saturday as he prepared to watch his new club, Southend United, play Wolverhampton Wanderers. He appeared before Newcastle magistrates on Monday on three charges following an incident in a wine bar two weeks earlier in which a club doorman, George Lumsden, received stab wounds to his leg and buttocks. Together with Brian Tate, he was charged with wounding

Steve Harper, Russ Wilcox and Ryan Kirby congratulate Mickey Norbury on his hat-trick at Scunthorpe United.

with intent to cause grievous bodily harm, possession of a firearm and violent disorder and was remanded in custody for seven days.

On a happier note, on that Monday Ian Measham made his long-awaited comeback when he played a full 90 minutes for the reserves against Stockport County and was well pleased with his performance despite losing 3–0. The following day, a meeting of supporters and shareholders was told by Chic Hicken, a shareholder and owner of Stainforth greyhound track who had been helping out at Belle Vue, that until the details were finalised the new stadium was a long way off. He also said that the club was heavily in debt and an increase in share capital was essential because £400,000 was needed before June to keep the club afloat. Yet after the Walsall game Mr Richardson talked of finalising a deal for the new stadium to be built when he met the council on Tuesday 11 April. Then the fine details would be gone through and hopefully full agreement would be reached. Mr Richardson stated that he did not foresee any late delays, saying the council had made a generous offer and, providing safeguards were written in to ensure the Rovers received a fair share of the income from the development of Belle Vue, he could not see a problem. He went on to say that a new stadium would secure the club's future and with that in mind plans were already underway to strengthen the team for next season. He then added that the club were nowhere near insolvent but an injection of cash was necessary, which he would provide once an agreement was reached. Finally, he said that he would personally guarantee to fund a reserve team, then under threat of being discontinued, in the Pontins Central League next season and was now much happier after the council's gesture and that all they required now was to reach the Play-offs. The chances of that receded, however, because that Saturday afternoon at Belle Vue they met Walsall, in third position, who were much the better team and went home with three points under their belt from a win by two clear goals. This dropped the Rovers down to eighth but only on goals scored because they had the same points as Scunthorpe United, who replaced them in seventh position. Yet they went to Glanford Park on the following Saturday and slammed five goals past the 'Iron' to leapfrog them into seventh place. They were three goals up at half-time through Mickey Norbury, Lee Warren and Steve Harper, the last two goals coming in the final two minutes of the half. Wayne Bullimore for Scunthorpe United put a penalty wide after 31 minutes but the Rovers were clearly on top by the break and Norbury scored twice in the second half to claim a hat-trick, his first goals for the club on his 18th appearance since signing from Preston North End. On Easter Monday second-placed Chesterfield came to Belle Vue and went away with a 3–1 victory. A crowd of 4,796 came to watch, the biggest for a League game at Belle Vue in 10 years. This defeat left the Rovers in seventh place, one place outside the Play-offs and five points adrift with three games to play. Although

Sammy Chung rolled out the battlecry 'we'll fight to the finish', it was obvious that the club had missed the boat, which was confirmed on the Saturday when they went down to Gillingham for a must-win game and suffered a 4–2 defeat.

The final home game of the season came against Scarborough but as the staff arrived for the game they were handed a letter containing their redundancy notices, which would take effect from the end of May. While the players were excluded, the manager Sammy Chung and his youth coaches Steve Beaglehole and Jim Golze also received redundancy notices. The letter, signed by Charles Dunn, stated: 'Due to financial circumstances beyond its control, the company has no alternative but to withdraw from the League at the end of the season. It had been hoped by the directors that some agreement could be reached with Doncaster Council as to the provision of a new ground. The new ground would provide the facilities needed to develop the club and improve its income stream. Despite entering into negotiations with the council, the council has failed to make any definite response and/or realistic proposals.' Of course, word soon spread to the 1,710 spectators at the match, so at half-time a small group of supporters marched to the centre circle to demonstrate against Mr Richardson, with shouts of 'sack the Board' also ringing round the ground. Graeme Jones scored what turned out to be the winner just before the hour mark and in injury time an altercation between Gary Brabin, just back from a five-match ban and Mark Calvert of Scarborough saw both of them red-carded, thus enabling them to have first use of the bath. Angry fans then demonstrated after the game, calling for Mr Richardson to go and the Board to be sacked.

On Wednesday 3 May the financial accounts for the year ending 31 May 1994 were published, showing current liabilities exceeding current assets by £910,593. The auditors' report to shareholders contained a note stating that the company might be unable to continue trading because of the debts. For the 12-month period covered, the first full year under the ownership of Dinard Trading Ltd, the accounts showed a loss of £647,297, mostly due to transfer fees and a big rise in wages and salaries, with Dinard Trading Ltd the major creditor, being owed £608,304. The profit and loss account showed operating costs and administrative expenses were up by more than 40 per cent to £903,166 on a much reduced turnover of £320,288. Total gate receipts were down slightly to £221,636 but wages and bonuses had increased from £439,257 to £610,305. The payment from the Football League showed Rovers receiving £44,734 less than the previous year, with the commercial account also down from £78,821 to £69,289. The total of transfer fees received amounted to £100,125 but the club paid out £303,620. Police and security charges almost tripled from £7,630 to £19,430. A total sum of £32,239 came from the Cup matches, although the club had exited at the first round. In comparison, the club had cut costs in 1992–93 and had actually made a profit of £45,229.

At a packed meeting of supporters held at the Park Hotel on Thursday evening, 4 May, an announcement by the Rovers representative, Chic Hicken, stated that at 4pm the previous evening a decision had been made that the club would develop Belle Vue bit-by-bit, providing planning permission was granted, with Ken Richardson agreeing to fund the proposals, which would cost around £2 million. This was because the club had become convinced that there would be no final agreement reached with the council over a new stadium. A leaflet handed out to the supporters read that the Rovers had been seeking a written binding legal agreement from the council about the new stadium so that funds could be made available to enable the club to stay solvent until it was built. However, they had received a letter on Tuesday 2 May from the council stating that there was no contractual agreement other than to carry out a feasibility study, which the club said had never been discussed at previous meetings and was something entirely new. The leaflet stated that the club were not seeking any confrontations with the council. A further announcement stated that redundancy notices issued to employees the previous weekend would now be reviewed and that the club would be staying in the Football League.

The final game of the season was played out at Springfield Park, the home of Wigan Athletic, on Saturday 6 May. With nothing at stake and the future of the club in the League settled, the match could be enjoyed simply as a game of football. Following his recovery from his broken neck, Ian Measham was selected to play for his first League game in 15 months and made captain for the day. An even first half showed at half-time with a goalless scoreline but with 20 minutes to go in the second half the Rovers held a 2–1 lead, Lyons netting for Wigan and Jones and Norbury scoring for the Rovers. Then two goals in five minutes from Wigan, the second a penalty by Lyons, gave them the win by 3–2. This left the Rovers in ninth place in the final table, their highest position in 11 years. Ian Measham arrived home that evening to find that his wife had given birth to a baby daughter.

Vandals hit Belle Vue over that weekend and caused some damage to the Main Stand but nothing major. While the club came ninth in the League, they were only four points adrift of the Play-off positions so it could be said that they had a good season. Actually they had been in the top six for most of the campaign, despite the shenanigans going on in the background over unpaid bills, disputes with the council and shareholders, the hiring and firing of three first-team coaches and the selling of star players, which says a lot about the character of manager Sammy Chung and the players. The following Tuesday the redundancy notices to the staff were withdrawn and more details were given about the proposed redevelopment of Belle Vue. To start with, a new Main Stand would be constructed and seating put on the Popular side to hold around 6,000 spectators and to include hospitality boxes, a bar, offices and changing rooms. The intention then was to resite the roofing from the Popular side over the Town End and make that end into a seated area.

At the club's AGM on 16 May at the Park Hotel the retained list was announced, which showed that 20 players had been retained, including teenagers Scott Maxfield, Kris Hoy, Lee Saunders and Chris Lee, with five players released: Darren Finlay, Steve Gallen, Lee Thew, Nicky Limber and Sam Kitchen. Shareholders were given details of the proposal to build a new two-tier stand on the Popular side, which would cost £1 million and be funded mainly by Ken Richardson, providing that minority shareholders contributed proportionately. However, it was also revealed that negotiations were ongoing with the council about a new stadium, with this being the preferred option. New auditors were confirmed as Lishman, Sidwell, Campbell and Price of Sheffield following the resignation of Arthur Wigglesworth and Co. The accounts that showed a record loss (as detailed above) were approved. Retiring directors Charles Dunn and Lisa Mabbett were re-elected.

Two days later the club's representatives, Ken Richardson and Charles Dunn, attended a special meeting with League officials in London to discuss the club's financial position. Mr Richardson explained later that the League were sympathetic but had wanted to know if the club could pay its way. Notification from the club that they could continue throughout next season was required to be with the League by the end of May, otherwise they had the power to expel the club before the start of the season. Mr Richardson also stated that he had decided to fund the £1.2 million cost of constructing a new stand at Belle Vue, providing the shareholders assisted in raising money to offset the running costs of the club. At least £350,000 fresh capital was required for next season, which would have to be raised by a new share issue. For this motion to be passed 75 per cent of shareholders were required to vote in favour. A new share issue had been blocked by John Ryan in December but his response was that he would have to consult with his business partner. But if Ken Richardson was putting in £1 million to build a new stand, he (Ryan) personally would not object to a new share issue, providing that it was for the purpose of putting fresh cash into the club. On 23 May Mr Ryan, after consultation with his partner, Lars Rydstrom, issued a statement to the effect that, 'I will not stand in the way of any share issue on one proviso that the money is cash only which will help the club. The reason I have held out until now was not to be obstructive but to prevent Mr Richardson and Dinard getting 75 per cent of the shares because I have grave concern for the well-being of the club when he gets total control. I hope my words will not be prophetic.' At the end of the month, with their Football League place secure for 1995–96, the club announced that admission charges would stay the same as the season just ended. This actually worked out cheaper because there would be two extra matches, with the Division increased to 24 clubs for 1995–96.

On the night of 28–29 June a fire broke out at Belle Vue Stadium in the Main Stand. It was soon established as arson because the arsonists had left a mobile telephone lying around and four people were charged with committing the offence. Two of them appeared in court on Thursday 6 July to apply for bail. Elaine Marie Wetherell, aged 20, of Newcastle-upon-Tyne, who was a student and a part-time soldier, was granted bail with conditions despite strong opposition from the prosecution. The alleged organiser of the crime, Alan Kristiansen, aged 37 from Hexham and the owner of a security and private investigation firm in Newcastle, was refused bail by the Stipendiary Magistrate, Mr Ian Pollard, on the grounds that he might not surrender.

The close season was not restricted to the changing of personnel on the field. Off the field Steve Beaglehole was appointed assistant manager, George Foster, former Mansfield and Telford United manager, became the first-team coach and Pete Schofield, a former manager of Bridlington Town, was appointed chief scout. Players were also signed, of course, namely Scott Colcombe on a free transfer from Torquay United; Darren Moore, 21, also from Torquay United for a tribunal-fixed fee of £62,500 plus 25 per cent of any profit made on a future transfer; Duane Darby, 21, from Torquay United for a tribunal-fixed fee of £35,000 plus £15,000 after 25 first-team games and 20 per cent of any profit on a future transfer; Kevin Noteman, released by Mansfield Town and signed by Rovers on a short-term contract after trials; Jason Knight, a former West Ham United trainee, from Hinckley Athletic; Mark McCluskie, a trainee from Crystal Palace; Paul Haywood on a free transfer from Nottingham Forest; Ian Clark from north-eastern non-League club Stockton; Hakan Hayrettin from Cambridge United and Mark Proctor, former Middlesbrough, Sheffield Wednesday, Sunderland, Nottingham Forest and England Under-21 midfielder on a free transfer from Tranmere Rovers. Pre-season friendlies were played at Boston FC, won 2–0; at Tamworth 2–2; at Goole Town 3–0; at Worksop Town 4–0 and at Hucknall Town 1–1.

Heading practice.

Kevin Noteman.

Because they were unable to attend the extraordinary shareholders' meeting called by the club on Tuesday 15 August, John Ryan and Mike Collett, former directors of the club, called an open meeting of shareholders at the Park Hotel for Wednesday 9 August and explained their stance regarding further share issues.

Steve Beaglehole and George Foster were in charge for the first match of the season, at home to Scarborough on 12 August, because Sammy Chung had been in hospital for 11 days with a viral illness before returning to his Wolverhampton home to convalesce on 5 August. While they had 26 professionals to choose from, Gary Brabin was not one of them because of a five-match ban carried over from the previous season. Due to the fire in June the middle section of the Main Stand was out of bounds for the start of the season, with season-ticket holders temporarily occupying Block C. Two and a half thousand fans turned out for the match, which also counted as the Yorkshire Electricity Cup Final. Rovers, with a second-half goal from Sean Parrish, won the three points and the Cup, which was presented to them after the match. Their next match on the Monday was also a Cup game, the first leg of the Coca-Cola League Cup at Belle Vue against Shrewsbury Town, in which two players, Steve Anthrobus for Shrewsbury and Sean Parrish for the Rovers, were sent off and five other players were booked in a hard-fought game. An early lead for the visitors was defended bravely after they went down to 10 men after 23 minutes. The Rovers, with a man advantage for over an hour, could only break through once in the second half, in which they dominated the play. Later that week there was one player out by mutual agreement, Mark Proctor and one in, Matt Carmichael, who had scored for Mansfield Town on Saturday but was playing as a non-contract player. Rovers moved in and signed him on contract. He was on the substitutes' bench for the next game at Torquay, with the Rovers including former Gulls players Darren Moore and Duane Darby. It was also Ian Measham's first return visit to the ground where he had suffered the horrific injury to his neck. For Darby it was not a happy return, because just past the hour he received his marching orders for using an elbow in a challenge on Ian Gore of Torquay. But for the Rovers, who scored the winning goal in a 2–1 win when they were down to 10 men, it was a great tonic, likewise for their manager, Sammy Chung, recovering at home from his illness. However, in midweek after this win they went to Shrewsbury in the League Cup second leg and, following a goalless draw after extra-time, were eliminated on the away-goal rule. This was despite hammering away for 102 minutes against a team reduced to 10 men. Two goalless draws followed in the League, at home to Cardiff City and away at Mansfield Town, where Kevin Noteman was sent off after 28 minutes for use of the elbow. The League table after four games showed the Rovers in third place.

The first day of September brought some surprises when Kevin Noteman was released from his short-term contract and Charles Dunn resigned from his position as managing director on the grounds of ill health. However, Steve Brodie, another forward, was brought in on loan from Sunderland. The first Saturday of the month saw Sammy Chung attend to see that season's team for the first time in the home game against Hartlepool United. Steve Brodie, on his debut for the club, scored the only goal of the game just before the hour, the three points pushing the Rovers into second place after five games. Meanwhile, Steve Harper was completing a move to Mansfield Town, with a tribunal later settling on a fee of £20,000 plus 40 per cent of a future transfer fee. This followed the recent announcement that the squad of 30 professionals had to be trimmed by a third. Duane Darby, suspended for three games after his sending-off, went to Burnley on a week's trial with a view to joining them if they liked what they saw. However, on the Saturday a visit to Craven Cottage to play fellow promotion candidates Fulham had the Rovers returning home empty handed after a 3–1 defeat had dropped them to fifth place, with the Cottagers moving up to third. To compound things further, Graeme Jones, who had replaced Norbury in the starting line-up, was sent off. In between losing at Home Park to Plymouth Argyle and then beating Northampton Town at Belle Vue, Rovers had signed Jamie Murphy, a 22-year-old defender who had been released by Blackpool earlier in the month. On Friday 22 September, however, came the bombshell that the Rovers fans had feared. Russ Wilcox, the outstanding figure in defence and captain to boot, had been transferred to Preston North End for £60,000. Sammy Chung later defended the decision by stating that he was the club's highest-paid player, who was out of contract at the end of the season and they could not afford to pay him the money he was asking for in a new contract. The following day, with Murphy making his debut, brought a resounding drubbing by three clear goals from Rochdale at Belle Vue, with the Rovers fans showing their displeasure at the display by booing the players off the pitch. Two days later the first game in the Auto Windscreens Shield was played against Bradford City at Belle Vue, ending in a 1–1 draw. This competition consisted of the teams in the bottom two Divisions playing in regional North and South Divisions in a preliminary round composed of three-team groups, each team playing the other two teams once. The winners of the North and South competitions would play in an overall Final at Wembley. Later that week Richie Barker, a reserve forward at Sheffield Wednesday, was brought to Belle Vue on loan but could not prevent the Rovers going down to a 3–1 defeat at Leyton Orient. The club now stood in 11th place in the table.

Action in the Plymouth Argyle match at Belle Vue.

On Thursday 28 September, following committal proceedings at Doncaster Magistrates Court, three men, Alan Cracknall of Ryton, Ian Hunter Hay of Gateshead and Alan Kristiansen of Hexham together with a woman, Elaine Marie Wetherell, a 21-year-old student, were committed to stand trial at Doncaster Crown Court charged with arson at Belle Vue in June.

The unpredictability of the Rovers was shown on the first Saturday in October when they went to second-placed Chester City and came away with the three points from a three-goal defeat of the Cestrians. A goalless draw at home to Hereford United was followed later in the week by the news that Warren Hackett had followed Steve Harper to Mansfield Town for a fee of £50,000 plus a percentage of any sell-on fee. The news also broke in the middle of the month that Darrell 'Chic' Hicken, the owner of the Stainforth Greyhound Stadium, had been appointed to the managing director post at the club after helping out behind the scenes in an unofficial capacity for the past several months. Back on the pitch, leaders Gillingham hammered the Rovers 4–0 at the Priestfield Stadium, dropping them to their lowest position yet, 12th. A late flourish from the team in the last three days of the month brought them four points from home games against Preston North End, a 2–2 draw and Cambridge United, who were beaten 2–1. An attendance of 4,413 at the Saturday match against Preston shrank to 1,657 two days later for the win over Cambridge. On the last day of October the management were busy bringing in two players from non-League football. Paul Robertson came from Conference side Runcorn and Stuart Doling, who was playing for Wessex League side Lymington even though Portsmouth held his League registration despite him walking out on them. The club forked out five-figure fees for each player. Both players had played in the League, Robertson with Stockport County and Bury and Doling with Portsmouth, then in Division One, the second tier of English football.

After a draw at Barnet on the first Saturday in November the Rovers travelled to play Carlisle United on the Tuesday in their final game in the preliminary round of the Auto Windscreens Shield. A 1–1 draw ensued due to a last-minute goal from David Currie for Carlisle. As the game between Carlisle United and Bradford City had also ended in a 1–1 draw, all three clubs had identical records!

Graeme Jones.

A drawing of lots was held to decide which two clubs would progress in the competition. The Rovers came out first and would therefore have a home game, while Carlisle United were the other team to go through. When the draw for the next round was held two days later the Rovers would have Notts County as their next opponents, at Belle Vue.

The following Saturday was FA Cup first round day and the Rovers travelled to Mansfield Town to meet two of their former colleagues, Warren Hackett and Steve Harper, who would play against them. In fact Harper scored the first goal for the home team, who were three goals up at half-time and four up before the Rovers, who had missed chances in the first half to establish a lead themselves, replied with two goals in the last nine minutes through a penalty from Graeme Jones and a goal from Matt Carmichael in injury time. This result led to Sammy Chung appealing to the fans not to desert the club, who needed their support because there was only Ken Richardson putting any money into the club. In midweek two youth members, Carl Lawrence and Darren Utley, were signed on one-year professional contracts but a week later Mickey Norbury was shipped out on trial to Linfield, the Irish League club. In between the Rovers had beaten high-flying Colchester United 3–2, despite being without key players Darren Moore (foot injury),

Jon Schofield (suspended) and Sean Parrish (groin injury). Injuries were now a real cause for concern. Hakan Hayrettin had not played since receiving a knee injury in a pre-season friendly, Stuart Doling had not played since signing because of injury and several other players were also out with a variety of injuries. The same line-up, with the exception of Perry Suckling, who had a back injury, played at Springfield Park on the following Saturday and lost by two clear goals to middle-of-the-table Wigan Athletic. Two days after the Wigan game the Rovers played their next round game in the AWS against Notts County, who were in a higher division. Darren Moore gave them a second-half lead but three goals in the last five minutes to the County team let them progress further in the competition, leaving the Rovers with just the League to play for. Even the visiting team's management admitted that the Rovers had been the better team on the night and the County had been lucky to get the win but goals count and Sammy Chung admitted that this was the area of the Rovers game that required sorting out.

As the Rovers were out of the FA Cup they brought forward the game against Exeter City from 23 December to 2 December, FA Cup second round day, at Belle Vue. However, only 1,429, the lowest attendance for six years, showed up to watch the Rovers win with goals from Gary Brabin and Graeme Jones and move up to sixth in the table. Then, in midweek, came good news from the youth team, who had gone to Derby County in the FA Youth Cup second round and come away with a 5–3 victory after being three goals down with 35 minutes left. Goals from James Hodgkinson, Darren Utley, Carl Lawrence, Mark Horan and Andy Hammond in the last half hour gave them the win and set up a home tie against Oldham Athletic in the next round. The following evening George Foster, the first-team coach, turned out for the reserves at Bury because of the number of injuries to the senior squad. Stuart Doling scored the Rovers goal in a 2–1 defeat. An announcement from the club on the Thursday apologised for the inconvenience caused by the fire to the Main Stand and stated that work would start in the next few days to repair the damage. Two days later Rochdale completed the 'double' over the Rovers with a single-goal victory to leave the Rovers in seventh place. Then, on Friday 15 December the club dipped into their coffers and paid out £40,000 for Colin Cramb, aged 21, a forward from Heart of Midlothian in Scotland. It was a return to English football by Cramb, who as a teenager had played for Southampton in the top division. The following day he made his debut in a 4–1 win over Leyton Orient at Belle Vue, with Graeme Jones getting a hat-trick and Scott Colcombe registering an early first goal. The following Tuesday came news that Mickey Norbury and Kris Hoy, both forwards, had been released by the club after agreement had been reached on the cancellation of their contracts but there was also news that Stuart Doling was to have a hernia operation and Hakan Hayrettin needed a major reconstruction of his knee, which ruled him out for the rest of the season. In the meantime it was learned that John Ryan and Mike Collett had sold their shares to Paul Theakston, a Yorkshire businessman and a Rovers season-ticket holder, who was prepared to put money into the club. The Christmas and New Year period was devastating for the club because of the snow and frost that led to the games at Feethams against Darlington, at Glanford Park against Scunthorpe United and at Belle Vue on New Year's Day against Lincoln City all being postponed.

When they resumed playing on 6 January, the Rovers took a 4–1 battering at Bury, a team above the Rovers in the table. On the Monday, Sammy Chung attended a meeting of the Doncaster Boys' League at the Earl of Doncaster Hotel, along with most of his youth-team coaches and outlined to the assembled boys' club officials that the Rovers wanted to forge a closer link with this thriving local boys' league. Well known for his development of youth players at his former clubs, Chung wanted the Rovers to benefit from the local talent rather than other clubs. He outlined the plans to reward clubs for informing the Rovers about any outstanding talent. The Rovers would pay clubs a £50 fee for recommending any youngster who went on to sign schoolboy forms and pledged a further £150 if the player was taken on a YTS placement. Also, if the player was signed as a professional Chung promised clubs another £200 and a further payment of £300 for five first-team appearances. It was an incentive for clubs to send the best young players in Doncaster to Doncaster Rovers, with the clubs receiving the money to spend on kit and equipment and help put

Jon Schofield and mascots before the Wigan Athletic game.

them on a sounder financial footing. The following evening the youth team took a five-goal beating at the hands of Oldham Athletic in the FA Youth Cup at Belle Vue. The weekend saw the Rovers regain winning ways with a Carmichael goal giving them a win over bottom-of-the-League club Torquay United at Belle Vue. They also signed goalkeeper Gary O'Connor from Heart of Midlothian and winger Mike Smith from Runcorn. Three days later they went to Darlington and collected another win, with an early goal from Parrish and a second-half goal from Carmichael that took them up to fifth in the League. Darlington had Sean Gregan sent off in first-half injury time but still managed to equalise three minutes into the second half. It was also announced that Gordon Gallimore, a former leader of Doncaster Council, had been appointed as chairman of the club, with Mr Richardson quoted as saying 'I am delighted that Gordon has joined the Board because he is such a well-respected figure in the town.' As chairman he would be in charge of the day-to-day affairs and he would make it his prerogative to attract more support through the turnstiles by providing better facilities. A third successive win, at next-to-bottom Scarborough by virtue of two goals from Colin Cramb and despite the sending-off of Gary Brabin for two bookings, took the Rovers to the dizzy heights of fourth position. The League match with Mansfield Town on the night of Friday 26 January was postponed as the frost and snow returned. The postponement of home games over the holiday period, followed by the Mansfield game, was not only hitting the club where it hurt in the cash accounts but also on the field, where their recent winning run had now been interrupted.

February began with a loss at lowly Cardiff City, for whom Carl Dale scored a hat-trick and although Graeme Jones drew them level just after half-time, a goal from Scott Colcombe three minutes from time was insufficient to gain any reward. Two days later the rearranged match against Lincoln City ended in a 1–1 draw when a penalty from Jason Minett two minutes from time cancelled out Sean Parrish's first-half goal. The Rovers then added another Torquay United player to their squad when David Byng was signed on a free transfer and a contract to the end of the season after trials at the club. The following Saturday the Rovers went down by a single goal at Belle Vue against middle-of-the-table Bury, followed a week later by a goalless draw at home to Plymouth Argyle, who leapfrogged the Rovers, now in seventh place in the table. A tale of two penalties on a freezing Tuesday night at Hartlepool gave the Rovers all three points and brought an end to their run of four matches without a win. A controversial penalty put away by Cramb, 16 minutes from time, gave the Rovers the win after Hartlepool had gone down to 10 men just past the hour when the referee refused them a penalty, with Damien Henderson taking his protests too far and getting his marching orders. A 3–3 draw followed at Sixfields against Northampton Town, managed by former Rovers manager Ian Atkins, on a mudbath of a pitch following heavy rain, which delayed the kick-off until 3.15pm to give the groundstaff more time to fork the pitch. An injury-time penalty won a point for the Cobblers but Cramb had a penalty saved in the 35th minute when the Rovers were two goals down. Consequently, when another penalty was awarded to the Rovers just before half-time Jon Schofield took the responsibility and made no mistake. Cramb redeemed himself with the other two goals. Two days later, at Belle Vue, struggling Fulham came and went away with all three points in a two-goal win, their first away from home, leaving the Rovers fans so disillusioned that they not only booed the players off the park but also had a go at the manager for the first time during his tenure. In the meantime, the merry-go-round of players continued. Matt Carmichael left the club by mutual consent but two players came in on loan: Nathan Peel, a forward from Burnley and winger Jermaine Wright from Wolverhampton Wanderers.

The first Saturday in March brought in-form high-flying Darlington to Belle Vue and, despite a Darren Moore goal, they went away with the points from a 2–1 victory. Ironically, Matt Carmichael came on as a substitute for Darlington and helped them to the win. This game was the Rovers' fifth home game without a win and dropped them to ninth, having consistently spurned the many chances to get into the automatic promotion positions in recent games. Early the following week an advert appeared in the *Financial Times* offering 'a football club within 25 miles of Sheffield for sale'. After Rotherham United and Barnsley said it was not them, all eyes turned towards Doncaster. An initial silence was followed by Mr Gallimore stating that he had been assured by Mr Richardson that it definitely was not Doncaster Rovers for sale and added that the club had a bright future. Meanwhile the club lost two more players. Nathan Peel's loan spell lasted just four days and one and a half games after he came off at half-time in the Fulham game with knee ligament damage and returned to Burnley for an exploratory operation, effectively ruling him out for the rest of his loan period. James Meara also left the club after making his first appearance of the season as a substitute against Fulham. His contract was terminated by mutual consent. On the Friday before the Exeter game, Mr Richardson had a go at

Sammy Chung and office girls.

Sammy Chung signs another Youth player.

the 'boo boys', who came to matches just to boo the players. Although sympathising with the supporters who witnessed the debacle against Fulham, he urged all supporters to get behind the team and lift them to promotion. However, another loss, by a single goal at Exeter City, shoved the Rovers down another place. A goal after 10 minutes was sufficient to give the Devonians the points, although Dean Williams, in goal for the Rovers, did his job a minute after the goal by saving a penalty from Mark Cooper. A return to winning ways came the following week at Belle Vue with second-half goals from Paul Marquis and Sean Parrish giving them the win over third-from-bottom Scunthorpe United, who had Mick Buxton in charge for the first time. The next player out of the door was 30-year-old Perry Suckling, whom the Rovers agreed to release from his contract so that he could go to Johannesburg in South Africa to study for a degree in sports-related psychology, while playing for the university and running a specialist coaching clinic for the most promising goalkeepers in that country. Lee Saunders, a young full-back, was also released. Then, on 21 March, came the announcement that Jimmy Neighbour was back at the club after being appointed first-team coach, with George Foster working more with the reserves and youth teams. Further transfer activity brought centre-half Ian Gore to the club from Torquay United for a nominal fee. However, the same line up against Scunthorpe United turned out the following week against Lincoln City at Sincil Bank and were thoroughly trounced by the struggling Imps by four clear goals, all of which came in the first 30 minutes, with Colin Alcide and Jason Minett getting two apiece. Then, on 37 minutes, Colin Cramb was sent for an early bath after kicking out at an opponent. Despite their disadvantage at being a man short, Rovers improved substantially in the second half and were unlucky not to get on the score sheet. Barry Richardson, in the Lincoln goal, kept them at bay.

Two days later the Rovers played a rearranged fixture against Mansfield Town at Belle Vue. The game was goalless, leaving the Rovers 11th in the table, six points away from a Play-off place. The real excitement was reserved for the final whistle, which heralded the police arresting Ken Richardson in connection with their investigations into the fire at Belle Vue in June the previous year. The police also took away a large number of files and documents from the club's offices. After two nights in a police station cell, Richardson appeared before Doncaster Magistrates charged with conspiracy to commit arson at Belle Vue, with another man, Alan Kristiansen, on or before 29 June 1995. The Crown Prosecution Service opposed bail but it was granted with conditions. They were: that he could not return to the Isle of Man, where his home was and had to live with his sister-in-law in Driffield, East Yorkshire; and that he report to the police every day and surrender his passport until another court appearance on 22 May for committal proceedings. Richardson failed to convince the court that he could provide a bail security of £240,000 but his sister-in-law and another person agreed to provide sureties totalling £250,000 to take effect on the following day. He was transferred to Marshgate prison for another night in a cell.

Transfer deadline day, Thursday 28 March, had some nasty surprises for the Rovers faithful. Duane Darby and Scott Maxfield went to Hull City for a combined fee of £25,000 and Gary Brabin left the club for Bury, who paid out

£120,000 for his services. In response to the expected outcry from the supporters at this news, Sammy Chung said it had been forced on the club because of poor support at the gate. Kevin Ashley, a full-back, was brought in from Peterborough United on a free transfer, Jermaine Wright was retained for a second month on loan and another loanee, 32-year-old Paul Williams, a 6ft 4in forward formerly with Sheffield United and West Bromwich Albion, came to the club from Rochdale. The month of March ended with the Rovers losing 2–1 at home to Chester City in front of 1,548 spectators. Chester scored in the last minute after the Rovers had led at half-time with a Paul Williams goal. A 700-word leaflet, which purported to give the facts about Ken Richardson's innocence in relation to the arson attack on the Main Stand, was distributed to the fans arriving at the ground. The club initially claimed not to have any responsibility for it, although the leaflet stated that people should read the club newspaper *Red all over*, which the club said was a supporters' branch publication. The official supporters' club secretary, Ken Avis, said he understood the magazine referred to was a club publication. All this led to Gordon Gallimore resigning from his post as chairman of the club during the following week because he had not been consulted about the leaflet and its contents.

The slide down the table continued at the beginning of April, with three successive single-goal losses in six days, at Hereford United, Preston North End and at home to Gillingham leaving them in 14th place in the table. Injuries were now taking their toll. A draw at Cambridge United, with debuts given to youth players Darren Utley and Martyn Speight, still saw them drop another place but an Ian Clark goal in the last minute at Belle Vue gave them the win over Barnet and halted the slide down the table. In between these games came the signing of youngster Adam Wheeler, a goalkeeper, from Newcastle United, the departure of Kevin Ashley by mutual consent and Graeme Jones handing in a transfer request. The Rovers finished the season with a draw at Scunthorpe United courtesy of two goals from Colin Cramb, despite playing with 10 men for the last 36 minutes after Sean Parrish had been sent off for a second booking. They then earned a win over Wigan Athletic at Belle Vue, with two goals from Jon Schofield and lost at Colchester United in the last match by a single goal. The Rovers' final position in the League table was 13th, a sad ending to a season that had promised so much before March, when the club had been in contention for a Play-off place. A total of 39 players took some part in the League games, which reflects the constant wheeling and dealing of players coming and going. It was Richardson's remit to bring in players. But it has to have made the jobs of the manager and coaches extremely difficult to weld a team together with a constant stream of new faces coming in. Of the first 14 players selected to play the first game, just six played in the last game, with Lee Warren, who missed just two games and Sean

Darren Moore, Supporters' Club Player of the Year.

Parrish, who missed four, being the most consistent performers.

Two days before the last game of the season at Colchester, on Thursday 2 May, Sammy Chung called a public meeting at the Earl of Doncaster Hotel at which the managing director, Chic Hicken, tried to put pressure on Doncaster Council by telling the meeting that the club needed a firm commitment within days in order to obtain a £1 million grant towards a new stadium from the Football Trust. He went on to say that if the deadline was missed they would be unable to apply again until January 1998. The following day it was announced that Jimmy

The Youth Team.

Neighbour would leave the club and that George Foster would resume as first-team coach. Later in the month the Stipendiary Magistrate at Doncaster, Peter Jones, eased the strict conditions for bail imposed on Ken Richardson. The new conditions were that he had to reside at his sister-in-law's house in Driffield, report to Driffield police station twice a week and was to be allowed to visit the Isle of Man after giving notice to the police. He also had to maintain his own bail security of £240,000 and provide two sureties totalling £250,000.

On 30 May it emerged that the Rovers would only have one team, the first team, in 1996–97, with both the reserve team and youth team not operating. Although Doncaster Council reiterated that their offer to build a multi-million pound stadium at Doncaster Leisure Park still stood, the club, frustrated at the lack of progress in talks with the council, decided to update the facilities at Belle Vue. Some £300,000 was required just to get a safety certificate for the next season but they would also build a new stand at the Town End, which would cost around £700,000. Mr Richardson claimed that he could not afford the improvements to the ground and the running of the other two sides. Consequently Steve Beaglehole was dismissed again, for the third time, along with Jim Golze, youth-team coach and Dave Dew, youth development officer. It was also a disappointing time for Sammy Chung, who had made the development of youth talent a cornerstone of his plans for the club, a strategy which was just beginning to bear fruit with two of the team breaking into the first team at the end of the previous season. At the supporters' club AGM at the Earl of Doncaster Hotel on Thursday 20 June disappointment was expressed at the failure of anyone from the club to attend, although it was pointed out that Sammy Chung and George Foster were on holiday. Ken Avis, the supporters' club secretary, said that many supporters were worried about the future of the club and wanted clarification about the new stadium and the proposed improvements at Belle Vue. He went on to urge club officials to improve their public relations by informing the fans of what was going on at the club. A surprise announcement on the following Tuesday informed the supporters that John Bird had returned to Belle Vue as commercial manager.

July saw the action on the player front warm up as players were shipped out and new ones brought in. Simon Black, a 20-year-old striker from Birmingham City, had already been brought in and two more strikers followed at the beginning of the month: Steve Piearce, 21, from Wolverhampton Wanderers and Martin Paul, 21, from Bristol Rovers, with 22 League appearances to his name. Two more former trainees, both 19 years of age, from Birmingham City, midfielders James Bunch and Ian Jones, were also given trials and experienced midfielder Paul Birch was signed from Wolverhampton Wanderers. Graeme Jones was transferred to Wigan Athletic for a Wigan club record fee of £150,000. The Rovers then spent the second week of July at a naval base in Plymouth honing their fitness levels ready for the start of a new season. On the 24th of the month it was announced that Mr Richardson had changed his mind and was now prepared to fund, out of his own pocket, the reserve and youth teams. Both were accepted back into their respective Leagues, the Pontins Central League and the Northern Intermediate League. As the previous incumbent as director of youth coaching, Steve Beaglehole, had moved on to Nottingham Forest, Pete Schofield, a former Halifax Town player and chief scout at the Rovers for the last three years was appointed to the post, which he combined with his scouting role. A general manager, Mark Weaver, was also appointed.

The pre-season friendlies began on 19 July with a game at Kettering Town but a 'jaded' (Chung's word after the week of training at the naval base) Rovers team were well beaten by three clear goals. Further matches were played at Harrogate Town, where a last-minute penalty by Jon Schofield gave the Rovers a 2–2 draw; at Worcester City, lost 1–0; at Bromsgrove Rovers, a 1–1 draw and at Hednesford Town, where the Rovers gained a 1–0 win with a goal scored directly from a corner kick by Mike Smith. A 2–0 win at Gainsborough Trinity and a 1–1 draw at Northwich Victoria completed the pre-season build-up. The phrase that had been bandied around at this time from the club was that quality would be the rule over quantity as regards the playing staff. As a witness to all these games the author was in a less than happy frame of mind about the season ahead. The fault could not be laid at the manager's door because he could only work with the tools provided by Mr Richardson, the man who brought in the players but the performances against non-League opposition were less than satisfactory, even allowing for it being a new set of players who had not played together before. Further signings had been made during this period: Steve Walker, a midfield player from Blyth Spartans; Alan Gray, a right-back, who had been playing in the US; striker David Larmour, a 20-year-old from Liverpool; Tim Ryan, 21, a left-back from Buxton and previously with Scunthorpe United and Martin McDonald, 22, a midfielder from Southport in the Conference. However, a fee of £35,000 plus two £5,000 payments for appearances and a 20 per cent share of a future transfer fee was fixed by a transfer tribunal on Sean Parrish's move to Northampton Town.

On the last day of July, Mr Richardson appeared before Doncaster Magistrates and successfully applied for a further relaxation of his bail conditions. The new conditions were that he only had to report to the police once a week and would not have to give 48 hours notice to the police before leaving his sister-in-law's house in Driffield on business. His passport, which had been stored at a solicitor's office in Ripon, was to be kept at a law firm in Driffield for ease of retrieval. The proceedings were then adjourned until 29 August.

On Thursday 8 August, Sammy Chung held the first of his regular public meetings at the Park Hotel, where he faced the fans and answered their questions, critical or otherwise. He stayed calm in front of a hostile meeting, even though some of the questions asked were on matters over which he had little control. A week later it was revealed that the Rovers were talking to Kerry Dixon of Second Division Watford, a former Chelsea, Southampton and England centre-forward but he wanted time to think over such a move. The following day, Mr Richardson attended Doncaster County

Jack Lester gets a shot in for the Rovers despite the attentions of the Chester City defenders at Belle Vue.

Court but the case brought by Ian Atkins, the former Rovers manager dismissed by Richardson in July 1994, was settled out of court after lengthy discussions between the two parties' legal representatives. The next day, Saturday 17 August, was the opening day of the Football League season, with the Rovers at home to Carlisle United, relegated from Division Two at the end of the previous season. But the match and the result were academic after the news got around that, 90 minutes before the start of the game, Sammy Chung and George Foster had arrived at the ground to be told that they had been dismissed and Kerry Dixon had been installed as player-manager on a two-year contract, signed just two hours prior to the match. Dixon was introduced to the players by Richardson at 1.45pm, which no doubt stunned the players, who would have been expecting Sammy Chung to walk through the door. The result was a win by a single goal over Carlisle United before a crowd of 3,000, a third of whom had travelled from Cumbria. Three days later, the club hosted York City in the Coca-Cola League Cup first round, first leg, before 1,800 spectators, earning a 1–1 draw, with Colin Cramb scoring his first goal at Belle Vue since he signed for the club. A loss to an early goal at Hereford United followed on the Saturday but on the Wednesday the team picked up their first League point at Exeter City with a terrific strike from Paul Birch in the second half to equalise the score on a rainy summer's evening.

Thursday 29 August was a busy day for Mr Richardson. First he appeared before Doncaster Magistrates, where his case was committed to the Crown Court in September. Then the annual shareholders' meeting was held that evening, at which it was proposed by the club to issue four million shares at 50p each to help fund a proposed new stand at the Town End and team building. These shares would be classed as 'B' shares, which would only carry one hundredth of the voting rights, to safeguard the interests of the existing shareholders of the 1.4 million shares already on the market, to be classed as 'A' shares. The other item of interest was a reported loss for the year ending 31 May 1995 of £350,611. It was also announced that Chic Hicken had resigned from his post of managing director earlier in the month. On the last day of August the Rovers gained their first League win of the season at Belle Vue over Darlington, in a match which finished 3–2. Dixon led the way with an early goal and Cramb and Schofield added the other two.

The Rovers' long and undistinguished run in the League Cup was prolonged on the following Tuesday evening with defeat by two clear goals at York City, although Andy Warrington in the York goal was called upon several times to save the day for the home club and York manager Alan Little was complimentary about the Rovers' exciting football skills, which could see them in with a chance of promotion. Over the next two weeks, Rovers had a goalless draw at home to bottom-of-the-table Mansfield Town, then lost at Scarborough, where Ian Clark was sent off in the last minute and again at Rochdale, against 10 men from the 15th minute and nine men for the second half, before hosting Swansea City in front of 1,391 spectators, who saw them beaten by a single goal, which plunged them down to last place in the League table. After the debacle at Rochdale, manager Dixon brought in Andy King, dismissed as manager of Mansfield Town just two games into the season, to help out on the coaching side. For the Swansea game Wayne Bullimore, a midfield player from Bradford City and Jack Lester, a striker from Sheffield United, were brought in on loan but a stunning strike from Dave Penney gave Swansea the points.

On Tuesday 25 September an advert appeared in a national newspaper, *The Daily Telegraph*, offering Doncaster Rovers for sale. For those who did not read the adverts in national newspapers, the *Doncaster Star* headline on the front page screamed 'Rovers for Sale'. When Saturday came the Rovers hit the local headlines again, or rather Martin McDonald did. As he parked his car at Belle Vue at 7.30am to catch the team coach for the trip to Colchester he was arrested by the local constabulary and taken to the town's police station before being driven to Southport to face questions about a £5,000 cheque that his girlfriend had allegedly banked. Although he had known the Southport police wanted to speak to him it had been difficult to fit it in and when he had a convenient date the police officer connected with the case was off duty. He was later released on bail after the club had arranged legal representation.

All this did not seem to affect the team, however, because they landed at Colchester and went away with a point. McDonald's replacement in the team, Scott Colcombe, played a starring role and scored the first goal, with Schofield netting a penalty just before half-time to put them back in front. All the goals came before the break and six minutes from time Dean Williams, in the Rovers goal, saved a penalty from Tony Adcock to preserve the draw and the point for the Rovers. Monday, the last day of the month, saw Mr Richardson again appear before Doncaster magistrates charged with conspiracy to commit arson. His bail conditions were altered to allow him to report to the police station

Action shot from Rovers' (in blue) pre-season friendly at Northwich Victoria.

in Douglas in the Isle of Man, where his home was and he was then told he would have to appear in court on 18 December at a special hearing to decide if there was a case to answer.

The following day, 1 October, the Rovers took all three points from highly placed Hartlepool United, whom they beat at Belle Vue with goals from Darren Moore and a penalty converted by Cramb. Schofield had a penalty saved early in the first half with the game goalless. This win, their first in six League games, lifted them off the bottom of the table. Later in the week eight players, Gary O'Connor, Steve Walker, Martin Paul, Simon Black, Alan Gray and youngsters Martyn Speight, David Byng and goalkeeper Gavin Leach were all placed on the transfer list in a bid to release funds for further signings. Another win followed, over Leyton Orient at home, on the Saturday, with Cramb and Lester netting in each half in a 2–1 victory. However, they were brought down to earth with a bump a week later, going down to the leaders, Fulham, at Craven Cottage after having Cramb sent off half an hour before time. This was followed in midweek by a visit to high-flying Torquay United and a one-goal defeat, which plunged them down to the next-to-bottom position. Two successive wins followed over bottom club Brighton & Hove Albion at Belle Vue and third-placed Cambridge United at the Abbey Stadium. Brighton were having a horrendous season and had garnered just eight points from 13 games before arriving at Belle Vue, where they suffered defeat by three clear goals. A Friday night game at Cambridge brought a first away win of the season for the Rovers and lifted them to the dizzy heights of mid-table. The last game of the month, in midweek, brought the club back to reality when Lincoln City visited Belle Vue and plundered three points with a 3–1 win after being behind at half-time.

On 30 October Mark Weaver, the Rovers general manager, announced that work on the new 2,000-seater stand at Belle Vue, housing new dressing rooms and hospitality suites, would begin in January. He stated that they had planning permission and had applied for grants from the Football Trust to go towards the cost of the £500,000 project. This effectively ruled out any new stadium being built away from Belle Vue in the near future because the conditions attached to the grants from the Football Trust committed the club to stay at Belle Vue for the foreseeable future.

November started with a home game against Chester City but it proved to be a second successive loss, this time to a late goal. However, two goals from Colin Cramb a week later gave the Rovers victory over Scunthorpe United at Glanford Park. A visit to Second Division Stockport County in the first round of the FA Cup followed and, although Cramb gave the Rovers the lead, it only lasted a few minutes before the home side equalised and they later scored the winning goal. Three days later, on a rain-soaked pitch, the Rovers, much to Dixon's chagrin, lost a third successive home game in the League, in front of a crowd of 1,030, the lowest-ever figure for a League game at Belle Vue. This time it was to Northampton Town under manager Ian Atkins, who was unhappy that his team had not scored many more than two goals, especially after scoring the first one after just 58 seconds. A loss by three goals at Barnet followed on the Saturday but on the last day of the month 1,600-plus fans turned up at Belle Vue to witness the Rovers beat second-placed Cambridge United and complete a League 'double' over the promotion-chasing side. Cambridge led at half-time but a penalty from Colin Cramb and a late winner from Simon Ireland gave the Rovers the points.

Early in December Andy King left the club, where he had assisted Kerry Dixon on a voluntary basis, because of his ongoing fight with Mansfield Town over his severance money. He was replaced by Graham Carr, a former manager of Northampton Town, Blackpool and Maidstone United, as assistant manager but he was dismissed on 28 December as an economy measure, with player-coach Jon Schofield taking over as Dixon's assistant.

On 6 December Ken Richardson and his two colleagues lost their long-standing battle against their conviction for conspiracy to defraud by substituting a three-year-old gelding in a five-furlong race for two-year-old horses at Leicester in 1984. Three appeal judges sitting in London's Appeal Court rejected their claim that their convictions were unsafe. Richardson was ordered to pay £50,000 towards the prosecution costs and would have to meet his own legal costs.

Four days later the Rovers went out of the last Cup competition open to them, the Auto Windscreens Shield, when they lost 2–1 at Belle Vue to Stockport County after leading at half-time through a Cramb penalty. It was little consolation for Dixon that his counterpart at Stockport, Dave Jones, was fulsome in his praise of the Rovers team, considering them unlucky to lose. Both Saturdays either side of this game were blank, the first one being FA Cup second-round day while the second, a home game against Cardiff City, was called off because of international call-ups to the Welsh team.

On Wednesday 18 December Mr Richardson appeared before the Doncaster Stipendiary Magistrate, Peter Jones, charged with conspiracy to commit arson at Belle Vue and was committed to stand trial at Doncaster County Court in 1997. He was granted conditional bail with sureties totalling £250,000. To compound Mr Richardson's problems, Sammy Chung had decided to take the club to an industrial tribunal, claiming 'unfair dismissal' from his post as manager at the beginning of the season.

The Saturday before Christmas had Rovers visiting Boothferry Park but Hull City proved to be too good for them by taking the three points with a 3–1 win and leaving the Rovers fourth from the bottom of the table. An attendance of 1,745 at Belle Vue on Boxing Day witnessed another defeat, this time at the hands of Scarborough but the games at Field Mill against Mansfield Town two days later, at the Vetch Field, Swansea on New Year's Day and at home to Rochdale on the first Saturday in January were all postponed because of the inclement winter weather. The Rovers were now really struggling financially and on the field of play. Dixon had trimmed his playing staff by offloading a dozen or so players but this had not led to him having any money to bring a few players in to lift them up the table.

On Tuesday 7 January Sammy Chung attended an industrial tribunal in Leeds with a claim for unfair dismissal against Doncaster Rovers. However, discussions held before the tribunal convened led to Chung withdrawing his unfair dismissal claim, having accepted an undisclosed sum of money in settlement. The following day George Smith, assistant manager and coach, who had been dismissed by the Rovers in September 1994, settled out of court just before going into the county court to give evidence in a case to resolve his claim for compensation. A further claim for unfair

Martin Pemberton challenges for the ball with Colin Cramb and Jon Schofield in attendance in the game against Fulham at Belle Vue.

Jon Schofield and Kerry Dixon with mascot against Darlington at Belle Vue.

dismissal was still to be held in regard to George Foster, formerly assistant manager to Chung, who had been dismissed at the same time.

The first action on the pitch in the New Year came on Saturday 11 January when a goalless draw was played out at Belle Vue against Colchester United in front of fewer than 1,500 fans. New player-assistant manager Jon Schofield was in charge of the team while Kerry Dixon stayed at home recovering from an illness. However, general manager Mark Weaver was noted by fans to be constantly tripping backwards and forwards from his seat in the stand to the dugout and was barracked by the fans, who obviously thought that instructions were being relayed from the directors' box. Later, Weaver explained that he was indeed relaying messages – from Kerry Dixon, with whom he was in contact throughout the game on his mobile telephone. Dixon was still missing the following week when the Rovers travelled to Hartlepool United and came away with a 4–2 victory courtesy of a goal from skipper Jon Schofield and a hat-trick from Colin Cramb. However, three games in a week were then lost, all away from home, to Mansfield Town, Lincoln City and Swansea City. The Rovers included two new signings at Swansea – Simon Ireland from Mansfield Town, on a permanent deal after a period on loan and Darren Esdaille from non-League club Hyde United – but lost a man when Colin Cramb was sent off after receiving two bookings. The month ended with the club's application for a Football Trust grant to help them build a new stand being put on hold because the Trust had been forced to put a moratorium on grants due to the uncertainty about funding. It hoped to release the funds in April. The club reiterated that the council's offer of a new ground was a non-starter, despite the supporters pushing for acceptance of the offer.

In January the Rovers management looked to the Northern Premier League for new recruits but only upset a number of clubs, with two of them, Hyde United and Droylsden, reporting the Rovers to the FA for alleged illegal approaches to players. Firstly they made an offer of £1,500 to Ashton United for Padi Wilson, which Ashton United turned down as 'derisory' (he went to Plymouth Argyle in the summer for £15,000) and resulted in angry words being exchanged between the two clubs. Then the Rovers signed Darren Esdaille on non-contract forms without, according to Hyde United, giving the required seven days notice of an approach. The non-League club claimed that the first they knew of the transaction was when Esdaille made his League debut at Swansea. However, even if the Rovers had given the required notice, the FA regulations stated that a notice of approach could not be served on more than one player at the same club in any period of 28 days. Before taking Esdaille the Rovers had served a seven-days notice to Hyde United for Val Owen, who declined the offer. The Rovers also gave the required notice for Demis Ohandjanian of Curzon Ashton but later served a seven-days notice on that club for Paul Edwards before the 28 days notice for Ohandjanian had passed. Edwards did join Rovers but it was a year later. Then, on 15 February Harvey Cunningham and Michael Beirne were waiting in the Droylsden car park having been selected to play for that club at Leigh RMI when both players were picked up by car and transported to Doncaster to play for the Rovers against

Barnet. Beirne, however, went back to Droylsden the following week and continued to play for them for the rest of the season. Esdaille and Cunningham signed two-year contracts for the Rovers. Then, in late March, Alan Fahy was signed from Barrow for the princely sum of £1,500.

The first day of February brought Scunthorpe United to Belle Vue, with Colin Cramb securing a 1–1 draw in an entertaining game played in front of a season-best crowd of 3,022. But a week later a depleted Rovers team visited the Deva Stadium at Chester and left after a six-goal drubbing against a club who had not scored a goal in their last seven League games at home. Dean Williams, the Rovers goalkeeper, was sent off for disputing the awarding of a penalty in the 88th minute, Chester having scored from the spot five minutes earlier, which had brought Williams his first booking for dissent. Colin Cramb went into goal and dived the right way to save from Jonathan Jones, who had scored from the first penalty. The Rovers were now second-from-bottom in the League, just six points above Brighton, who were in the throes of a revival in a desperate attempt to stay in the League.

On 11 February Mr Richardson appeared at Sheffield County Court for a pre-trial hearing but the judge was told that the case would not be heard until some time in 1998, at least a year away. He would continue to be under bail conditions until the trial commenced. Meanwhile, it came out that the Rovers had not paid Sammy Chung the five-figure sum of money, about £25,000, that had been agreed in the previous month to obviate the case going to an industrial tribunal and he had now issued a winding-up order against the club. Mark Weaver admitted they had not paid a penny of it for the simple reason that the club had no money.

At the same time Brighton had won in midweek and closed to within three points of the Rovers and, if they won an appeal against the deduction of two points for a pitch invasion by their fans during a match against Lincoln City earlier in the season, that would come down to a one-point deficit. Other clubs, Hereford United, Exeter City and Darlington in particular, were also in the danger zone but they had a four, three and two-point advantage over the Yorkshire club. At this time just one club went down to the Conference at the end of a season and, with the current run of form, it could be the Rovers. Mr Weaver had called for the fans to back the team at the next game against Barnet instead of demonstrating against Mr Richardson and himself and just over 2,000 turned up to witness a 1–1 draw against a team whose last win had been over the Rovers back in November. The club had distributed 5,000 tickets to local schools for the match so this could well have bumped up the attendance by a few. The Rovers team, short of six regular players through injury and suspensions, included four new signings: Harvey Cunningham and Michael Beirne from Northern Premier League club Droylsden and two loan signings, Simon Weaver from Sheffield Wednesday and Adie Mike from Stockport County.

Early the next week came more adverse publicity for the club when they admitted that Jim Golze, the youth-team coach, had been suspended while the police investigated allegations of assault following complaints from some members of the team. It would be Easter before the Crown Prosecution Service told him that there would be no charges brought against him. Troubles continued to pile up against the club when, in addition to the winding-up order from Sammy Chung, others were received from George Smith, Steve Beaglehole and TOFFS, The Old-Fashioned Football Shirt Company of Gateshead, who were owed a total of £1,400. When they threatened the club with legal action to recover the debt they had been told 'to join the queue'. This led to Mark Weaver issuing a strident appeal to the town's business community to back the club or lose it.

Against this background the team travelled to Northampton, where the local Town club beat them by two clear goals. The Rovers had skipper Jon Schofield back from suspension but were still without Colin Cramb and had to include teenage 'keeper Adam Wheeler for his League debut because Dean Williams was suspended and Gary O'Connor was injured. The anger of the fans was shown at Sixfields when three supporters of the club went on to the pitch at half-time to orchestrate shouts of 'sack the Board' and 'Weaver out'. The club, who struggled to find the money to pay for the coach that took them to Northampton and had not paid their players and staff in the previous week, were now in dire straits financially and on the pitch, as the results that weekend showed. Brighton won, Exeter City beat Darlington and Hereford United got a point at Lincoln, which left the Rovers just one point in front of Brighton but four points adrift of Darlington, the nearest club to them in the table. Further pitch protests were promised by fans at the home game against Wigan Athletic but Mr Weaver was quoted as saying that the demonstration was pointless because Ken Richardson had already agreed to sell the club if someone came in with the money. Walking away from the club at this point would see it go under, because he was the only one putting any money in. The wage bill was £20,000 a fortnight and the income £20,000 a month, so the money had to come out of his own pocket.

Then, at a supporters' meeting at the Park Hotel on Thursday 27 February, came the confirmation of something that the supporters had always suspected. Kerry Dixon admitted to the assembled fans (so many that they had to move to a larger room) that 'I'm not the manager of the club. I'm the trainer, coach and friend to the players. Who picks the team? I advise Mr Richardson, that's all.' He went on to say that Paul Birch, one of the club's best players, was not even allowed to play for the reserve team because of a falling-out with Mr Richardson, who took offence to Birch arguing with him and making his opinions known in front of the other players. As Mr Richardson was the boss and paid the wages, he ultimately made all the decisions. The fans did not blame Dixon for the club's plight and made that clear to the manager but Mark Weaver received a hostile reception when he spoke. His overall message to the fans was that he would plead with Mr Richardson to play Birch against Wigan but his advice to the beleaguered owner would be to sell the club and give it back to the town. It was also revealed by the shareholders' group spokesman, Alan Criddle, that one group of people had made an offer for the club and another had asked for further talks with the council.

Mr Weaver's pleading must have been eloquent because Paul Birch started the game against Wigan Athletic that Friday night and inspired the team to a two-goal win, their first in eight games, through goals from Colin Cramb, who outshone former Rovers player Graeme Jones and Adie Mike. This win took the Rovers on to 33 points, a four-point advantage over Brighton but they were three points adrift of the next club, Hereford United, who were one point behind Hartlepool United and Darlington.

Rovers players celebrate Colin Cramb's goal against Hull City at Boothferry Park.

Gary O'Connor.

An unchanged team represented the Rovers on the first Saturday in March against Hull City at Belle Vue in front of the biggest crowd of the season, 3,274, of which 1,200 came from Hull. A goalless draw represented the one point that kept the Rovers in front of Brighton, who had won and cut the deficit to the next club, Hereford United, to two points. The next match was on a Friday night at Ninian Park against a team in a Play-off place, Cardiff City. However, despite Paul Birch being left out of the team, an early goal by Darren Moore set the tone of the game for both teams. The Welshmen grew increasingly nervous as the game went on, with the result settled in the 62nd minute when a 40-yard up-and-under from Darren Utley went into the net off the underside of the bar, much to the amazement of the player himself but admired by his team mates, who bowed in supplication to him. The following day Brighton & Hove Albion, Hartlepool United and Exeter City lost, Darlington drew and Hereford United won at top-of-the-table Carlisle United. The bottom of the table read: Darlington 37 games/39 points; Hereford United 38/39; Exeter City 38/39; Hartlepool United 38/38; Doncaster Rovers 36/37; Brighton & Hove Albion 38/33.

The Rovers were struggling with injuries, especially in the forward department. Kerry Dixon had not played since Boxing Day because of injury, Steve Piearce had a knee injury, Adie Mike was injured against Cardiff and Colin Cramb was struggling to be fit for the game against Hereford United. Consequently the club tried to bring in a player on loan but several Rovers players had not received the stage payments of their signing-on fees and had taken the case to the Professional Footballers' Association, who had slapped a transfer embargo on the club. Mr Richardson then had to pay out £23,000 in unpaid wages, stage payments and medical bills so that the PFA embargo on signing players was lifted. Kerry Dixon, Paul Marquis and Gary O'Connor signed a waiver to allow unpaid amounts due to them to be paid after Easter. The lifting of the embargo enabled the club to bring in Martin Pemberton on a free transfer from Oldham Athletic and former Wrexham player Lewis Coady came in on a non-contract basis. Both went straight into the team for the match against Hereford United on the evening of Friday 21 March. Colin Cramb came through his injury problem and early in the second half headed the goal that gave the Rovers the three points. The following Tuesday they ran in three goals without reply against Rochdale at Belle Vue. This fourth win in the last five games moved the Rovers up to 18th place, seven points in front of bottom club Brighton and with a game in hand over all of the clubs below them.

The following day, Wednesday 26 March, the club survived the winding-up order brought by Sammy Chung and heard at the Courts of Justice in Manchester. The Rovers asked for 28 days to put their financial affairs in order and

Chung instructed his legal representative not to raise any objection. Thursday 27 March was transfer deadline day, with the Rovers shipping out Paul Birch on a free to Exeter City and Tim Ryan going to Altrincham on loan to the end of the season. The Saturday brought the Rovers a visit to Cumbria to meet the League leaders, Carlisle United. Contrary to all expectations, they got a point from a goalless draw but on Easter Monday their unbeaten run of six games came to an end when Exeter City, below the Rovers in the table, came to Belle Vue and went back to Devon with all three points from a 2–1 victory. Schofield had given the Rovers a half-time lead but two goals in 10 second-half minutes from Glyn Crowe settled the Rovers' fate. They had not conceded a goal in those six unbeaten games and had gone 606 minutes before Crowe broke that record. This defeat plunged the team back into the relegation mix, two points behind Darlington, who had 46 points but three points in front of Hereford United and Hartlepool United, with Brighton & Hove Albion two points further back.

The first Saturday in April brought another crucial six-pointer against Darlington at the Feethams ground. Kerry Dixon took a place on the bench but did not come on. Goals from Martin Pemberton and a brace from Colin Cramb meant that the Rovers took the honours and a jump up the table to 19th place, level on 47 points with Exeter City, leaving Darlington with 46 points, Hereford United and Hartlepool United with 42 and Brighton with 39. The Rovers and Darlington had five more games to play, the others just four. The following Tuesday the Rovers entertained Cardiff City, who were in the last Play-off place, at Belle Vue. A crowd of 1,989 were entertained to a feast of goals, with the teams sharing six goals. The visitors took a two-goal lead before Darren Moore pulled one back and Jon Schofield equalised 10 minutes from time. In a frenetic finish, the Welshmen took the lead again after 88 minutes but Ian Gore powered in a header in the next minute to give the Rovers a much-needed point. This took them above Leyton Orient on goals scored but Darlington, also playing their game in hand, beat third-placed Carlisle United and jumped above both clubs. The next game had the Rovers visiting Brisbane Road, where the Orient took the points with a 2–1 win, thus taking them to safety. The clubs below them were still not mathematically safe with just three games to go – Darlington 49 points, Torquay United 49, Doncaster Rovers 48, Exeter City 48, Hereford United 45, Hartlepool United 44, Brighton & Hove Albion 42. A goalless draw at home to second-placed Fulham before a near 3,000 crowd put the Rovers on the brink of safety because Brighton only drew at Cambridge. This meant that the Yorkshiremen were six points in front of the Seagulls with two games to go and the next game was a meeting of the two clubs at the Goldstone Ground at Brighton.

This was not just a meeting that would decide who went down, it was also the last-ever game at the Goldstone Ground, which had been sold to developers by the club's owners. With no provision for a new ground, this factor drew the ire of the Seasiders fans, who, together with the Rovers fans, had had a traumatic season. In the meantime Scott Colcombe and Stuart Doling, both of whom had been dogged by injury, were released with the cancellation of their contracts by mutual consent. Thus the last Saturday of April produced a tense afternoon at Goldstone Road before a big crowd, 11,341, although the fans of both teams saluted each other in their common cause of acrimony towards their club's owners. In the 19th minute, a clash between Darren Moore and Ian Baird resulted in blows being struck and the inevitable red card was shown to both of them. Then, halfway through the second half, the home team struck a decisive blow when Stuart Storer scored from close range following a corner. Brighton held their lead to the end and set up a thrilling finale for their last match, against Hereford United at Hereford, who had just replaced Brighton at the bottom of the League after losing at the Orient. For the Rovers, despite losing, it meant safety. They still had 49 points but both Brighton and Hereford had 46 points and, as they had to play each other, the Rovers could not finish at the bottom of the pile.

While they were safe on the playing side it came to pass on Monday 28 April that they were still in danger of going under financially. John Bird, the commercial manager, had been dismissed a week earlier as an economy measure, while Stuart Doling, Scott Colcombe and Tim Ryan had their contracts cancelled 'by mutual consent'. So on the aforementioned date, at a court hearing in Manchester, the Inland Revenue demanded a sum of £190,000 towards a total bill of £250,000, otherwise they wanted the club to be wound up. Other unnamed creditors supported this action, which Sammy Chung had asked to be adjourned because he had received a large payment towards what the club owed him. Maynard Connor, the Rovers' lawyer, suggested that the sale of players would bring in enough money to pay the debts but under FA transfer rules this could not be done until June. The judge adjourned the hearing until 23 May to allow the club to submit evidence that enough money could be raised through the sale of players.

The final game, at home to Torquay United, could have been played in a celebratory atmosphere with the club escaping relegation but an article in the programme for the match incensed the supporters. Written under Mark Weaver's name, the article made an attempt to put before the fans exactly what Ken Richardson had done for the club. The article branded the club's record under Dixon a 'disaster' and handed the credit to Richardson for saving the club from relegation by taking over the team towards the end of the season. Supporters at the match chanted throughout the game for the removal of Richardson and Weaver while giving their backing to Kerry Dixon but Weaver said the chanting and demonstration was pointless and uncalled for because if Richardson walked out it would mean the end for the club. He was the only one putting any money in and there was nobody else interested in taking over the club. The two groups that had expressed an interest earlier in the year had lost interest after being told by the council that there was no prospect of a new ground being built in the near future. In addition, the club had been told by the Football Licensing Authority that they would have to supply a written assurance before the end of May that ground improvements totalling £100,000 would be carried out before the next season started, the inference being that if the club failed to meet the deadline they would not be included in the fixture list. Weaver finished by saying 'Once again, it is down to Ken Richardson to save the day.'

And so to the match against Torquay United. The result was incidental but it ended in a win for the Rovers with two goals, from Simon Ireland and Martin McDonald, to one for Torquay. Before the match Darren Moore was presented with the supporters' club Player of the Year Trophy for the second year running, finishing a long way in front of anybody else. Kerry Dixon also started a game for the first time since Boxing Day. The win left the Rovers in 19th place on 52 points, five more than Hereford United, who were relegated because they had scored three goals less than Brighton & Hove Albion, who also had 47 points. A total of 39 players were used in the Football League matches, a situation that speaks for itself. Only six players played in 30 or more games, so the scale of player turnover was not conducive to good results. The average attendance at Belle Vue was 1,993, helped considerably by the policy of handing out tickets to local schools.

With the season ended, five players, Alan Fahy, Lee Anderson, Lewis Coady, Adam Wheeler and Demis Ohandjanian were given free transfers and six more, Darren Utley, Mark Hawthorne, Steve Piearce, Ian Clark, Mike Smith and David Larmour were put on the open-to-transfer list. Later, Paul Marquis refused a new contract and left the club and Gary O'Connor's contract was terminated 'by mutual consent'. This clear-out of players made the supporters wonder whether they would have a club to support for the next season. Would Mr Richardson take umbrage at the treatment he had received during the last match (he was reported to have been very angry) and refuse to put money in to bring new players to the club? Mr Richardson had said that the youth team cost about £150,000 to run and that the money could be spent better somewhere else, so once again the youth policy at the club was at risk. But he left the final decision to his general manager, Mark Weaver. Kerry Dixon wanted the youth team to continue because it represented the future of the club and so passionate was he on the subject that he went out to find sponsorship. He succeeded in getting financial pledges from prominent local businessmen and firms to a total of £70,000. Meanwhile public relations, which had been a disaster since Dinard took over, were not helped by Mark Weaver accusing the people of the town of failing to support the club. He apologised later when he found out the amount of financial support given to the club by people buying lottery tickets for the Alpha Tote draw, which he had little knowledge of because it was run by the supporters' club to raise money for the football club. The other news coming out of the club was a statement to the effect that the club would attempt to stand on their own two feet because, as Mark Weaver pointed out, every time he went to Mr Richardson with a begging bowl it increased the size of the financial debt owed to the main shareholder, who would expect to be repaid when he left the club. Consequently, the Rovers' offer to meet Doncaster Council in a bid to restart the talks about a new ground was largely welcomed by the fans.

On Friday 23 May, at the High Court in Manchester, the club faced a winding-up order over unpaid monies. The judge rejected a request for another adjournment to give the club time to sell players but agreed to adjourn the hearing so that an application for an administration order under the Insolvency Act 1986 could be made. Another hearing would take place on 12 June. The financial position of the club had recently worsened because Mr Richardson had announced that he would no longer put any more money into the club. Mark Weaver urged people to come forward and buy the B issue shares issued the previous August. Very few of the £2 million worth of 50 pence shares had been sold. With the club now being run by an administrator, whose main job was to clear the club's debts, primarily by selling players or releasing them, the question arose as to whether he would sanction the safety work needed on the ground to enable the club to obtain a safety certificate. The Football Licensing Authority had told the club that 2 June was the latest date for the receipt of details of the £100,000 of safety work needed for a safety certificate. Although the Football Trust would pay 75 per cent of the cost, the club had to find the money first and the contractors had to be paid before the club could claim the money back. Without the necessary certificate the club would not have a ground to play on in 1997–98, which threw into doubt their status as members of the football league.

The *Doncaster Free Press* of 29 May carried a front page banner headline 'ROVERS: IS THIS THE END?', under which the paper, after outlining the position of the club, quoted fans urging the owners to sell their shares and allow a takeover. The following day it was reported in the *Doncaster Star* that former player-manager of the Rovers, Dave Cusack, had expressed an interest on behalf of a consortium headed by Anton Johnson, who had previously been involved at Rotherham United and Southend United. Mr Cusack said that they had made an offer the previous year when the club was advertised for sale but had never had a reply. The continuing problems at the club had hit season-

Jon Schofield challenges for the ball in a Rovers attack on the Brighton goal in the last match at the Goldstone Ground.

ticket sales and Mark Weaver reported that his appeal to supporters and businessmen to buy shares had fallen on deaf ears, with no donations coming in either. He was also finding it difficult to find accountants to take the administrator's job because they feared they would not get paid! Eventually a Preston-based accountancy firm, Buchler, Phillips, Traynor, who were experienced in football administration orders, having dealt with Millwall, Tottenham Hotspur, Barnet and Darlington, were appointed, with John Eddleton and Andrew Dick as joint administrators.

On Thursday 12 June the Rovers appeared at Manchester High Court, where the administrators applied to oversee the Rovers' affairs. They also hoped to persuade the Inland Revenue not to wind the club up. The judge adjourned the case for a further fortnight to give the administrator more time to turn things round. It also emerged that day that Mr Richardson's lawyer, Paul Dumbleton, had left his home in Ripon, which had been repossessed by a building society and left his staff unpaid, along with various creditors. The following Monday the club were told that they had to guarantee to cover the next season's projected losses or face being wound up. The administrators said guarantees were needed to a total of £250,000 in order to satisfy the High Court and the Football League.

The Football League had included Rovers in the 1997–98 fixtures, their first fixture being at Shrewsbury Town on 9 August. But the financial situation of the club meant that the only players they would be able to sign were free-transfer men and as one player came in another would have to move out. Earlier in the month Mark Weaver had tried to bring down the wages bill but after agreeing details with several players he was told that there was no money available to pay them off. Ten days later, at Leeds High Court, the winding-up order was dismissed in favour of an administration order granted to the club, which protected the club from its creditors. The hearing was told that the club was worth £700,000 but had made losses last year totalling £800,000, to give an overall deficit of £2.6 million. However, Mr Richardson said that he was willing to put in £80,000 of his own money to keep the club going. It also emerged at the hearing that Doncaster Council, who leased the ground to the Rovers, would assist with the building of a new stadium if the club's directors thought that was the only way to survive. The hearing was told that the current site was valued at £150,000 but if a change-of-use application was successful so that retailers could use the site it would be valued at around £2.5 million. The players at the club were valued at £1.3 million, with the transfer fee for Darren Moore, who had joined Bradford City, due to be decided by a Football League Tribunal. The appointment of Andrew Dick and John Eddleton of Buchler, Phillips, Traynor as joint administrators of Doncaster Rovers was confirmed. With the official confirmation of administrators, the first job for Andrew Dick was to go with Mark Weaver, on the following day, to a

Martin Paul.

Martyn Speight.

Colin Cramb with mascot.

Football League meeting in Newcastle to give an update on the club's situation. The administrators later issued a statement revealing that the club had debts totalling around £3.9 million but said they were confident that, with the support of various parties, including the Football League and the local authority, a rescue package could be formulated for the benefit of the club's creditors and also to ensure professional football continued in Doncaster.

A few days later, the administrator, John Eddleton, said that scrapping the youth policy at the club was one of three options that he was considering to stem the club's losses. Any benefits from the youth policy were long term and his priority had to be the immediate future of the first team. He had to give assurances to the Football League that the club would be able to fulfil their fixtures in the coming season and scrapping the youth team would have less effect on the first team than some other measures. However, if anyone wished to put money into the youth programme he urged them to contact him at the ground without delay. He had eight days to come up with a package to satisfy the creditors, so he needed to make some big decisions over the following two

Kerry Dixon feels lonely among the Rochdale players at Spotland.

days. If the club raised £45,000, which would attract a similar sum from Sportsmatch, the youth policy could then be administered by the Doncaster Youth Trust. Kerry Dixon backed this approach and met with the businessmen who had previously pledged financial support for the youth team.

One piece of good news came late in July when the transfer embargo on the club was lifted, although the financial conditions put on the club by the administration order did not allow the signing of a lot of players. In the meantime Colin Cramb had moved to Bristol City in Division Two for a fee fixed by a transfer tribunal of £150,000, plus 25 per cent of any future transfer fee, a decision that the club were not very happy about, having valued Cramb at £750,000 against an offer of £50,000 from Bristol City. Meanwhile, the supporters' club held their AGM at the Park Hotel, at which they expressed dissatisfaction at the uncertainty and total confusion at the club. Vice-chairman Ken Wilkinson said that they were concerned about the club's situation and he personally could not see any light at the end of the tunnel under the current regime. Having lurched from one crisis to another, the only hope was a change of ownership. The secretary, Ken Avis, said in his report that recent years had been traumatic for the club and last season had been no exception. The comings and goings of players and backroom staff had not been a recipe for success and supporters had become disillusioned, leading to a drop in membership from 425 a year ago to 295. He also criticised the club for the way the supporters' club had been treated. Geoff Wilson of the Football Licensing Authority attended as a guest speaker and told the meeting that the club were proceeding with essential ground improvements and safety work. The supporters' club were in favour of a takeover and expressed a desire for a delegation to meet the administrator.

With the club in administration, thoughts turned to the new season. Colin Richardson, a former manager of Bridlington Town and a man renowned in the North East for winning trophies in non-League football, was appointed assistant manager by Ken Richardson without the knowledge of Kerry Dixon. Towards the end of July, Darren Brookes, a centre-back from Worksop Town, was signed on a two-year contract as a full-time professional and Gary Ingham, a goalkeeper from Gainsborough Trinity, signed a one-year contract as a part-time professional. A series of pre-season friendlies were played, with the team made up of contracted professionals, youth-team players and trialists. A goalless draw at Northern Premier League club Guiseley was followed by a hammering by four clear goals at Morecambe, who were in the Conference. Two 1–0 defeats followed, at Northwich Victoria of the Conference and at Belle Vue to Premier League newcomers Barnsley. The match against Barnsley was Jon Schofield's last game in a Rovers shirt because he was transferred to Mansfield Town later in the week. As one of the club's highest-paid players he simply had to go. A win did come at Halifax Town, another team from the Conference, against whom they would win by a good margin in the forthcoming season, with a goal from Paul Conlon but they followed this with a loss by two clear goals at Belle Vue against a second-string Sheffield Wednesday side.

Then, at the end of July, Brent Peters, who had been brought in by Ken Richardson as a coach in March but had left the club at the end of the season, went public about the footballing side of affairs at the club during his short time there. He predicted that the Rovers would drop to the Conference if Ken Richardson continued to interfere in team matters. He said that Mr Richardson had regularly overruled Kerry Dixon's decisions, claiming that Mr Richardson wanted to pick the side, decide the tactics, do the team talks and make the substitutions. The team did well at the end of the season because they had responded to Dixon's calls for them to be professional despite the situation. Even the administrator andrew Dicks, said a manager should be allowed to manage, which included supervising training, deciding the tactics and selecting the team. Mark Weaver, the general manager, responded by saying that the club depended on Mr Richardson's involvement. If Ken Richardson did not pick the team he would lose interest and if he did that then the town would not have a club, because they had yet to see the colour of anybody's money regarding any takeover. If football was to continue in the town then they needed Ken Richardson.

August came and the team travelled to Shrewsbury, where they were beaten 2–1, the Rovers goal scored by Paul Conlon. Shrewsbury missed a penalty just after half-time when Paul Evans hit the bar and on 54 minutes Darren Esdaille received his marching orders after a second booking. However, the ugly side of football showed itself when some fans, on the way home from Shrewsbury, stopped at the home of Mark Weaver in Stockport issuing threats, banging on doors, threatening to break the windows and terrifying the residents of the neighbourhood. The next game, a League Cup first-round first-leg tie against Nottingham Forest, a team just relegated from the Premier League to Division One, had been eagerly anticipated and an attendance of 4,547 came to see the Rovers humiliated 8–0 by a team containing the likes of Steve Chettle, Geoff Thomas, Pierre Van Hooijdonk and Dean Saunders. The crowd chanted continuously throughout the game 'Richardson out' and 'Sack the Board'.

In a national newspaper Richardson was quoted as saying that Dixon had asked him to pick the team in the previous season but Dixon replied that he had taken the job in the first place because he thought he had something to offer, so why would he hand over the job of selecting a team to someone else? This war of words fought out in the national newspapers caused Mark Weaver to step in, bring the warring parties together and read the Riot Act, because the battle to save the club needed everyone to pull together. He also dismissed the speculation that Dixon would be leaving, insisting that he would still be at the club at the end of the season.

Two days before the visit of Peterborough United to Belle Vue Martin McDonald signed a new two-year contract to the end of 1998–99 but despite a hard-working display from the midfield man the Posh smashed five past the unfortunate Gary Ingham without reply. The chants against Richardson and Weaver were heard again but as the goals flowed past the Rovers 'keeper in the second half some mounted police stationed themselves at the end of the Popular Stand when a pitch invasion looked likely, with other police taking a position around the directors' box, where the fans demonstrated after the match for about an hour. Police had advised both men not to leave the ground until the demonstrators had dispersed. On Thursday 21 September Kerry Dixon left the club after agreeing a settlement figure with the administrator for the 11 months left on his contract. Leaving the club was not what he wanted and neither was the financial settlement but enough was enough so he accepted what was offered and walked away. This left Mark Weaver to run the day-to-day team affairs, Colin Richardson doing the coaching and Ken Richardson selecting the team. A visit to Macclesfield Town two days later included Jim Dobbin, signed the previous day after his release from Rotherham United but it ended in a three-goal defeat, with the Rovers fans at the match expressing their views about Richardson, sat in the dugout, throughout the game. After the match they waved banners in front of the Rovers team coach, which the police escorted away from Macclesfield for a good eight miles. The Rovers gained some respect in the second leg of the League Cup game at Nottingham Forest, where they went down to defeat by the odd goal in three but two home defeats followed to Exeter City and Leyton Orient in front of crowds of 1,186 and 1,098 respectively. Before the Exeter game Ken Richardson made an appeal to supporters through the local media to put their dislike of him to one side and get behind the team. The appeal obviously went unheard because many of the fans demonstrated continuously on the terracing in front of the directors' box. Exeter moved to the top of the table with this win, leaving the Rovers stranded at the bottom without a point to their name after four games. In the Orient game the crowd got behind the team in the first half and the Rovers went in at half-time leading by a goal from Prince Moncrieffe but the second half was a totally different story. The Orient got their nose in front with two goals before the hour when Martin McDonald was sent off for a foul on the goalkeeper. Two more goals for the Orient settled the issue and gave the fans an excuse to resume their chanting for Richardson to go. The local evening and weekly papers were full of readers' letters demanding that Mr Richardson sell up and go for the benefit of the club, because his intransigence over the amount of money he wanted and his handling of the club was driving it into the ground and, along with the 'Donnygate' political situation, was making the town a laughing stock to the rest of the country.

The next game was at Field Mill against Mansfield Town on the first Friday in September, the match having been brought forward from the Saturday, which was the day of Princess Diana's funeral. Here the Rovers gained their first point with a second-half equaliser from Prince Moncrieffe. The following Monday's evening paper carried the story that Ken Richardson and Mark Weaver had decided to stay on until a new stadium was built 'to show the fans that we are genuine and not just looking to make a financial killing as has been claimed'. This news took the Anton Johnson consortium by surprise, leading to their advisor, Clive Purdy, seeking urgent talks with the administrators. He told the evening newspaper that the consortium had made an offer to the administrators who were currently considering their response. The offer in writing was £1.5 million to cover the money owed to the creditors. The administrators, after consultations with Mr Richardson, had indicated that he was looking for a higher fee, so the consortium was considering the position. He went on to say that an offer had been made to the shareholders, of which Dinard and Mr Richardson were the biggest holders of shares as well as the biggest creditors but there had been no response. The supporters' club hierarchy, Ken Wilkinson and Charles Walker, publicly called for Mr Richardson to go as he had lost all credibility with the club's fans and the club were now in a worse position, financially and on the field of play, than when he took over four years previously. Then came news that the only consortium bidding for the club had made an increased offer, which was accepted by the administrators and the small shareholders but blocked by the main shareholders. The week of activity off the field ended with the Rovers going to Scunthorpe and picking up another point with a goal from Martin

Ian Gore and mascots before the match against Nottingham Forest at Belle Vue in the League Cup.

McDonald, a result that stopped the Iron going top of the division. A goalless draw at home to Cambridge United followed with the now customary verbal abuse directed at Richardson and Weaver, who were both escorted away in the last minute of the game.

On the morning of Friday 26 September, at the Moat House Hotel, Warmsworth, a creditors' meeting was held to hear proposals outlining a repayment plan. The main creditors, Dinard Trading and Mr Richardson, agreed to defer their debt of £850,000 but other creditors could not agree on the package of measures put to them, so a further meeting would be held a week later. This meeting, on Friday 3 October, turned out to be rather heated, as minor creditors voted against accepting an offer from Dinard Trading of £350,000 to be paid to them at 18 pence for each pound they were owed. However, the major creditors – Richardson, Dinard and the Inland Revenue – had a controlling vote which was enough to push the offer through. Many of the shareholders said they would rather see the club go under than see it continue under Mr Richardson. Undaunted, Mr Richardson stated afterwards that if fans did not come to games they would still play, even if there was no one there. It was also revealed that a £1.85 million offer from the Johnson consortium had been rejected by Mr Richardson. Mr Weaver later said Mr Richardson would not sell for less than £3 million.

The following day, Brighton & Hove Albion, who were experiencing the same problem as the Rovers and had had their ground sold from under their feet, were visitors to Belle Vue. Joining together with the Rovers fans, they subjected Messrs Richardson and Weaver to sustained verbal abuse throughout the first half, with Mr Richardson leaving the ground altogether during half-time. A minor pitch invasion at half-time was cleared by police and stewards, with several people ejected from the ground. After the game, which Brighton won by 3–1 to register their first away win for 11 months, the fans gathered in front of the Main Stand to protest noisily but peacefully. The Rovers team included a goalkeeper, David Smith, from Bramhall who played in Cheshire local football and Rod Thornley from North-West Counties team Warrington Town, while half the team came from non-League football below the Conference.

The follow-up to Saturday's protests by the club was to announce the closure of the Main Stand terracing on the grounds of safety after reports of coins being thrown at the directors' box. But Mr Richardson decided to give up his role in charge of team affairs for the next game against Hartlepool United at Belle Vue in a bid to quell the dissatisfaction of the fans, because all that had been going on off the field was affecting some of the players, who preferred to play away from home. However, this gesture was nullified with news that the supporters' club, who had had an office at the ground since their inception in 1921, had been unceremoniously thrown out because Weaver said they were the hub of the protests during games. As for the game itself, the Rovers held a two-goal lead, both scored by Prince Moncrieffe, with seven minutes to play but were held to a 2–2 draw. Whether the fans' walkout after 75 minutes had much to do with it was open to conjecture. The following week's match at Darlington saw the Rovers go in at half-time all square at one apiece thanks to a goal from Prince Moncrieffe on the stroke of the break but the second half was a different story as four goals by the home club completed a rout by 5–1. This defeat was, apparently, the last straw for Mr Richardson. Mark Weaver stated that the major shareholder would no longer pick the team, or loan any more money to the club, although he was not going to recall his loan. He would not be attending any more matches because he had been badly let down by the players at Darlington. The following Tuesday came the announcement that Dave Cowling, a former Huddersfield Town winger and director of youth at the Rovers for the past 12 months, had taken over the previous day as the first-team coach in charge of team affairs, with Colin Richardson as his assistant. His first task was to pick a team to go to Colchester United that night and win some points, having received assurances that he would have a free hand in team selection. They lost by two goals to one from Martin McDonald after going two down in the first six minutes. Sat in the stand with Mark Weaver were Anton Johnson and Dave Cusack, who were negotiating a takeover with Mr Richardson. They also appeared in the directors' box alongside Mr Weaver at the next game, at home to Swansea City and saw another woeful loss by three clear goals, which Cowling described as the worst performance he had ever seen from a Football League club. Dave Cowling, who had said that if the terms of his appointment were changed he would walk away, did just that on the morning of Wednesday 29 October after nine days in the job, citing interference in selecting the team. Matters had come to a head when Mr Weaver handed him a list of names, saying that that was the team to play in a reserve match against Scarborough that night and the same team would play the following Saturday at Scarborough in the first-team League match. Cowling immediately quit his post.

Instead, Danny Bergara, who had left Rotherham United in April, was invited to watch the reserve team and agreed to help the club out for the next few games. This was because a deal had been agreed between Mr Richardson, Dinard Trading and Anton Johnson, subject to the solicitors drawing up the necessary papers. Mr Weaver stated that Mr Richardson and his family had decided to leave

Defender Steve Sanders throws the ball in at Shrewsbury Town's Gay Meadow ground. Notice a lack of sponsors names on shirts.

their money as an interest-free loan to the club until Anton Johnson could pay it back. While the fans celebrated the news at a meeting held in the Park Hotel, there was just one fly in the ointment. The Football League intimated that if Anton Johnson took an active role in the management of the club they would investigate him. In 1984 the Football League had been all set to investigate Mr Johnson for having an interest in two clubs, which was against League rules but he had left the game before it could be carried out, prompting the League to say that if he ever entered football again he would be investigated.

Danny Bergara.

On 1 November the Rovers suffered another heavy defeat when they lost by four clear goals at Scarborough. They were bottom of the division, seven points behind the next team, Brighton & Hove Albion, after 15 games. Three days later, just 1,004 fans turned up at Belle Vue to see the Rovers get a 1–1 draw against Cardiff City, with Prince Moncrieffe getting the Rovers goal to put them in the lead, which only lasted five minutes. In the directors' box were Anton Johnson and Kerry Dixon, who would be the new manager when the takeover went through, with John Ryan taking over as chairman. The following week the Rovers got a point at Barnet from a 1–1 draw but it meant that they had gone 17 League games from the beginning of a season without a win, a new record in the Football League.

In midweek, after contacting Dinard's solicitors, who said they had not heard anything from the Johnson consortium, Mr Weaver offered Danny Bergara a 12-month contract, which he accepted. This immediately brought a reply from Mr Johnson, who castigated the club for giving Bergara a contract when the takeover was imminent and they had a manager ready to step in. He claimed it had thrown a spanner in the works but he and other members of

Photo by Sean Flannery

Despondent Doncaster Rovers fans held a 'mock' funeral procession prior to the team's game with Rochdale, protesting at the delay in the proposed takeover of the club.

Prince Moncrieffe outnumbered by Darlington players at Feethams.

the consortium held talks with Doncaster Council about the redevelopment of the Belle Vue site and the plans for a new stadium, failing to come to any agreement.

FA Cup first-round day had the Rovers leading Second Division Preston North End at Deepdale by an Adie Mike goal after six minutes but three goals in the second half from the home club gave them the win, despite a late goal for the Rovers from youth-team player Andy Hammond. Hammond, along with two more youth-team players, goalkeeper Gary Hoggeth and full-back Maurice Hilton, started the midweek game at Lincoln City, who were unbeaten in 12 games. They extended that record with a 2–1 win over the Rovers, who were at the other end of the scale with a winless run of 18 League games. Hoggeth had to take over in goal because Dean Williams arrived late after going to the police to report being attacked in his car at a set of traffic lights in Nottingham on his way to the game at Lincoln from his Tamworth home. This caused a difference of opinion with Danny Bergara that never healed and saw Williams moved out of the club. As Gary Ingham had already been moved on it left the club with just 18-year-old Gary Hoggeth.

Then came a new dimension to the demonstrations by the fans, who were disgruntled by the drawn-out saga of the takeover. Before the match at home to Rochdale on 22 November the Rovers supporters marched from the Park Hotel to Belle Vue, with six mourners carrying a black coffin to symbolise what they saw as the death of a long-established club. A man dressed as an undertaker led the procession and a banner proclaiming 'Doncaster Rovers is dying' was carried by two fans. They arrived in the Belle Vue car park, dispersed and took their place inside the ground, where hundreds of black balloons were released.

The terraces in front of the Main Stand were closed after an inspection by the council found some faulty barriers. Throughout the first half the chairman, Ken Haran, was verbally abused as he sat in the directors' box and did not appear after half-time. Mark Weaver suffered the same abuse throughout the game until leaving just before the end. The fans also turned on Danny Bergara by calling for the reinstatement of Dean Williams. A three-goal defeat seemed somewhat incidental with everything else going on but it was the 22nd competitive game without a win for the Rovers, setting a new club record.

The week that followed had Mr Weaver outlining the state of the club's finances and, with the exception of Simon Ireland, Martin McDonald and Ian Gore, all the professional players would be allowed to leave the club on free

Adie Mike leads a Rovers attack against Exeter City at Belle Vue.

transfers. Also, the club's glossy programme would no longer be produced in colour but would be replaced with a black and white one. On the last Saturday in November another 3–0 defeat came at Hull City, with the Rovers having a former Rotherham United trainee in goal. Craig Davis had been signed on a non-contract basis but it turned out later that he was not even paid for playing. With Bergara suffering more abuse at Boothferry Park he took the decision to stay away from future games but would carry on with training the players. Mr Weaver then decided that a manager could not manage if he did not see the team play, appointed Bergara as director of coaching so that he continued to coach the team during the week along with Dave Cowling and appointed himself to the manager's job, complete with title, selecting the team with the aid of the senior professionals.

The evening of Tuesday 2 December 1997 was a heart-warming evening for Doncaster Rovers supporters, even if it was the coldest night of the year so far. Chester City visited Belle Vue for the Rovers 21st League match of the season and went away with their tails between their legs, beaten 2–1. A goal from Ian Helliwell after 14 minutes, in reply to a John Jones goal for Chester a minute earlier, seemed to give the team some confidence. Mike Smith then scored a winner after 83 minutes. The only discordant note of the evening was an attendance figure of 864, the lowest in Rovers' Football League history.

Tempering the fans' euphoria over their first win was the news on Sunday 7 December that former manager Billy Bremner had died. Two days later the Rovers came back to earth when they lost in their Auto Windscreens Shield game at home to Rochdale by a single goal before an all-time low attendance for a competitive match of 580. Adding to the Rovers' playing problems was the sending-off of Harvey Cunningham for elbowing. Coupled with the sale of Martin McDonald, the club's best player by far, to Macclesfield Town for £20,000, it had been a poor week for the club. The money raised from McDonald's transfer was not to be used to bring new players in, so they would have to soldier on with what they had. This meant throwing in the youngsters again but through no fault of theirs the next game at Notts County was lost by a 5–2 margin. Darren Utley, who had been out of favour when Richardson picked the team, was re-called and had a memorable game. He conceded a penalty after eight minutes for County's second goal, scored an own-goal for County's third and had a goal put past him after he took over in goal for the last 13 minutes from the injured Gary Hoggeth, whose heroics had kept the score down.

When the news broke that a fans' group was calling for a boycott of games, Mr Weaver came out and described the harsh reality of what would happen if gates continued to be below a thousand. The club needed gates of 1,900 to break even, so the income from gates less than that was insufficient. This meant selling players, with McDonald being the most recent example. His fee kept the club going through December. Weaver went on to say that there was a possibility that the club might have to go part-time in January.

Ten days before Christmas there seemed to be movement on the takeover by the Johnson consortium. A letter was received from Dinard's solicitor in answer to the several letters they had sent to the club's owners. Although it was querying a couple of points, which Mr Johnson responded to, he was satisfied that the deal for the club was back on.

On the Friday night before Christmas a good following from Rotherham increased the attendance at Belle Vue against the Millers to 3,533, the best for about two years. They came, they saw and they conquered, did Rotherham United, with a 3–0 victory but they acknowledged they had had to battle for it. More bad news hit the Rovers the following Monday when Harvey Cunningham received a six-match ban for his recent sending off, it being the second time he had been sent off in the season. With such a small squad the Rovers were struggling to put out a team as it was, without having players suspended. Boxing Day was another sickener because the home game against Mansfield Town was postponed because gale-force winds had ripped a 10-foot hole in the roof of the Main Stand and there had not been time to repair it. Traditionally, Boxing Day crowds are bigger than normal so the Rovers' already depleted coffers suffered again. On Sunday 28 December they travelled to Leyton Orient, a mid-table team who had won 4–1 at Belle Vue earlier in the season. In the first 65 minutes Orient doubled that score to run out victors by eight clear goals. The Orient evidently thought they had humiliated the Rovers enough because they took off both their strikers and their playmaker at around this point. Five youth-team players took part in the game for Rovers, either starting or as substitutes, so it really was a case of men against boys. Thus, at the end of 1997 the League table showed the Rovers at the bottom with nine points from 24 games, having scored 16 goals and conceded 65. The gap to the next-placed team, Brighton & Hove Albion, was 12 points.

The Rovers' scheduled match at Peterborough United on the first Saturday of the New Year was postponed because of Peterborough's involvement in the FA Cup third round. The hot topic of the moment, which was fast fuelling the regard, or lack of it, in which Mr Richardson was held, was the takeover of the club. Facts kept coming out piecemeal but it seemed an agreement had been reached between the Rovers' owners and Anton Johnson for the sale to go through for a fee of £2 million. The sticking point was about a further payment of £1.7 million in relation to the length of the lease on the Belle Vue ground, which the owners wanted when Belle Vue was sold for development. Richardson wanted a guarantee that the money would be paid but Johnson preferred to wait for planning agreement before paying it.

At a public meeting in town Mr Weaver came under fire from supporters for not naming another bidder, which led to supporters believing that no bid existed but despite this Weaver refused to give their identities. Another welcome three points for the Rovers came on 10 January when Moncrieffe's 75th-minute goal gave them the win over Shrewsbury Town at Belle Vue but, with some supporters boycotting the game, the attendance was just 1,116, of which about 300 came to support the visitors. Also in attendance were members of three consortia interested in acquiring the club, Johnson's and two mystery consortia, whose identities were under wraps. During the week Danny George, a defender, was signed on loan from Nottingham Forest and joined the squad for the trip to Devon for an overnight stay before playing at Exeter City. A 5–1 drubbing from the highly-placed Devon side was the result. In the days that followed, striker Padi Wilson was signed from Plymouth Argyle on a free transfer and made his debut against newcomers Macclesfield Town, who were in mid-table and were visiting Belle Vue for the first time, although Martin McDonald, in the Macclesfield team, was no stranger to the place. A three-goal victory gave Macclesfield the 'double'. Dave Cowling, the first-team coach, took over in the dug-out from Danny Bergara, who was still director of coaching but would have more involvement with the youth team. On Thursday 29 January, while Anton Johnson and his group were meeting with Dinard's solicitor, Reg Ashworth, in York, the mystery bidder was meeting Mr Richardson in Zurich, Switzerland. Splashed across the front page of the local evening paper was the banner headline 'AT LAST! Rovers are sold'. They had agreed on the £3.75 million asking fee and it was expected the deal would go through quite quickly. That night the team had a game at home to Scunthorpe United, which they lost 2–1, with Adie Mike scoring the Rovers goal.

At a press conference on Sunday 1 February Mr Chris Plumtree, a former Scunthorpe United director, announced himself as the chairman-elect of the club when the Irish group that had agreed the deal with Mr Richardson in Zurich finally took over. The group had been in talks with the council over the previous six months and had a good relationship with them and once the deal was completed Mr Richardson would have no further involvement. However, all parties concerned had signed a confidentiality clause agreeing not to say anything until everything was finalised.

The trial of Mr Richardson in connection

Darren Moore receives Supporters Club Player of the Year award from Dr Erskine.

with the fire at Belle Vue should have started on 2 February but was adjourned until January 1999 after defence counsel applied successfully for more time. A rearranged game at Belle Vue in midweek against a Mansfield Town team containing Steve Harper, who scored a goal and Jon Schofield, was watched by more than 1,500 fans, who saw their team capitulate to a defeat by three clear goals. However, hope sprang eternal and when the Rovers went a goal up through Padi Wilson a minute from half-time at Cambridge United, three points looked on the cards. Cambridge snuffed that hope out by scoring twice in the second half. After 30 games the Rovers were 10 points adrift in bottom place.

Then, in midweek, the fans' hopes were raised when the Rovers went to third-placed Peterborough United and came away with a win by a single goal, scored by Mike Smith in the last minute, to give the club their first away victory of the season at the 16th attempt. St Valentine's Day, designated as Fans United Day 2, fell on a Saturday, with the Rovers playing Brighton & Hove Albion at their new 'home', the Priestfield Stadium at Gillingham. Nearly 6,500 people from about 40 Premier and Football League clubs turned up with placards, scarves and banners to show their support for all clubs, like Brighton and the Rovers, who were in trouble. The Rovers had a new loan signing from Burnley, former Spurs 'keeper Tony Parks, in goal. He kept a clean sheet and so did the forwards as the game ended goalless.

Meanwhile, the silence continued as regards the takeover by the Irish-based consortium, who were supposed to finalise the deal by 11 February, while Anton Johnson's consortium waited in the wings. Before the next game, at home to Torquay United, Danny George was signed on a free transfer from Nottingham Forest, Steve Hawes came in on a free from Sheffield United and striker Zeke Rowe was brought in on loan from Peterborough United because Prince Moncrieffe was injured and Padi Wilson had a suspension coming up. A goal four minutes from time took the points back to Torquay. Mr Weaver upset the fans again during the week when it was made known that he had signed on at the club as a non-contract player, with his stated aim to help out the reserves if they were short and save the club a fine, while Ian Gore had been made available for transfer. Another midweek game at Belle Vue provided Darlington with their first away win of the season by two clear goals. This was followed at the weekend by a 3–1 loss at Hartlepool United, with Zeke Rowe getting his first goal for the Rovers. The police had to hold back the Rovers fans, who tried to get to Mr Weaver as he left the ground after the match.

March began with a Tuesday night game against Barnet in front of 739 spectators, the lowest-ever assembly for a Rovers home League game. A 2–0 result in favour of Barnet was the Rovers' sixth consecutive home defeat. Mr Weaver thought that the end of his Rovers career was nigh and thought that the takeover by the Irish consortium would go through but not until the end of the season, leaving him to take the flak. After the match he met a supporters' club delegation, who pulled no punches with their questions. He admitted to some mistakes, such as forcing the supporters' club out of their office but also put over his points of view by explaining the reasoning behind some decisions. Two days later, on 5 March, the 'Save the Rovers' group, together with the official supporters' club, held a meeting with the Government's Football Task Force, making them aware of the condition that the club was in and how they were operating. At the same time, Mr Ian Green, a spokesman for the Irish consortium, confirmed that the takeover would not take place until the end of the season because of all the delays in finalising the details. He said that they were not part of the problem and as relegation was looming they needed to take a good look at things but relegation, although a factor to be considered, would not stop the takeover. While waiting for the takeover to be finalised the group would be talking to the Doncaster Council in a bid to get them on their side.

The Saturday game at home to Scarborough was called off because of a waterlogged pitch but it gave more time for the many injured players to get fit for the game to be played on the following Tuesday. Zeke Rowe scored an equaliser for the Rovers but a goal six minutes from time condemned the team to a seventh successive home defeat before more than 1,100 fans. Padi Wilson did not play for the Rovers because he was facing the magistrates at Plymouth after being caught driving while disqualified the previous October. The player pleaded guilty and was sent to jail for three months. Meanwhile, Mr Weaver confirmed that Mr Richardson had provided £35,000 to keep the club going.

Beware the Ides of March! On Friday 13 March, the club laid off coaches Dave Cowling and Paul Ward and terminated the contracts of Simon Ireland and Darren Utley. The first-team players would continue to train under Danny Bergara for three days a week. Mr Weaver justified the move by saying there was a lack of money available to carry on as before. The following day the team travelled to play Cardiff City at Ninian Park only to suffer a hammering by seven goals to one, the Rovers goal scored in the last minute by Adie Mike. The Rovers were severely hampered by goalkeeper Craig Davis being sent off for a professional foul on the hour when they were only three goals down. Davis was only playing because Tony Parks had been recalled by Burnley before the Cardiff game. A certain Dave Penney scored the fifth goal for Cardiff.

The following week the Rovers were fast running out of players when Ian Gore, Steve Sanders, Martin Pemberton and Jim Dobbin were all paid up and left the club and Zeke Rowe returned to Peterborough United at the end of his loan period. However, unbeknown to the fans, Lee Warren was offered a new two-year contract, which he accepted and signed.

Photo by Sean Flannery

Doncaster Rovers' Adie Mike in action v Colchester.

Then, on Thursday 19 March, a heated public meeting at the Earl of Doncaster Hotel gave Mr Weaver a hard time. A motion paper was handed out to the fans, which stated that the public meeting:

• Condemns the manner in which Doncaster Rovers Football Club has been run since Mr Ken Richardson and Dinard Trading Ltd of the Isle of Man became its major shareholders.

• Condemns the deliberate running down of the club, which sees it at the bottom of Division Three of the League without any attempt to achieve an acceptable playing standard.

• Strongly objects to the decision brought upon the Metropolitan Borough of Doncaster by the policies of the major shareholders and the Board of Directors.

• Urges Mr Ken Richardson and Dinard Trading Ltd to conclude a takeover deal consistent with the principle that the Doncaster Rovers Football Club is a part of the local community.

• Urges the Football Association to work towards the speedy introduction of a Code of Conduct for the game of football and a monitoring and compliance unit with adequate powers to oversee and regulate effectively the conduct of clubs.

• Urges the Government's Football Task Force to address the issues highlighted by the current administration of Doncaster Rovers Football Club and formulate appropriate recommendations in its Report to Government.

The first motion was withdrawn because of possible movement on the Johnson takeover but some of the meeting called for it to be reinstated. Ray Gilbert, a leading supporter in opposition to Richardson and Dinard, opened the meeting with an impassioned speech in which he spoke about Richardson's appointment of friends and relatives to the club's Board of Directors and his removal of the club's registration from Belle Vue to the office of a Harrogate solicitor, who was later suspended by the Law Society. The supporters' club chairman, Chas Walker, criticised the town's MPs and councillors for not accepting the invitation to attend. But Anton Johnson was in attendance and confirmed that they would pay £2 million for the club immediately, with a further £1.75 million for any development that went ahead on the Belle Vue site. Mr Weaver, also on the stage, then stated that the asking price was £3.85 million, to which Mr Johnson replied that that was not the figure agreed at a previous meeting with Mr Richardson. He added that Mr Richardson had twice agreed to sell but had changed his mind within hours. They would not buy at a £3.85 million one-

Photo by Sean Flannery

Doncaster Rovers fans protest at the end of the Colchester game.

off price but he said if they took over the club they would, irrespective of any planning deal, redevelop Belle Vue if necessary as well as investing in players. Also in attendance was Mike Clynch, the council's Economic Development Officer, who told the meeting that a site for a new stadium had been earmarked but they would not deal with Mr Richardson. However, they had met with both the consortia in contention to take over the club. A planned meeting the following day between Messrs Richardson and Johnson did not materialise after the consortium received a message that the asking price was now £4 million.

On the Saturday, the Rovers team that lined up at Belle Vue against Lincoln City contained seven teenagers: Gary Hoggeth, Rob Debenham, Paul Edwards, Danny George, Mark Donnelly, Robert Pell and Gary Messer, plus two more on the bench, Mark Hawthorne and John Borg. Prince Moncrieffe, on the bench, was only 21 and the four remaining in the starting line up were Lee Warren 29, Adie Mike 24, Darren Esdaille 23 and David Esdaille 34. They went two down in the first 10 minutes but scored twice in two minutes just before the break through Danny George and Mark Donnelly. Well as they played, they were beaten by a further two goals in the last 18 minutes. However, the attendance of 2,357 was well above average. With these youngsters playing in the first team the youth team was left a bit threadbare and eventually they could not fulfil their fixtures. The next first team game was away at Rochdale, with John Borg going into the starting line up to replace the suspended Darren Esdaille. Matthew Russell, aged 20, signed on loan from Scarborough on transfer deadline day, replaced Borg on the bench and youth team player Domenico Tedaldi came on to the bench for Prince Moncrieffe. Tedaldi also got on the field and scored the Rovers goal on 80 minutes in a 4–1 defeat. The Rovers were now 13 points behind Brighton & Hove Albion with just six games to play.

Jim Dobbin.

The first match in April was a home game against a struggling Hull City side. A crowd of 2,500 attended, with the Hull fans joining the home fans in protests about the running of their respective clubs. A peaceful sit-down protest in the centre circle in the first half caused Ken Leach, the referee, to take the players off the pitch for 11 minutes while the fans were ushered back onto the terraces. A last-minute goal from Adie Mike gave the Rovers a win and a stay of execution but they were 12 points behind the next club, Hull City. A week later, on 11 April, the Humberside team won their next match, Brighton drew and the Rovers lost 2–1 at Chester City, despite the magnificent backing of their travelling supporters. Thus were the Rovers relegated, being now 14 points behind Brighton with four games and just 12 points to play for. The end of the game brought tears and fears — tears because of relegation and fears for the future of the club.

However, there were still three games to play to complete the season. Two days later, on Easter Monday, 2,500 people turned out to see the champions, Notts County, go away with a 2–1 win, the Rovers goal scored in injury time by Gary Messer. At Rotherham on the following Saturday, the Rovers replaced Messer with Padi Wilson in the starting line up, just 24 hours after his early release from Exeter prison but all to no avail as the Millers scored three goals in the last 14 minutes without reply. Coming off the bench for the Rovers on 81 minutes was 16-year-old Robert Betts, the grandson of Maurice Setters, for his first taste of senior football, having received permission from his school headmaster to take part. For the next game at Swansea on the last Saturday in April Betts was selected to replace Matthew Russell, whose loan spell had ended, in the starting line up and acquitted himself well, as did the five other youth-team players who took part in a goalless draw.

The last match of a traumatic and dramatic season was at Belle Vue on Saturday 2 May, against Play-off contenders Colchester United. On police advice it was made all-ticket for a crowd of 5,500. Weeks before the game Mr Weaver indicated that he would not attend the last game so as not to inflame the passions of what was hoped would be a capacity crowd. Before the match, a ceremony was held by the supporters in the centre circle of the pitch in which a bugler, Ken Hawley, sounded the *Last Post* as the supporters laid a number of wreaths behind the Town End goal before a minute's silence was held. There was an official attendance of 3,572 spectators in the ground at the start, some of whom, after 12 minutes of play, went on to the pitch and sat down in the centre circle, chanting 'Weaver out' and 'Sack the Board' as word got out that Mr Weaver, despite his publicly stated intention not to attend, was actually at the ground. The referee immediately took the players off the pitch for a period of 14 minutes as appeals went out from the supporters' club secretary, Ken Avis and the 'Save the Rovers' group chairman, Richard Haley, for the fans to go back to the terraces. Mr Weaver left the ground before half-time. Colchester's Neil Gregory scored after 57 minutes, which brought another invasion and again the referee took the players into the dressing room. With a cacophony of booing coming from the Rovers fans in the Main Stand and the Colchester fans at the Rossington End, the intruders were quickly ushered off the pitch by the police and the game restarted and went to its conclusion without interruption. The players were applauded off the pitch and when they appeared in the Main Stand they received a welcome fit for heroes, which brought tears to the eyes of some of the players, never mind the supporters. For the record, the Rovers team was: Craig Davis, Mark Donnelly, Maurice Hilton, Lee Warren, Danny George, Mark Hawthorne, Harvey Cunningham, Prince Moncrieffe, Robert Betts, Adie Mike, Padi Wilson, with Robert Pell replacing Donnelly after 86 minutes and Rob Debenham and Darren Brookes being unused substitutes. Thus 75 successive years in the Football League came to an ignominious end, with a new Football League record set by the club of 34 defeats sustained in a season.

The Rovers' playing record for 1997–98 was: played 46, won 4, drawn 8, lost 34, goals scored 30, goals against 113, points 20. A total of 45 players played in the Football League, with just six topping 30 or more games. Lee Warren appeared 44 times, Adie Mike 42, Prince Moncrieffe 37, Simon Ireland and Harvey Cunningham 33 each. The top scorer was Prince Moncrieffe with eight League goals, followed by Adie Mike with four. Eleven players scored one goal.

Action from the last match against Colchester United at Belle Vue.

The retained list made stark reading. Only five players: Lee Warren already under contract, Danny George with a clause in his contract that he could leave in the event of the club's relegation, Darren Brookes, Harvey Cunningham and Prince Moncrieffe, would be offered deals to stay at the club. But within days Prince Moncrieffe decided that he did not want to stay at the club and left. The youth policy was

Left to right, back row: Danny Bergara (Coach), Danny George, Lee Warren, Craig Davis, Darren Brookes, Harvey Cunningham, Robert Pell, Mark Hawthorne, Maurice Hilton. Left to right, front row: Rob Debenham, Prince Moncrieffe, Mascot Natalie Greenwood (4), Robert Betts, Mark Donnelly, Padi Wilson, Adie Mike.

to be discontinued, so all the teenagers who had helped the first team out were released, with the exception of Robert Betts, who was offered a YTS place along with three other 16-year-olds, an offer he did not take up, joining Coventry City the following month.

To make matters worse for the fans, it soon became public knowledge that the Football Conference had written to the Rovers, after the Chester City game confirmed their relegation, wanting to know if the club was going to take their place in the competition for 1998–99. If so, they needed to know before 31 May but the Conference confirmed on 4 May that they had not had a reply so far. Then, on 13 May the Conference stated that they had received a fax from the club intimating their desire to join the Conference, with their application being sent in after the next Board meeting. The cost of joining the Conference, £1,600, would have to come out of Mr Richardson's pocket, said Mr Weaver, thus adding to the asking price for the club. The Conference received the club's application and registration fee on Monday 25 May.

On 3 June the news broke that the Irish consortium claimed to have bought the club but could not take over while the club was in administration. The club came out of administration towards the end of June, having paid off their debts under a creditors voluntary agreement but still the sale of the club had not gone through. Meanwhile, there were only four players signed up and Mr Weaver would not sign any more because he was continually told that the club was to be taken over. Obviously a new manager would want to bring in his own players but time was getting short and the best players would have been signed up by other clubs and players were due back for pre-season training in the second week of July.

To further aggravate their standing with the supporters, it was announced that the shareholders' annual meeting, always held in Doncaster, would be held at the Southlands Hotel in Stockport. Mr Weaver, who lived in Stockport, claimed it was not his decision but had been taken for the safety of the directors. Despite fervent condemnation from all and sundry, it was not changed.

The story of Doncaster Rovers and their relegation from League to non-League football was featured in a documentary film on Channel 5 television on Sunday 5 July. But that phase of the club's history was on the way out.

The following Friday, the 10th, the annual shareholders' meeting was held at the Southlands Hotel, Stockport. If Mr Weaver and Mr Richardson thought people would not attend they were to be sadly mistaken. A coach was chartered to take everybody to the meeting. Reg Ashworth, Dinard's solicitor, told the meeting that Mr Richardson would not be involved once the sale of the club went through. Unfortunately, some people travelling home from the meeting turned up outside Mr Weaver's house, causing his family some distress and upsetting the other residents of the street.

During the week that followed, a joint statement by the club and the new owners, Westferry Ltd, signed by club chairman Ken Haran and Ian Green, a Watford-based businessman for Westferry Ltd, announced the takeover. The statement read that the majority shareholders, Dinard Trading Ltd and Mr Richardson, had entered into an unconditional binding contract to sell their shares, with the transaction being completed by the end of July. Of course, scepticism was rife among the Rovers supporters, as once again secrecy was the order of the day with regard to the people behind the takeover. Mr Green answered the sceptics by saying that when the deal was finally completed then names would be divulged, a local businessman of some standing would be appointed and a public meeting for supporters and minority shareholders would be held. Meanwhile, Westferry appointed Manchester-based sports management agency Premier Crew, a FIFA licensed company, to recruit a new manager. They had been given details of the budget available for management and players but time was short.

The fixture list for the Rovers' first season in the Conference was issued, with their first game being at Dover Athletic on 15 August. On Tuesday 14 July the players, all five of them, reported back for training. They were: Lee Warren, David Esdaille, Danny George, Harvey Cunningham and Darren Brookes. In the meantime Ian Snodin had been approached about whether he would accept a job as player-manager. Following negotiations with Scarborough, where he had another year to run on his contract as a player, the Rovers agreed a nominal fee for his release.

On Wednesday 22 July a press conference was held at which Ian Snodin was unveiled as the new player-manager of Doncaster Rovers on a two-year contract. A new chief executive was also introduced – former Oldham Athletic

Shaun Goodwin leads the team out for the first match in the Conference at Dover Athletic.

Shaun Goodwin on the ball at Dover.

player Ian McMahon. Both men would start their jobs on 1 August when the takeover was officially completed. Ian Snodin, knowing time was short to assemble a team, had spent his time looking for likely players since he was first approached. But so late on in the close season, most good players had already fixed themselves up with clubs. A pre-season friendly arranged by the previous regime for Tuesday 28 July at Worksop Town was used to give the five professionals on the books a game so that Ian Snodin could evaluate their potential. The rest of the team was made up of guest players and it was the last match played under the old ownership. Snodin attended the game, which ended 2–2, as a spectator but could not make any definitive assessments of players who were chopped and changed throughout the evening.

A further announcement was made by the new owners in late July, naming Ian Green as acting chairman and Paul May as finance director. Ian Snodin started work on Monday 3 August, knowing he had less than a fortnight to gather a team together for the first match at Dover. He had already signed Shaun Goodwin, who had been released by Rotherham United at the end of the previous season, despite several League clubs being after his signature. Snodin followed this with the signing of Mark Hume from Barnsley, Scott Maxfield, released by Hull City and Colin Sutherland from Scarborough. The following evening he took a team of trialists plus Maxfield, Sutherland and Cunningham to play Brighouse Town, with the manager playing in the second half for the first time in a Rovers shirt for 14 years. The Rovers XI won by a single goal scored by trialist Steve Elmberg, a trainee released by Huddersfield Town.

On the Wednesday evening, a team comprising signed players Hume, Sutherland, Goodwin, Warren and Simon Shaw, a new signing from Darlington, started with a number of trialists against Gainsborough Trinity at the Northolme, with other signed players Darren Brookes and Danny George coming on as substitutes. Snodin had already said that the players had to impress him because there were only 10 days to the big kick-off and he wanted to sign at least eight more players. A 1–1 draw ensued, with former Barnsley player Duane Beckett scoring the goal.

The following day, Thursday, the prices for season tickets were released. It would cost adults £135 to sit in the Main Stand, while the unemployed, juniors and pensioners paid £67.50. A family package for the Main Stand would

Dave Penney and mascots photographed before the match against Cheltenham Town at Belle Vue.

cost £330 for two adults accompanied by three children. Season tickets for the terrace were priced at £100 for adults and £50 concessions. The terrace family package would cost £245 for two adults and three children. Also on that day, the industrial tribunal hearing over the dismissal of coaches Dave Cowling and Paul Ward was opened in Sheffield and adjourned to a later date.

On Saturday 8 August the team travelled to Bacup Borough where Brent Peters, former assistant manager to Kerry Dixon, was manager and came away with a 1–1 draw, followed by a 2–2 draw at Eastwood Town in Nottinghamshire on the Tuesday. After a good showing in the two matches, Tunisian Dino Maamria, who had played with Ayr United the previous season, was signed and Tommy Wright, 32, a former Leeds United player who had been at St Johnstone the year before, was signed the next day on a month's trial. A game at Denaby United followed on the Wednesday evening and non-League trialist striker Lutel James stood out above the rest. Snodin wanted to see how he performed against a team of higher calibre before he signed him but James wanted an immediate answer as to whether he would be signed so he could go elsewhere. Snodin could not give that assurance so James went back to Hyde United and two months later Bury snapped him up.

The big day arrived on Saturday 15 August. For this first-ever game in the Conference, the team travelled down on the Friday and stayed overnight before turning up at the quaintly named, picturesque Crabble Stadium, halfway up a hill and surrounded on two sides by tree-covered slopes. Snodin was unable to play because of a one-match ban carried over from the previous season but his team included two loan signings – Kevin McIntyre from Tranmere Rovers and Mark Bradley from Heart of Midlothian, signed the day before they travelled. The team that took to the field for this historic match was: Andy Woods, Simon Shaw, Kevin McIntyre, Lee Warren, Mark Hume, Colin Sutherland, Mark Bradley, Shaun Goodwin, Tommy Wright, Dino Maamria and Scott Maxfield. Jason Minett replaced Bradley for the second half, Duane Beckett took over from Maxfield nine minutes from time and Danny George had to be content with a place on the bench. The Rovers lost this first game by a single goal scored after 34 minutes by Daniels, with a header from close range following a free-kick. However, after 83 minutes Dover were awarded a penalty when McIntyre was adjudged to have brought down Clarke in the area. This prompted a pitch invasion by about a dozen so-called Rovers fans. An altercation developed between the invaders and the Dover goalkeeper, Charlie Mitten, who had gone to the assistance of a steward. The police were called but no arrests were made and the pitch was eventually cleared. Budden took the penalty-kick, only to see Woods dive to his left and save. Drink was blamed for the behaviour of the people who went on to the pitch, as they had been drinking in the clubhouse until well after the game had started and Ian McMahon was quick to announce that anybody identified for that incident or any more like it during the season would be banned from attending games. Two minutes from time McIntyre was sent off, apparently for having too much to say to the referee. On the long journey home Snodin had a lot to think about and knew that he had a big job on his hands. The next game was only three days away, at home to Southport.

On the Monday the club announced that a full and final settlement had been reached with Mr Richardson and Dinard Trading Ltd, leaving Aidan Phelan of Westferry Ltd as sole owner of the club with 96.6 per cent of the shares. The remaining 3.4 per cent were held by supporters. Of more importance perhaps to the fans was the follow-up announcement that Manchester-based, Doncaster-born businessman John Ryan, managing director of the Transform Medical Group, had accepted the post of chairman of the club, with Ian Green as vice-chairman. To the supporters, this was a sure sign that Mr Richardson was not involved.

Meanwhile, volunteers had painted the ground and generally spruced it up for the first home game of the season against Southport on Tuesday. The admittance for under-16s at this game was set at £1, with face painting and free sweets given out in a carnival atmosphere. Former Everton and Wales goalkeeper Neville Southall, at the time a goalkeeping coach at Tranmere Rovers and Huddersfield Town, was signed on the morning of the match on a week-by-week basis. A month short of his 40th birthday, he certainly had the experience that Snodin wanted in his team. So

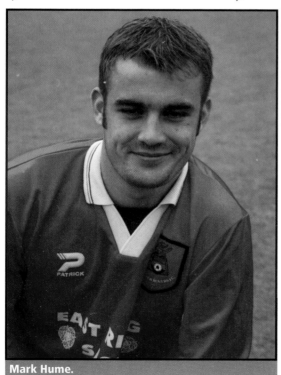

Mark Hume.

Southall replaced Woods, Snodin came in for Warren, who dropped to the bench and Minett started in place of Bradley, who had returned from whence he came. A single goal, scored on 24 minutes by O'Reilly, was sufficient to take the points back to Southport. Unfortunately for the Rovers, their captain, Goodwin, was sent off after 79 minutes for a second booking, the second offender in the first two games. The attendance for this first home game of the new era was an encouraging 3,663. The fans believed that things would only improve now that local people were running the show.

Two days later Ray Green, the marketing manager of Doncaster Dragons Rugby League club, was brought in to help set up a commercial department. The next day Snodin signed striker Glenn Kirkwood from Eastwood Town on a two-year contract for a fee of £15,000. Saturday 22 August brought another home game, against Kidderminster Harriers, with under-16s being let in free, bringing in another gate over the 3,000 mark. When Wright was brought down, the crowd saw Goodwin's penalty after 49 minutes give the Rovers their first three

Simon Shaw.

points to get off the mark in their third game, which had another sending off – Webb of Kidderminster, for going over the ball on McIntyre after 44 minutes. This prompted the question, did any Conference game finish with all 22 men on the pitch?

The following Tuesday the team travelled to Barrow – old foes from earlier days in the Football League – who had lost all three games at this point. The only change in the line up was Lee Warren replacing Snodin, who had injured his ankle against Kidderminster. Barrow took an early lead from a Sutherland own-goal when he sliced the ball into his own net trying to clear but Maamria equalised on 27 minutes. A penalty by Goodwin seven minutes from time put Rovers in the lead but Barrow equalised five minutes later.

Ian Snodin made another foray into the transfer market two days later, pulling out a real plum signing that would have a resounding effect in seasons to come. Dave Penney, Cardiff City captain in the previous season, had moved his family back to his home territory at Castleford earlier in the year and, at 34 years of age, was seeking a more local club at which to ply his trade. Rochdale and Scarborough offered him League football but he chose the Rovers. However, Snodin's other target, big striker Andy Saville (also at Cardiff City), decided to go on loan to Hull City and signed for Scarborough early in the New Year despite Snodin's persistent attentions. The manager had better luck though with John Sheridan, the former Leeds United and Sheffield Wednesday midfielder, who had been released by Bolton Wanderers in the summer. He signed on a non-contract week-to-week basis.

Both new players made their debuts on Saturday 29 August at Kingstonian, a club that had been promoted from the Isthmian League while Rovers were falling out of the Football League. McIntyre was suspended after his earlier sending off and Minett dropped to the bench along with Warren, who was replaced by Snodin. Playing in a new strip of yellow shirts and black shorts, the Rovers warranted at least a point, with Minett having equalised in the 79th minute, 14 minutes after full-back Mustafa, making his debut, had given the home team the lead. Unfortunately for the Rovers, Holligan scored for Kingstonian in the last minute, leaving the Rovers to travel back home empty-handed.

A fine, sunny bank holiday Monday brought high-flying Kettering Town to Belle Vue. Snodin, Penney and Goodwin were out injured and were replaced by Warren, Minett and debutant Kirkwood. And a good debut it proved to be when he scored after 20 minutes by chasing a long ball that looked like a lost cause. The Kettering 'keeper was slow to react and Kirkwood got there first, easily shooting into an empty net. A minute before half-time Hume received a second booking and was despatched from the field of play having conceded a penalty. Norman equalised for Kettering from the spot, giving Southall no chance of saving. Down to 10 men, the Rovers had their fair share of play and chances in the second half but the match ended all square at one goal apiece.

The first day of September brought some good news for Ian Snodin and the supporters when his brother, Glynn, finally joined the club as head coach, with Scarborough receiving a settlement. This signing eased the burden on Ian, who had been doing the coaching with the assistance of John Stiles, helping out as a favour and Jon Bowden, the physiotherapist. Now he could concentrate more on his own fitness to carry on playing. For Glynn it was straight into the daily grind of coaching in the morning and going on the road scouting for players but he was happy to be back at his old stamping ground alongside his brother.

On the following Saturday, the Rovers met Forest Green Rovers, making their debut in the Conference following promotion from the Southern League. Kevin McIntyre was available after suspension and replaced Scott Maxfield, who dropped to the bench – the only change in the team from the last match. Ian Snodin, Dave Penney, both with ankle injuries and Shaun Goodwin, suspended, were all unavailable. Alick Jeffrey, the club's most famous player and hero of John Ryan's since his younger days, was presented to the fans at half-time as the new honorary president of the club. A presentation of a silver salver by former Manchester City and England player Mike Summerbee was made on the pitch on behalf of the club, followed by a parade of former stars individually introduced to the crowd.

The Rovers turned out in a new red strip with black lines on the shoulders, with the logo of shirt sponsors Transform etched in black on the front. The proper new strip of plain red body and a blue collar was modelled by Page 3 girl Amanda Robins but they would not be ready until October, due to the deal with manufacturers Asics being finalised only three weeks previously. This game was a classic case of one team – the Rovers – having more than 90 per cent of the play throughout the game but losing by a single goal scored just past the hour on the counter-attack by Hunt, the Forest Green forward. Goals win matches not possession and the Rovers were unable to put the ball into the net. This scenario was to become a familiar lament throughout the season. Seven games played, five points gained, just five goals scored as they slid to 18th in the table, ironically one place in front of Forest Green on goal difference. However, the attendance was standing up, as a healthy 3,400 turned out.

In midweek the club announced that four players, defenders Darren Brookes and Danny George and midfielders Harvey Cunningham and David Esdaille, had been transfer listed. Meanwhile, the hunt for new players, particularly a goalscorer, went on apace. In successive evenings, the Snodins watched games as diverse as Frickley Athletic against Emley and Huddersfield Town Reserves against Sheffield United Reserves. Steve Nicol, the former Liverpool and Scotland star latterly with Sheffield Wednesday, was signed on a week-to-week basis the Friday before the away game against Hayes, signing a two-year contract later in the month.

Once again injuries dictated the selection of the team, with Tommy Wright, Dino Maamria and Duane Beckett out with hamstring problems, Dave Penney still out with an ankle injury and Kevin McIntyre also injured. However, Ian Snodin and Shaun Goodwin reported fit and with Steve Nicol making his debut in defence the team was as strong as any put out so far. On the bench, though, were transfer-listed players Harvey Cunningham and Danny George, with the former coming on halfway through the second half but then being replaced by the latter because of injury near the end. Although the Rovers largely dominated the game they still lost it by two clear goals; the first as early as the sixth minute, the second just past the halfway mark in the second half. Although Hayes manager Terry Brown was quite effusive in his praise of the Rovers, it was something that

Ian Duerden watched by Lee Warren in the FA Cup tie against Guiseley at Belle Vue.

Rovers fans at Dover for the first match in the Conference.

Ian Snodin was getting tired of hearing because it did not make up for the fact that the team lay next to the bottom of the League. The injury list also got longer, with Simon Shaw suffering a groin strain and John Sheridan, Harvey Cunningham and Steve Nicol also receiving injuries.

Tuesday 15 September and a visit to Southport loomed, with the team virtually picking itself because there were only 13 players fit and available. To make the required number of substitutes on the bench Glynn Snodin was registered as a player and the other two were the transfer-listed pair of Darren Brookes and David Esdaille.

Danny George made his first start of the season and Ian Snodin played at right-back. Kirkwood put the Rovers in the lead after three minutes and Guyett made it 2–0 when he turned a shot from Warren into his own net after 16 minutes. Guyett headed in at the right end for Southport on 69 minutes and was then adjudged to have been fouled by George in the area three minutes later, when everyone in the ground thought the free-kick was the other way. Gamble put the penalty past Southall to equalise. Two clear-cut penalty appeals by the Rovers had gone unheeded during the game, although the referee put his whistle to his mouth for the second one and then changed his mind. Southall, who had been hobbling since the 10th minute, was taken off on 80 minutes after Southport scored a third goal. Brookes, already on the field, went in goal and Glynn Snodin came on as a substitute. The Rovers had been trying for some time to have Southall substituted but the referee had ignored them, resulting in a frustrated Ian Snodin venting his displeasure to the referee, who issued a second yellow card, the first one having come as early as the ninth minute, followed by the red after 81 minutes. After holding a two-goal lead until the 69th minute, the Rovers eventually lost by the odd goal in five after a whole series of controversial decisions by the referee. They were now bottom of the pile. Added to the injury list were Southall, Wright and Ian Snodin, who would also have a suspension to serve. Physio Jon Bowden would have more work to do.

Top-of-the-table Rushden & Diamonds, owned by Doc Marten's boot manufacturer Max Griggs, were the visitors to Belle Vue the following Saturday. Andy Woods was back in goal, with Southall not having recovered and, as it turned out, having played his last game for the Rovers. Hume was available again after suspension and Nicol, Sheridan and Penney returned after recovering from injury. Despite three successive defeats, another good attendance of 3,768 turned up to see substitute Hume, playing as a striker, snatch a point in the 89th minute, the Diamonds having scored early in the second half.

The series of two matches a week continued on the Tuesday, with a long trip to Morecambe. This time the Rovers travelled home with three points from a 2–1 victory. Kirkwood put the Rovers in front after 18 minutes, Hume added a second eight minutes from time and Morecambe got a consolation goal in injury-time. The last Saturday in September was another long trip, this time to the south west, to Yeovil. The Rovers were leading 2–0 after 60 minutes through Hume and second-half substitute Goodwin. However, Yeovil fought back well and a penalty after 70 minutes and a goal eight minutes from time gave them a point. The Rovers had now moved up to 20th place in the table.

Late in September Ray Green was able to concentrate solely on the Doncaster Dragons' commercial activities after the Rovers appointed Nigel Reed as their commercial manager. The first game in October was a home game against Farnborough Town, who were at the bottom of the table. The Rovers had signed former Frickley Athletic and Rotherham United striker Andy Hayward on loan from fellow Conference side Hednesford Town in time to make his debut. The team sported a new strip of red shirts with a broad white stripe across the shoulders and without a sponsor's name on but nothing went right for them. Farnborough went two goals up in the first 27 minutes and the Rovers could only pull one back in injury-time at the end of the game, with a Sutherland header. It was interesting to see the captain's armband worn by four different Rovers players during the game. Captain Shaun Goodwin was substituted on 29 minutes with a hamstring problem, Dave Penney took over but was sent off after 39 minutes for the use of his elbow on Baker of Farnborough and Steve Nicol took the armband and was substituted with eight minutes left. The last captain was Lee Warren, who managed to survive to the end of the game. This first away win for Farnborough Town in 11 months lifted them over the Rovers, who dropped a place to 21st on goal difference, below Woking but above Barrow, all on 10 points.

The hectic life for the Snodins continued as they went out scouting on Monday following the poor display against Farnborough, after which Ian was scathing in his match comments. The following evening Ian attended a fund raising evening and football memorabilia auction at Clay Lane Social Club. Included was a football signed by Paul Gascoigne and his Rangers teammates, which fetched £30. One of the Rovers away shirts signed by the team brought in £55 and Duncan Ferguson's Everton shirt fetched £50. The evening brought in £550 for the Rovers. Meanwhile, Glynn was at Stalybridge Celtic watching a player recommended to Ian by Graeme Sharp, a former teammate at Everton.

Ian Snodin wanted a full-time squad at his disposal, so on Thursday 8 October Andy Woods, who had impressed in Southall's absence, was given a one-year contract which effectively ended Southall's time at the club because he had other commitments. Tommy Wright and John Sheridan were offered contracts instead of their week-to-week arrangement; Tommy signed his two-year contract but John needed time to think it over and as a result left the club to later sign on at Oldham Athletic. Ex-Blackpool midfielder David Jones, 20, was also given a two-year contract.

On the Saturday, another bottom-of-the-table game was played at Belle Vue against Woking. The Rovers lost by a single goal scored by West five minutes from time and dropped to the bottom of the League after Barrow picked up a point. The match was not a dirty game, yet bookings were handed out to six men from each side. The attendance of 2,833 was the lowest of the season but a counter attraction was a televised European Championship qualifier at Wembley between England and Bulgaria, which ended goalless. Ian Snodin had wanted six points from the home games against Farnborough Town and Woking, struggling at the bottom end of the table but it was not to be. After these games Kevin McIntyre was recalled by Tranmere Rovers from his loan spell.

A midweek game played behind closed doors against Mansfield Town Reserves included a trialist who had been training with the club for the past few weeks. Matthew Caudwell, a 19-year-old from Hallam FC, scored a goal and impressed the Snodin brothers enough to warrant them signing him on a two-year contract. Tommy Wright also came through the game without any problems following his recent hamstring injury. Striker Ian Duerden was signed on the Thursday from Halifax Town on a one-year contract but was not eligible to play in the FA Cup on the Saturday, having been signed after the deadline for that round of the competition.

The FA Cup third qualifying round was next and a home game against Northern Premier League side Flixton had come out of the draw. The Rovers won by two clear goals in atrocious weather conditions of heavy rain before 2,048 spectators. Flixton fought hard and it was 70 minutes before Kirkwood broke the deadlock with a header. Hume added a second four minutes from time to record the Rovers' first win in the competition after going 12 games since their last win in November 1989.

In mid-October a club shop was opened in a portable building at Belle Vue under manageress Tracey Fernie. Between October and Christmas they sold more merchandise, replica shirts, polo shirts, baseball jackets, hats and training tops than in the previous four years, which all added to the club's kitty.

In the week after the FA Cup tie the Rovers tried again to sign Andy Saville from Cardiff City and received some encouragement but he was out of the game at that time with an injured back. At the same time enquiries were made about signing Kevin McIntyre but Tranmere Rovers put a £25,000 valuation on him with further stage payments, which put it in abeyance for the time being. However, a week later the Rovers agreed a flat fee of £10,000 with Tranmere Rovers but then found that McIntyre had had an apparent change of mind and wanted to stay at the Wirral club. Early in November the Rovers tried again and offered him a very good contract but he turned them down.

As a non-League side, the Rovers were required to play in the Sheffield Senior Cup, run under the auspices of the Sheffield and Hallamshire County FA. They had been drawn to play away at works team Avesta, a County Senior League team from Sheffield, on a date to be agreed before 15 November. The rules stated that clubs had to play their best team and play on a Saturday, which meant the Rovers postponing a Conference fixture. The Rovers wanted to play it midweek and at Belle Vue, because Avesta had not got floodlights but Avesta were adamant that they wanted to play at home. Thus a date could not be agreed.

The next game, on Saturday 24 October, was a big test for the Rovers – an away game against the leaders Cheltenham Town. On a rainy day the Rovers, with Ian Duerden making his debut, more than matched their opponents but after 42 minutes a bizarre decision by the referee stunned the crowd and even the home fans and players, when he awarded a penalty to Cheltenham for handball by Maxfield following a corner to the home team. Maxfield was stood on the goalline holding on to a post with one hand and his other hand was at his side away from the line of the ball, which hit him in the face. Despite vociferous protests the referee adamantly stuck to his decision and sent Maxfield off. Woods saved the penalty from Eaton and minutes later the referee waved away a far clearer claim for a penalty to Rovers when Hume was brought down in the area. The Rovers dominated the second half even though they had only 10 men but lost again by 2–1. All the goals were scored in the first half hour of the game; Brough, for the home team, scored on six minutes, Hume got the Rovers goal on 29 minutes to make it 1–1, then Duff scored two minutes later for what turned out to be the winning goal.

On Thursday 29 October a gentleman's evening was held at the Earl of Doncaster Hotel as a fundraiser for Rovers. The cost of £25 included a meal, with entertainment from comedian Martin Gold and after-dinner speaker Stan Taylor. Charlie Williams and Alick Jeffrey attended, along with current players and the chief executive, Ian McMahon.

The last day of October brought a fourth-round FA Cup tie at Belle Vue against Guiseley, a Northern Premier League team. The Rovers won comfortably enough by 3–1, with two goals from Duerden and one from Kirkwood. The following Tuesday, a behind-closed-doors friendly against Rotherham United included Dave Penney, back after a three-match suspension, Mark Hume in the middle of a two-match suspension and several trialists, including Ignacio Linares-Ybarra, aged 26, who had played for Real Zaragoza in Spain and was currently studying law in Leeds. Ybarra impressed sufficiently to be offered a one-month deal, which he accepted.

The Rovers' first match in November was at high-flying Stevenage Borough. Out injured were Jason Minett (torn thigh muscle), Shaun Goodwin (torn hamstring), Duane Beckett (knee injury), Scott Maxfield (knee injury and suspension) and Mark Hume (suspended). Dave Penney was back after suspension and Natcho Ybarra made his debut for the Rovers. But it was an all too familiar story when, after matching the new leaders in every aspect except scoring, they lost by two late goals. The Rovers were now four points adrift at the bottom.

On Monday 10 November the Rovers took the unprecedented step of withdrawing from the Sheffield Senior Cup after failing to agree dates with Avesta. Sheffield and Hallamshire FA fined the Rovers £2,000 but they had a far more meaningful Cup competition to occupy their minds that weekend. They had come out of the hat with an away game at struggling Third Division side Southend United in the FA Cup first round. The Rovers caused the surprise of the round by winning with a stunning low drive from Penney after 12 minutes. It was a superb performance from the Rovers, startling their opponents by continued attacking in the first part of the game and then, when Southend came back at them, particularly in the latter part of the game, they defended magnificently. Had they turned the corner and were they able to climb the table?

They started to answer that question the following Tuesday, 18 November, when they entertained Barrow. A goal in each half from Kirkwood and Maamria before Barrow hit back with a goal 10 minutes from time gave the Rovers the three points that they needed so badly. However, Ian Snodin aggravated the ankle injury that had caused him to miss a number of matches and Duerden injured a groin.

Another Cup tie was next, this time at home in the FA Trophy second round. During the week the club had agreed a sponsorship deal with Beazer Homes and would wear a strip bearing their logo against Frickley Athletic. A week earlier they had been the giant-killers but this time they found out what it was like to be on the receiving end of a giant-killing act, when Frickley won 2–0, with goals from Fuller either side of half-time. The Rovers were reduced to 10 men after 48 minutes when Ybarra was sent off for a foul but they did not perform well enough, even with 11 men, to get anything from the game.

On Thursday 26 November Colin Sutherland was placed on the transfer list and suspended by the club until 8 December after missing training a fortnight earlier and ruling himself out of the FA Cup game at Southend because of personal problems. Two days later the club journeyed down to Hereford to take part in a game in which the match officials hit the limelight rather than the players. Shaw was sent off after 44 minutes for bringing down Leadbeater as the last man. Nothing wrong with that, because as last man it was the law but Leadbeater was clearly offside to the

Team picture prior to the Woking home game. Left to right, back row: Scott Maxfield, Andy Hayward, Andy Woods, Lee Warren, Kevin McIntyre, Colin Sutherland, Simon Shaw. Left to right, front row: Steve Nicol, Jason Minett, Dave Penney, Dino Maamria.

Dino Maamria against Crook Town in the FA Cup.

spectators at that end of the ground, although the man that mattered – the linesman – did not signal it. The game was then won by Hereford United when they were awarded a dubious penalty on 80 minutes after Evans fell down in the area following a corner. Leadbeater slammed in the penalty-kick for the only goal of the game.

Tuesday 1 December brought Southport to Belle Vue in the Endsleigh Trophy, the Conference League Cup. Both sides had weakened teams because of the FA second round due to be played but the Rovers won 2–0, with goals from Hume either side of the break. Included in the starting line up was Sutherland, released from his club suspension and three YTS lads – Robert Wild, Richard Powell and Mark Ridley – came on as second-half substitutes before a crowd of 949.

The aforementioned FA Cup second round was played at home against Rushden & Diamonds on the Saturday. The match ball was delivered by a helicopter piloted by Sgt Tom O'Malley, a Rovers fan and a former resident of Rossington (now based at Wattisham in Suffolk). Schoolgirl Anna Gray of Sprotborough was judged by Mike Davies, *Doncaster Star* office manager and Rovers' chief executive, Ian McMahon, to be the winner in the competition to design a club mascot. Her winning entry of a cartoon dog dubbed 'Donny Dawg' earned her a signed ball, a Rovers shirt and a season ticket. The match itself ended in a goalless draw before an attendance of 5,396, the highest crowd figure for four years. A week later came a visit to the south of London to play Welling United, in which a goal by Hume after 23 minutes was equalised on 79 minutes by Adams. The Rovers were still bottom, with 14 points from 19 games, one point behind Welling United.

The FA Cup replay on Tuesday 15 December at Nene Park meant that the winners knew who their opponents would be: Premier League Leeds United. The match started badly for the Rovers when Hume was sent off for a two-footed tackle after just four minutes. Rushden were then awarded a penalty on seven minutes, from which Hampsher scored. The Rovers equalised on 18 minutes when Sutherland took a pass from Penney and shot past the 'keeper. Rushden then scored three goals in 22 minutes just past the hour, with Maamria getting one in the last minute for Rovers to make the score 4–2 in favour of Rushden & Diamonds.

The following Saturday, the Rovers were at home to Dover Athletic. And what a match that turned out to be. Three goals in the first 27 minutes for Vansittart of Dover had the lowest League crowd of the season turning on the Rovers players and management for the first time. Kirkwood pulled one back on the half-hour mark but Rovers went in at half-time with boos ringing in their ears. The fans had turned up in their thousands until now and had backed them even though they had been losing games and were bottom of the table. But they expected to see some effort put in and fortunately they got just that in the second half. On 52 minutes a Penney special, a low drive from 25 yards, blasted past the Dover 'keeper. Maamria shot in for an equaliser on 75 minutes but Hynes put Dover back in front four minutes later. Two minutes on, a cross from Duerden was turned into his own goal by Budden and five minutes from time Kirkwood hit the winning goal to round off a sensational second half and take the match by five goals to four. This win took the club up to third from bottom.

The weather was atrocious on Boxing Day for the home game against Leek Town, a game the Rovers dominated but lost to a single goal scored by Hawtin after 41 minutes. The Rovers' best chance came in added time at the end of the game when they were awarded a penalty. Penney took the kick but hit a post, the whistle went and another three points were lost against a team they should have beaten.

Two days later came a trip to Hednesford Town in the West Midlands. The Rovers were totally dominant in the first half and scored through a great volley by Hume on 42 minutes. But following a corner to the home team on 78 minutes the Rovers cleared the ball and pushed out of defence, leaving several Hednesford men in the penalty area who were clearly offside when the ball was played back in, although the linesman did not raise his flag. Andy Woods parried Comyn's header but the ball hit Lee Warren, who had got back to defend and bounced back into the net. Even the home supporters, while cheering the goal, were shaking their heads in disbelief. But the goal counted, leaving the Rovers with one point instead of three.

The new year of 1999 opened on Saturday 2 January with another away game at Leek Town and yet another 1–1 draw, with goals from Kirkwood for the Rovers after 11 minutes and McAuley with a penalty after 56 minutes for the home team. Included in the Rovers team was Kevin McIntyre, back at the club on loan.

Matty Cauldwell in action against Crook Town at Belle Vue in the FA Cup.

Steve Nicol is presented with a thank you award.

During the week the Rovers signed Steve Rimmer, a centre-half from Manchester City, on a month's loan. He made his debut against second-placed Cheltenham Town on their visit to Belle Vue on the 9th. Again the Rovers had a poor first half, going two down in 35 minutes. McIntyre brought Watkins down in the area, with the Cheltenham player scoring from the spot after 28 minutes and adding another seven minutes later. The second half produced a goal from Goodwin after 51 minutes and a header by Duerden to level the score four minutes later. Cheltenham had Brough sent off after 78 minutes but they held on for the draw.

The next game a week later was at home to Morecambe, who were comfortably in the top half of the table. The club allowed under-16s into the ground for just one penny, which no doubt helped to bring in a crowd of 4,251. This was a game of two halves, with the Rovers behind at half-time to a ninth-minute strike by Lyons. No doubt fired up by the half-time pep talk, the Rovers came out in the second half and made their presence felt with two goals from Penney in two minutes: a volley from 25 yards in the 70th minute and the second slotted in from close range to complete their first 'double' in the Conference.

Having hit the winning trail, they followed up in the next game at Rushden & Diamonds with a tremendous 3–1 win. An own-goal by Nicol four minutes before the break gave Rushden the lead at half-time but a second-half hat-trick by Duerden took three well-merited points back to Doncaster. The Rovers were now up to 18th with 26 points from 26 games. However, Ian Snodin missed the game as he was out on a scouting mission in Scotland and again on Monday at Northampton.

The last match of January was at top-of-the-table Kettering Town. It was a hard-fought game with defences on top but two minutes from time Duerden volleyed in from a cross by Wright to add a further three points to Rovers' total and move them up another notch in the table. On the evening of 4 February, another gentleman's evening was held at the Earl of Doncaster Hotel to raise funds for the club. A Newcastle United shirt autographed by Alan Shearer was auctioned for £350. The Snodin brothers, chairman John Ryan and the players were in attendance.

The match against Northwich Victoria two days later, on the Saturday, was postponed because of Northwich's involvement in the FA Trophy. However, the next Saturday (13 February), at home to fourth-placed Yeovil Town, the Rovers reverted to inconsistency, losing by two clear goals rattled in by Patmore after three minutes and Pickard on 59 minutes. Hume came on as a substitute for Kirkwood after 71 minutes but was on his way back to the dressing room three minutes later after being sent off for use of his elbow on Hannigan. This was his third dismissal of the season and his tally of missed games rose after each one. Also, manager Ian Snodin had been sent to the stand in the first minute of the second half by the referee. The referee was roundly booed at half-time and full-time by supporters and objects were thrown around the tunnel area. After the match John Ryan issued an appeal to fans to control their behaviour despite feeling aggrieved at decisions given by the officials. One statistic issued after the game was the fact that the 14,000th under-16 person had passed through the turnstiles.

The next game was an away game against Forest Green Rovers. This meant getting the maps out – where was Forest Green? One season, Worksop Town turned up at Forest Green near Gatwick Airport but those in the know were aware that the actual club was a village of that name situated in Gloucestershire on top of a hill above the town of Nailsworth and nowadays a suburb of that town. The game itself was sterile in the extreme, producing a goalless draw at the Lawn Stadium on a poor pitch, with the chips from the refreshment kiosk being the only thing keeping the Rovers spectators warm.

The following Tuesday, the 23rd, a home game against Telford United brought another welcome three points for the Rovers, with goals from Goodwin after four minutes and Kirkwood on 73 minutes. Telford pulled one back in the last minute but could not prevent the Rovers taking the 2–1 win and moving up to 15th in the table. Later that week Ian Snodin signed Jamie Barnwell-Edinboro, a former Cambridge United and Stevenage Borough striker, on a non-contract basis to cover for Hume, who was ineligible for selection for the next five games – the length of his suspension for his latest misdemeanour. He made his debut as a substitute on the last Saturday of February at Belle Vue as the Rovers demolished Hereford United with two goals from Duerden (at 14 minutes and 50) and a penalty from captain Penney after 56 minutes when Caudwell was chopped down in the penalty area.

The Endsleigh Trophy quarter-final on Tuesday 2 March was played at Belle Vue against Northwich Victoria. The Rovers struggled to put a team together because, for a variety of reasons, they had 10 players out. McIntyre was Cup tied, having played for Barrow in a previous round; Hume and Sutherland were suspended; Shaw was on international duty with the England semi-professional squad for the game against Italy; and Maxfield, Wright, Goodwin, Minett, Brookes and Warren were injured. A second-string team managed to win by the odd goal in five, with all the goals coming in a 20-minute period in the second half. Barnwell-Edinboro (66) started the rush, Tait scored for the visitors a minute later, George (69) gave the Rovers the lead and Barnwell-Edinboro increased it after 76 minutes. Vicary scored for Northwich four minutes from time but only an inspired goalkeeping exhibition from Greygoose really denied the Rovers a more emphatic win with their depleted side.

Even with half a dozen of the missing players back, the Saturday after produced a poor display at Woking as they went down to two goals from Hay. Another midweek game at home to Northwich Victoria on the Tuesday had to be called off because of snow and rain causing the pitch to be waterlogged. The following night the Retford Branch of the supporters'

Ex-Liverpool star Steve Nicol gets the player of the month award at the Woking home game.

club, under the able stewardship of the irrepressible Paul Mayfield, staged a fund raising race night at the Earl of Doncaster Hotel to help swell the Rovers coffers.

Saturday 13 March proved to be unlucky when fourth-placed Hayes visited Belle Vue and went away with a single-goal victory. This was another case of the Rovers dominating a game without being able to find the net, only to be hit on the break after 72 minutes when a cross from the right was fired into the net by Randall to drop the Rovers to 16th place.

The following Tuesday the Rovers faced Northwich Victoria at the Drill Field. In a torrid first half, only the brilliance of Woods in goal, with the help of the woodwork on occasion, kept the score goalless at half-time. The second half was a different story. Three minutes in and a Duerden shot following a corner put the first score on the scoreboard. On 61 minutes the same player added a second goal, with a low shot that goalkeeper Key made a mess of, allowing the ball to go through his hands into the net. However, minutes later came drama when the floodlights on the big new stand went out. But the fears that the game would be postponed, causing an already crowded fixture schedule to be overloaded, were alleviated after seven minutes when the electricians got the lights back on.

The break seemed to have a singular effect on the home team. After 75 minutes Nathan Peel was sent off for elbowing Maxfield and two minutes later the home captain, Steve Walters, followed him after a wild challenge on the unfortunate Maxfield. This did not stop Northwich, who pulled a goal back two minutes from time when an Illman shot was parried by Woods only to roll over the goalline, despite desperate efforts by McIntyre to clear. A penalty shout by the home team in added time was dismissed by the referee, who then awarded a penalty to the Rovers seconds later. Duerden took the kick, much to the chagrin of manager Ian Snodin, who wanted the regular penalty taker, Penney, to take it. After being informed that there was less than a minute to go, Penney let Duerden complete his hat-trick and complete a victory for the Rovers, which took them to the dizzy heights of 13th.

During the week that followed, Simon Shaw retained his England place when he was selected for the match against Holland and also signed a new two-year contract for the club. Andy Watson from Garforth Town had had trials at Huddersfield Town but Ian Snodin stepped in with a £25,000 cash offer and brought him to Belle Vue.

A home game against Welling United followed on 20 March. The Rovers had Lee Warren, Kevin McIntyre and Scott Maxfield out through suspension but new signing Andy Watson was on the bench. Welling, at the bottom of the table, should have been dead and buried in the first 20 minutes but the Rovers only had Duerden's ninth-minute strike to show

Alick Jeffrey and Gina Maxwell.

for it. Then, after 22 minutes, Zeke Rowe went on a brilliant run and provided the cross for Trebble to equalise. Two minutes before the interval Wright ran on to a Sutherland pass and shot past the advancing 'keeper. Welling centre-half Skiverton was to the fore in organising the resistance and would have equalised before half-time but for a fingertip save by Woods. The Rovers finally broke the dogged resistance of the bottom club two minutes from time when Watson, who had replaced Wright just past the hour, intercepted a clearance from Knight in the Welling goal and shot in for the third goal. In added time Penney hammered a cross from Shaw into the net to give the Rovers their biggest winning margin of the season, taking them 10 points clear of the relegation zone with seven games to go.

In midweek Ian Duerden signed a new two-year contract – a reward for his goalscoring exploits since he joined the club. With transfer deadline day (Thursday 25 March) looming, the Snodin brothers were out scouting for fresh talent at as many games as they could fit in. They did not get any joy from their endeavours but did make one signing on the recommendation of Eddie Gray, a former colleague of Ian Snodin at Leeds United. The player in question was Martin Foster, a former Leeds United player who had been released by Scottish club Morton. He was signed on a non-contract basis to the end of the season, giving him a chance to earn a contract. The club also registered Jamie Helliwell, a former Halifax Town player who was on trial with the club from local football. This was to ensure that he would be eligible to play in the Conference if it was decided that he was good enough during his trial period.

The Rovers played their next match on a Friday evening on 26 March because England were playing Poland in the televised European Championship the following day. The visitors to Belle Vue were Stevenage Borough and the Rovers' biggest League gate of the season, 4,629, witnessed a firework display before the match and a terrific game despite being goalless. It was Steve Nicol's last game in a Rovers shirt before he moved to Boston in the USA to become coach of New England.

Dave Penney lifts the Endsleigh Challenge Cup in front of 9,000 fans after beating Farnborough.

The Endsleigh Trophy semi-final first leg was played on the following Wednesday at Morecambe. An extraordinary match ensued as the Rovers scored first on 12 minutes when Duerden took a through ball from Goodwin and shot into the Morecambe net. The same player added a second after 33 minutes from a terrific cross by Watson. Although Morecambe had a shot cleared off the line after just five minutes, the Rovers were certainly the better team in the first half. But Morecambe came out in the second half clearly determined to do something about the scoreline. On 51 minutes Minett was adjudged to have pushed Keeling in the penalty area. Lyons took the penalty-kick but Woods dived the right way and pushed it round the post. A minute later Minett was penalised again for bringing down the same player on the edge of the box, with the referee pointing to the spot and then sending Minett off. Norman, Morecambe's leading scorer, took over the duty of penalty-taker, only to see Woods repeat his earlier feat. It was now backs to the wall for the Rovers' 10 men, as the trophy-holders staged a tremendous effort to keep the trophy in their sights. Apart from Keeling getting through to score on 70 minutes and despite losing Sutherland – with a shoulder injury – and Caudwell – suffering from cramp – the Rovers defence kept Morecambe out, with goalkeeper Woods in particular thwarting them with some fine saves. They held on to take home a 2–1 lead.

The first Saturday in April was not April Fool's Day, it was the 3rd but you could have been forgiven if you thought it was when the Rovers visited Kidderminster Harriers for the very first time. The Rovers had to borrow a set of blue shirts from the home club after the referee ruled that their white shirts clashed with Kidderminster's red and white. Constant pressure from the kick-off by the home team was crowned on 13 minutes when they finally breached the Rovers goal through a Druce volley from a cross by Hinton. Five minutes later the Rovers levelled the scores when Sutherland headed in a corner from Minett. Hadley put the home team in front with a glancing header on 53 minutes but again the Rovers hit back four minutes later when a 50-yard run by Penney ended with him giving the ball to Barnwell-Edinboro to slot home for a second equaliser. Back came Kidderminster to take the lead again after 75 minutes with a Hadley header but they received a setback four minutes later when Shaun Cunnington was sent off after receiving his second booking of the game. Seven minutes from time Maxfield volleyed in from a cross by Shaw to gain a point for the Rovers from a very entertaining 3–3 draw. Shaun Goodwin was taken to Kidderminster hospital after injuring his little finger, which he had to have pinned at Rotherham Hospital the following day.

Easter Monday followed quickly, too quickly for the Rovers, who succumbed at home to Hednesford Town by a single goal scored after 32 minutes by Kimmins. The Rovers had dominated the game in the first half hour, so much so that they should have been several goals in front. But 'keeper Morgan had kept the Pitmen in the game with a string of fine saves and continued to do so for the rest of the game.

Tommy Wright went into hospital on the Wednesday to have rough edges smoothed on a bone in his foot, while Dino Maamria went into hospital on the Friday to have an exploratory keyhole operation to check for suspected cartilage damage on his knee. Both were out of action for the rest of the season.

On the Thursday came the second leg of the Endsleigh Trophy semi-final against the holders Morecambe. The Rovers won on the night, with a goal from Watson after 64 minutes giving them the tie with a 3–1 aggregate score. Despite their heavy schedule of two games a week, the Rovers sent a full strength side to play a testimonial game for long-serving Mark Hancock of Frickley Athletic on Monday 12 April. The Rovers won 2–0, reversing the FA Trophy result from earlier in the season, with goals from Duerden and Kirkwood in the first 14 minutes as the rain teemed down, with thunder and lightning overhead.

Two days later, a rearranged League game took place at Belle Vue against Northwich Victoria. Glenn Kirkwood and Jason Minett were out through suspension but Scott Maxfield and Mattie Caudwell were back after injury. Hume, making his first appearance since February, scored after five minutes. Seven minutes later Northwich's Peel intercepted a ball from Shaw and went on to equalise. Ten minutes into the second half Duerden headed in a free-kick from Foster but Tait netted after Woods had blocked a shot from Illman to give Northwich a deserved point 14 minutes from time.

The weekend game was a dress rehearsal for the first leg of the Trophy Final against Farnborough Town three days later. A 65th-minute goal by Robson gave the bottom club the points but it did not stop them being relegated that day. Results elsewhere meant that Farnborough went down and, despite losing, the Rovers were safe from relegation in 16th place with two games to go.

On Tuesday 20 April the Rovers made the long trip to Farnborough again for the Endsleigh Trophy Final first leg. Heavy rain earlier in the day put the match at risk but despite the pitch being waterlogged in places the match went on. The home team were reduced to 10 men after 57 minutes when Harte was sent off after a second booking. It was not a great game, as much because of the playing conditions as anything but the Rovers did enough to get a win, confirmed by Penney volleying in at the far post from a cross by Shaw in the last minute. The Rovers team was Andy Woods, Simon Shaw, Scott Maxfield, Lee Warren, Dave Penney, Colin Sutherland andy Watson (Matt Caudwell, 80 minutes), Shaun Goodwin, Ian Duerden, Glenn Kirkwood (Jamie Barnwell-Edinboro, 46 minutes) and Jason Minett. The substitute not used was Martin Foster.

On a hot sunny day the following Saturday, over 800 Rovers fans, constituting half the attendance, had to queue to get through one turnstile at Telford United. This meant delaying the start of the match by 15 minutes to allow them to get in. Eventually they saw a hard-fought and entertaining contest that was not settled until the last five minutes. The three Rovers substitutes introduced during the second half combined to score twice and win the game. Five minutes from time Caudwell put over a cross for Beckett to head in his first Conference goal for the club and in the last minute, from a low cross by Caudwell, Penney curled in a left-foot shot past the man who had defied them throughout the match, former Rovers goalkeeper Dean Williams.

Dino Maamria celebrates winning the McMillan Trophy.

On Wednesday 28 April the Rovers' first annual awards night took place at the Earl of Doncaster Hotel before a packed audience. Lee Warren won the players' Player of the Year award, Ian Duerden took the Young Player of the Year award, Dave Penney won the club's Goal of the Season for the first of his two goals against Morecambe on 16 January and Simon Shaw received a special award from Charlie Williams for his selection for the England semi-professional team. Colin Sutherland was voted the *Doncaster Star* Readers' Player of the Year and was absolutely thrilled with winning his first-ever award. Then, to great applause, John Ryan announced that he and Peter Wetzel had agreed a deal with Westferry Ltd to acquire control of Doncaster Rovers Football Club. They would officially take over as the club's new owners on the day of the second leg of the Endsleigh Trophy Final.

The first day of May was the last League game of a hard, demanding season. The Rovers, safe in 16th place, rested several players for the home game against FA Trophy finalists and eventual winners Kingstonian. After a minute's silence had been observed in memory of the 1966 World Cup-winning manager of England, Sir Alf Ramsay, the game was played out at a slow tempo, with a headed goal by former Spurs, Oxford United and Reading striker Leworthy in the 24th minute taking the points. This left the Rovers with a playing record of: played 42, won 12, drawn 12, lost 18, goals for 51, goals against 55, points 48.

On the evening of Monday 3 May a capacity crowd of 7,160 (far exceeding the expected 5,000), with many more unable to get in, witnessed the Rovers ending the season on a high by collecting their first piece of silverware for many a year. It was the biggest attendance at Belle Vue since the FA Cup win over Queen's Park Rangers in January 1985. The same 14 players turned out for the Rovers, the only alteration being Jamie Barnwell-Edinboro starting in place of Glenn Kirkwood, who replaced him on the bench. All three substitutes came on: Caudwell for Watson after 80 minutes, Kirkwood for Barnwell-Edinboro on 69 minutes and Foster for Minett in the 77th minute. Sutherland set them on their way after seven minutes, with a cracking effort from 12 yards and Duerden finished the job with two goals either side of the break to send the Rovers fans into delirium. The idea of doing a lap of honour after the match had to be abandoned when the fans invaded the pitch but the players appeared in the Main Stand to a mighty welcome as Dave Penney received the trophy. It gave Ian Snodin as much pleasure as winning the League Championship with Everton when he saw the team that he had gathered together from scratch finally taking a trophy. 'It might only be the Conference League Cup but try telling that to the fans. You can see what it means to them. To attract over 7,000 for a game like this just shows what the potential is in Doncaster for a successful football team,' said Ian Snodin.

However, when the retained list came out later in the week there was at least one big surprise when Andy Woods found himself on the released list. The hero of a number of games andy had saved two penalties in the Endsleigh Trophy semi-final against Morecambe. As the club could only use one 'keeper on the books, Ian Snodin wanted a more experienced man in the job. Others released were Duane Beckett, Jamie Barnwell-Edinboro, Harvey Cunningham, Darren Brookes, Danny George, Richard Powell and Robert Wild.

A civic reception at the Mansion House was accorded to the Rovers Cup-winning team on Thursday 13 May by the Doncaster Metropolitan Borough Council, who applauded the club's regeneration and the plaudits that a successful football club can bring to the town. For the supporters of the Rovers, they were just happy that the recognition by the council of the football club meant that the Rovers were well and truly back

Disgraced boss 'left in tatters'

Ex-Rovers chief 'a sorry figure' as he goes to jail

BY JANE STAPLETON

MILLIONAIRE business-man and former Doncaster Rovers supremo Ken Richardson's mental state was in tatters today as he began a four-year jail sentence.

The 61-year-old tycoon became psychotic and paranoid while waiting to be sentenced for plotting to burn down part of the Belle Vue soccer ground, Sheffield Crown Court was told.

He suffered hallucinations and delusions after being convicted of conspiracy to burn down the club's main stand four years ago.

Judge Peter Baker, who is considering making Richardson pay the £75,000 trial costs, told him: "You present us with a sorry figure in the dock today. But in 1995 you were able to exercise great influence on the destiny of Doncaster Rovers football club.

"In my judgement this calls for not only an immediate prison sentence but for a substantial one."

He said Richardson's legal applications had delayed the case for years and caused suffering to his co-defendants.

Richardson hired former SAS man turned investigator Alan Kristiansen, aged 41, to torch the ground for £10,000. Kristiansen pleaded guilty to conspiracy and was jailed for a year. Ian Hunter-Hay, 54, and Alan Cracknell, 32, like Kristiansen also from the

North-East, both admitted arson and were each given suspended nine-months jail sentences.

Richardson's jail term was today welcomed by the club and fans alike. Supporters had blamed him for the club's demise from the Football League.

Doncaster Rovers chairman John Ryan said: "I am just pleased that the whole thing has now been concluded and hopefully we can continue with the club turning over a new leaf."

Fans

Fan Richard Haley, who was chairman of the Save the Rovers action group last season, said: "I think everyone in Doncaster will be delighted. I think he has got what he deserved and I don't think there will be many tears shed in this town.

"He destroyed the club and destroyed our lives for a long time. I think a lot of people will be in a mood to celebrate at the Woking game at Belle Vue on Tuesday."

Gilbert Gray QC, in mitigation, had told the court how Richardson's mental state had deteriorated in the hospital wing at Doncaster Prison and he was suffering from a classic psychotic disorder.

He has been subjected to threats inside and his business affairs had suffered.

The Star newspaper cutting from 6 March 1999.

in business. The fans backed the club by taking advantage of the reduced prices for season tickets taken up before the close of the offer on 28 May, leaving the previous season's total for season tickets way behind. They also snapped up over 700 videos of the second-leg trophy success.

For Ian Snodin, the hard work was just beginning all over again. The team wanted strengthening for the new season so new players were needed to push for a return to the Football League and this time he had three months to find them.

The end of May 1999 had Ian Snodin delving into the transfer market in a bid to recruit skilful, experienced players before they got fixed up elsewhere. His first new recruit was goalkeeper Andy Warrington from York City on a free transfer, followed by former striker turned centre-half Dean Walling, signed from Lincoln City for a fee of £25,000. As the close season went on he added left-back Mark Barnard, a former teammate of Simon Shaw at Darlington, who turned down Mansfield Town to join the Rovers and Mike Newell, Alan Shearer's partner at Blackburn Rovers when they won the Premier League in 1992–93. The club also appointed Mickey Walker, a former Leeds United and Nottingham Forest youth-team coach, as coach to a new youth set-up.

A tough pre-season was on the cards with friendly games against Premier League Sheffield Wednesday (Reserves) behind closed doors, Sheffield United from Division One, old rivals Rotherham United from Division Three and Manchester City (Reserves) from Division One, all in the space of 10 days. Two single-goal losses to the Sheffield clubs, a goalless draw against Rotherham and a 2–2 draw against City were the results but an ankle injury to Glenn Kirkwood in the Manchester City game would prove problematic. The day after playing Manchester City Reserves in scorching hot weather they met Third Division Darlington in the semi-final of the Minster Carpets' Cup Tournament at Seamer Road, Scarborough and won by a goal scored by Duerden after 27 minutes. A day later they beat Scottish club Airdrieonians in the Final by two brilliant goals from Caudwell (2) and Maamria (89) to one by the Scots from Forrest after 65 minutes. Thus the Rovers started the new season with a piece of silverware.

With very little respite, further friendly games followed. A hard and not too friendly battle against Scunthorpe United at Glanford Park, with Newell scoring twice for the Rovers as Scunthorpe netted three, was followed by a testimonial match for former Rovers youth coach and manager Steve Beaglehole against Premier League side Leeds United, which drew a healthy crowd of 4,500 on a hot and sunny Sunday afternoon. They saw Leeds stroll to a two-goal victory, with £5 million signing Michael Bridges getting their second goal. At the time, Steve Beaglehole was with Leeds United as a coach and, although billed as his testimonial, shared the receipts from the game with the Rovers youth policy, which was operating with no funds from any grants but would be financed by the club.

Two games against lower non-League clubs – Andy Watson's old club Garforth Town helped officially open their new stadium along with Mattie Caudwell's old club, Hallam – rounded off the Rovers' pre-season work. During this pre-season period, Caudwell's displays since he had been at the club had attracted attention from other clubs but he readily signed a year's extension to an improved contract until the summer of 2001. Only days after signing Mike Newell, Ian Snodin received an offer from a Second Division club for him but when he passed it on to Newell it was turned down flat.

For this season the Conference had introduced five substitutes on the bench, from which three could be chosen to play at any time during a game. The season began on Saturday 14 August with a home game against Forest Green Rovers. There was a strong, blustery wind and driving rain at the start of the match, although it did not last too long. Before the match a minute's silence was held in memory of Ray Gilbert, a leading figure in the opposition to Mr Richardson in 1997–98, who had died recently. The football part of the season started well, with a goal from Duerden after just three minutes. But two goals from McGregor in the three minutes before half-time sent Forest Green in for a cup of tea with a 2–1 lead. Ten minutes into the second half and Duerden added a second to equalise for the Rovers and then he got his hat-trick 17 minutes before time to set the Rovers on their way with three points. The bad news was that Simon Shaw received knee ligament damage that would keep him out of the game for nearly the whole season.

Two days later the Rovers were rudely brought down to earth at Stevenage Borough, with a three-goal hammering after Newell had been sent off for receiving two bookings after 50 minutes. A half-time pep talk inspired the Rovers to fight back but all to no avail. Ian Snodin accepted the blame because he had changed the team after winning against Forest Green and played a three-five-two system, which he accepted had not worked.

The long-running saga of Robert Betts and his signing by Coventry City was finally settled on 18 August after an adjudication by an FA tribunal hearing at Walsall. Betts, who played for the Rovers' first team in the ill-fated relegation season as a 16-year-old schoolboy, was a product of the Rovers' Centre of Excellence and therefore commanded a compensation fee when he joined Coventry City on a youth training scheme that summer. The Midlands side offered the Rovers £5,000 plus a further £50,000 in staged payments as compensation. The Rovers turned this down and the judgement by the FA tribunal justified their stance. A five-figure sum had to be paid immediately and a further five-figure sum was to be paid after 10 first-team games, plus a six-figure sum to be paid after 40 first-team appearances. Betts had already played for the Coventry first team in the Premier League at this point and went on to make five starts and eight substitute appearances altogether in the League team.

The following Saturday the Rovers went to Woking and came away with a 3–1 win courtesy of a goal from Newell after 24 minutes and two from substitute Maamria in the last minute of each half, after being down to a penalty goal on 10 minutes. A 1–1 draw followed on the Tuesday at Belle Vue against the previous season's bogey team, Southport, with Rovers going one down on the hour and Hume equalising 14 minutes later. Hume's goal galvanised the Rovers, who threw everything at the opposition but failed to find a winning goal. In the dugouts, the importance of gaining points was made clear as Ian Snodin and Paul Lodge, the assistant manager of Southport, exchanged words and stood face-to-face with each other before being separated. So after four games the Rovers had scored seven goals, had seven goals put past them and had earned seven points to sit in seventh position. Injuries had once again reared their ugly

Mark Atkins takes on the Dover 'keeper.

head, with Watson, Caudwell, Shaw, Goodwin, Kirkwood, Wright, Maxfield and Duerden all on the injured list at various times over the first four games. Meanwhile, Mickey Walker's youth team began their Northern Youth Academy season on Wednesday 25 August with a game at Selby Town Youth, which they won 3–1.

The loss of two points from a goalless draw at home to Hayes dropped Rovers to 11th place, followed by a further drop of two places after losing at Northwich Victoria two days later on August Bank Holiday Monday. Two goals in the first half for the Victoria gave them a half-time lead, although Goodwin of the Rovers hit the bar with a penalty-kick just past the half-hour. Foster registered on the score sheet after 65 minutes but the Rovers returned home empty-handed. Manager Ian Snodin was deeply unhappy at the way his full-time team were outfought by a couple of part-time teams. After he read the Riot Act at half-time at Northwich, the team did perform better but Snodin wanted such performances on a more consistent basis.

The following evening, the Rovers youth team made their first entrance onto the national stage since their re-formation in the FA Youth Cup first qualifying round at Blackpool Mechanics, taking the tie by a two-goal margin with goals from Danny Martin and Duncan Milligan.

On the first Saturday in September the Rovers were involved in an extraordinary match at Hereford United, where eight goals were scored. Unfortunately for the Rovers they only got three of them on what was a scorching summer's day. Ian Snodin made a comeback in the starting line up. A goal in the first minute by Elmes gave the home team the early lead but McIntyre equalised three minutes later. Newell put the Rovers ahead after 29 minutes so that the teams went in at the break with the Rovers leading 2–1. Four minutes into the second half the home team levelled and on 56 minutes McIntyre was controversially sent off after a second booking. Two minutes later Hereford took the lead with a hotly disputed penalty. An own-goal by Hereford full-back Sturgess brought the Rovers level at three goals each but their 10 men were overwhelmed in the last eight minutes when Hereford scored twice to make their score five to the Rovers' three. The Rovers did win the cautions count, however, by six to one and one sent off.

At the beginning of the week the Rovers signed right full-back Simon Marples from Stocksbridge Park Steels after a brief period on trial. Scarborough had wanted to sign him and had him on trial for three months but they could not afford the fee of £15,000. Tuesday 7 September brought another home loss, to Altrincham, with Walling scoring an own-goal in a header intended for Warrington in the Rovers goal. Although they had played well the Rovers had failed to find the right net and lost. The Rovers' slide took them down to 15th place as Shaw, Kirkwood, Maxfield, Duerden and Sutherland stayed on the injured list.

A sweltering summer's day for the next match at Dover Athletic brought a win, after Dover had taken the lead on 24 minutes through Vansittart. Goals from McIntyre (26) and Hume (27) gave the Rovers a half-time lead, which could have been greater if Penney had hit the net instead of shooting wide from a penalty on the stroke of half-time. Penney did make up for it, however, when he rattled in a third goal six minutes from time as the Rovers dominated the second half. Unfortunately the Rovers injury list grew by two when Shaun Goodwin, with a hamstring problem and Mattie Caudwell, who was only on the field as a second-half substitute for 23 minutes before being substituted with a groin strain, were added to it.

The midweek game that followed against Hednesford Town at Belle Vue brought another win by the odd goal in three. The Rovers started at full tilt and registered two goals through McIntyre, who fired the Rovers in front in the first minute and Penney, with a second after 10 minutes. The Hednesford reply came in the 24th minute but really they were outplayed in the first half. A good display from the Rovers in a cracking game was marred in the last two minutes when the Rovers' Andy Futcher was sent off, after a second booking, on 88 minutes and Jimmy Kelly of Hednesford was also sent off after a second caution in added time.

A third successive win made September a very good month for the Rovers. This time it was Kettering Town on the receiving end at Belle Vue, when Maamria and Penney scored in the second half for the Rovers and Setchell pulled one back two minutes from time for Kettering. The Rovers had now elevated themselves to seventh position even without the injured personnel: Shaw, Kirkwood, Maxfield, Duerden, Sutherland, Goodwin and Caudwell, plus McIntyre under suspension. This list meant the Rovers could only field four substitutes.

In midweek, the youth team played their FA Youth Cup second qualifying-round tie at Belle Vue and beat Selby Town Youth convincingly by six goals to one. Skipper Jonathan Greenland got two, with Aaron Johnson, Kevin Leighton, Duncan Milligan and Paul Green supplying the other goals. Meanwhile, the last Saturday of September broke the Rovers' winning run when they went down by a single goal at Kidderminster Harriers. Although the Rovers started the game well, they faded badly and let the Harriers take over but despite the Harriers' domination they could only manage a single goal, scored after 32 minutes by Ian Foster.

Welling United were the visitors to Belle Vue on the first Saturday in October and they were struggling in the relegation places. However, despite the Rovers taking the lead 14 minutes from time when Minett converted a penalty and then seeing Warrington save a penalty taken by Hanlon after 85 minutes, the Kent team managed to rescue a point two minutes from time through Bailey.

On Wednesday 6 October the Rovers youth team took on Emley Youth at Belle Vue in the third qualifying round of the FA Youth Cup, winning a hard-fought match by the odd goal in five, with goals from Gary Lynch, Duncan Milligan and Kevin Leighton. The following Saturday the Rovers entertained new opponents in Nuneaton Borough, in third place despite being newcomers to the Conference. A goal after 20 minutes from O'Connor secured the three points for the Midlands team.

Saturday 16 October saw the FA Cup fourth qualifying round and the Rovers faced Crook Town from that hotbed of football, the north-east of England. Unfortunately the Northern Leaguers found that they were no match for the Conference side. The Rovers were four goals up in 16 minutes, through Newell after just 32 seconds and a hat-trick from Kirkwood (6, 12, 16). Three more in the second half from Caudwell, Kirkwood again and McIntyre completed the rout.

Six days later, on a Friday evening, the Rovers followed up with a two-goal victory at Telford United in a blood-and-thunder game that had four men, two from each side, sent off. The first to go was Telford's Maurice Doyle for a second booking after 35 minutes, with the Rovers capitalising on their extra man four minutes later when Caudwell scored with a good 20-yarder. In spite of only having 10 men, Telford gave it a real go in the second half and were the better side overall but they missed the best chance they had to get on the score sheet when they were awarded a penalty after 66 minutes. Murphy took the kick but Warrington beat it away. Two minutes later the game erupted when a two-footed tackle by McIntyre on McGorry saw both men sent off when McGorry retaliated. Eight minutes on and another flare-up occurred, resulting in Sutherland being sent to join the others in the bath. With nine-a-side there were gaps all over the place and it was the Rovers that took advantage when transfer-listed substitute Maamria added a second in added time. The Rovers were now in ninth place.

On Monday 25 October the youth team travelled to the JJB Stadium to play Wigan Athletic Youth in the first round proper of the FA Youth Cup. The Rovers, who had barely played a dozen games together, put on a magnificent performance against an older and more experienced team, scoring twice through strikers Danny Martin and Darren Fell in the last quarter of the game to win the tie. Despite Wigan throwing everything at the Rovers' defence in the last 15 minutes, they held out superbly. The Rovers team that night was Denis Kindel, a Canadian Youth international, Jamie Price, Aaron Johnson, Jonathan Greenland, Paul Robinson, Kevin Leighton (Craig Edwards), Duncan Milligan, Lee Snodin, Danny Martin, Darren Fell and Steven Beck (Paul Green).

The last Saturday in October was first-round day in the FA Cup, with the Rovers at home to the club that had replaced them in the Football League, Halifax Town. Played before the BBC *Match of the Day* cameras and a crowd of 5,588, the team held their own in the first half but Halifax took over in the second half, with Tate and Paterson putting the result beyond doubt and progressing to the next round.

At the beginning of November it emerged that Colin Sutherland wanted to leave the club, as he and his girlfriend were homesick for their native Scotland. Ian Snodin did not stand in his way, because he did not want unhappy players at the club and Sutherland was to miss the next three matches anyway because of suspension. The Rovers had also advertised the availability of Mark Hume after cutting short his loan period at Gainsborough Trinity with a week still to go, rendering him out of the Rovers squad. Thus the Rovers team were short of Sutherland, Kevin McIntyre, suspended for four matches and Jason Minett, suspended for one match, as well as a number of injured players. Clubless Mark Atkins, the former Scunthorpe United, Blackburn Rovers and Wolverhampton Wanderers defender, lived in Doncaster and had been training with the Rovers to keep fit. Ian Snodin agreed week-to-week terms with him and signed him to play with the Rovers while he waited for offers from Football League clubs. Snodin also indicated that Mirsud Bubalovic, who had played for Sochaux in France the previous season, was to be released at the end of his short-term contract in December.

The next match, on Saturday 6 November, found the Rovers so short of players for the trip to Sutton United in South London that they could only name three substitutes and two of those were Ian and Glynn Snodin. Shaw was out with a long-term injury and Watson, Wright, Foster and Newell were also injured. Barnard had stayed at home because his wife had gone into labour and Hume was still technically on loan at Gainsborough Trinity. Oh, the match? It was poor in the extreme, with Sutton taking the points from a Watson goal after 20 minutes. Ian Snodin was not impressed by the quality of the opposition and even less impressed by his team's lack of passion and commitment. After all, he had gone on as a substitute halfway through the second half and had been booked for a foul within 60 seconds!

The following Tuesday was the first match in the Conference Trophy, now named the McMillan Trophy. The Rovers came in at the second-round stage and were at home to Nuneaton Borough. Having got Jason Minett back from suspension, Mark Barnard back from the birth of his child and Martin Foster back from injury, the Rovers could still only field three substitutes; it would have been four but Shaun Goodwin, selected in the starting line up, was injured in the warm-up and replaced by Foster. Ian Snodin missed the game as he was away scouting for players, leaving brother Glynn to take charge of the team. Nuneaton only had two substitutes so they were also in dire straits. The upshot was that the Rovers won at a canter, with goals from Foster and Walling in the first half and Duerden and Maamria in the second.

The next evening the youth team travelled to the Deva Stadium to play Chester City Youth in the FA Youth Cup second round. While not playing up to the standard they set at Wigan, they had sufficient chances to have brought the tie back to Belle Vue for a replay. But it was not to be on the night and they had done extremely well to have got as far in the competition as they had. Darren Fell scored for the Rovers in between the home side's two goals.

Twenty-four hours later came the Rovers' debut in the Sheffield Senior Cup, from which they had withdrawn in the previous season. They were entered at the first-round stage and played Brodsworth Welfare of the Northern Counties East League at Woodlands. The Rovers' starting line up contained eight senior players, including Glynn and Ian Snodin and three youth players, who had played for the youth team 24 hours earlier. Also, five youth players were on the bench but only two (Lee Snodin and Darren Fell) were called upon. In dreadful wet weather it took the Rovers 33 minutes to register the first score, a penalty dispatched by Glynn Snodin after he had been brought down. Maamria scored on the stroke of half-time and added another two late in the second half for his hat-trick. Lee Snodin got the other goal in a 5–0 win. It was the first time a father and son, Glynn and Lee Snodin, had played in the same Rovers competitive match and both scored.

A goalless draw followed on the Saturday against Woking at Belle Vue, with the Rovers managing four substitutes on call. It was a game of two halves for the Rovers, which showed how inconsistent they were. A poor first half led to an all-action second half that had the visiting team rocking on their heels but the decisive blow would not come. Even though the under-16s were let in free and tickets were distributed around the local schools, the attendance was only 1,920 – the main reason being England's clash with Scotland at Hampden Park in a European Championship qualifier, televised live on Sky Sports. For the record, England won 2–0.

A week later, a visit to leaders Kingstonian brought three points for the Rovers, with a goal after 59 minutes by Duerden being sufficient to take the win. Only the brilliance of goalkeeper Farrelly and the Rovers' failure to put away other chances saved the home team from a heavier defeat. During the week, Colin Sutherland came back from Airdrieonians, where he had been on trial with a view to signing permanently but the Scottish club were not in a position to sign him until they had moved other players on. Mark Hume went out on loan again, this time to Barrow, initially for a month.

A 1–0 scoreline suggests a close contest and indeed Ossett Town made it hard for the Rovers to get the victory on Saturday 27 November but again the Rovers did not capitalise on the chances they had. The FA Trophy second-round tie at Ossett was played before a record attendance in a competitive match of 1,360 for the home club. The decisive goal was scored by Kirkwood after 58 minutes. During the following week the Rovers notified clubs about Shaun Goodwin being available. Because he was starting a business he had asked to go part-time but Ian Snodin refused such a request, requiring all players to be full-time so that they were available every day.

The first match in December was against Stevenage Borough at Belle Vue and the Rovers had Mike Newell and Jason Minett back, although Lee Warren failed a late fitness test on a groin injury picked up in training. The Rovers led, with a goal from Atkins after 26 minutes, until the 83rd minute when Stevenage equalised – the first goal against the Rovers in six competitive games – and then got a winner four minutes later.

The second round of the Sheffield Senior Cup occupied thoughts on a very cold evening the following Tuesday at Belle Vue. Just six senior players turned out, including Glynn Snodin playing alongside his son Lee and the rest included five substitutes from the youth team. Glynn was also in charge of the team because Ian was away on a scouting mission, taking in a couple of Central League games. A hard-fought match against Wombwell Main from the Sheffield County Senior League was won by a goal scored after five minutes by Wright, in front of an attendance of 769. Meanwhile, the Rovers received the thumbs down from Morecambe when they made a £30,000 offer for their leading scorer, Justin Jackson. He

Dave Penney in action against Sutton.

had cost Morecambe that much in the summer from Halifax Town. Morecambe were only four points behind leaders Yeovil Town, so obviously did not want to lose their top scorer, who was leading the way with 12 goals in the season at that stage.

On the last Saturday before Christmas, just 20 more people than the figure recorded against Wombwell Main turned out to see the Rovers beat relegation-threatened Welling United at Welling, with a diving header from Barnard after 11 minutes. It was a hard, tough game, which led to four bookings apiece for each side and one or two players were lucky to last the course.

In the week leading up to Christmas, Mark Atkins signed a contract with the club, having previously played on a week-to-week basis. The chairman then followed this with an increased offer of around £40,000 for Jackson from Morecambe but again this did not match their valuation of £70,000 and was turned down. The Christmas fixture on Monday 27 December was a Yorkshire derby against Scarborough at Belle Vue before a good crowd of 4,706. A stunning goal from 30 yards by Tate, re-signed by Scarborough from Halifax Town for £80,000, after five minutes took the points for the Seasiders, who were in the middle of the table with the Rovers. Despite having a good proportion of the play, the Rovers rarely troubled former 'keeper Andy Woods in the Scarborough goal.

On Monday 3 January the return fixture against Scarborough at the seaside resort ended goalless, with each side having a man sent off – Matthew Russell for Scarborough and Mike Newell for the Rovers – following an altercation between the two after 51 minutes. An even if full-blooded game, with both sides boasting good defensive records, ended as predicted before Scarborough's biggest crowd of the season (3,510), swelled by over 1,000 Rovers supporters.

On the Thursday of the following week Ian Snodin signed Doncaster-born striker Neil Illman, who had been released by Northwich Victoria, on a short-term contract. Two days later the Rovers took revenge on Sutton United when they visited Belle Vue by exactly the same score of a single goal, scored by Kirkwood after 23 minutes. Sutton had a chance to score after five minutes when they were awarded a penalty but Warrington dived the right way to save Newhouse's kick. A blow to the Rovers was an injury to Mark Atkins, who suffered a torn calf muscle.

A week later the Rovers, who had received a home draw in the third round of the FA Trophy, entertained Halesowen Town from the Southern League, who included former Rovers player Paul Birch in their team. The match ended in a 1–1 draw but it was touch and go for the Rovers, who went behind on 54 minutes thanks to former Aston Villa striker Ian Olney on his debut for Halesowen. Andy Watson equalised nine minutes later to take the match to a replay, which led to a most extraordinary evening for fans and players alike on the following Tuesday. The kick-off time at Halesowen was set at 7.45pm and the buses carrying the Rovers supporters had the fans clock-watching as they found themselves in a horrendous hold-up on the M1 motorway following two accidents. Some of the coaches left the motorway and meandered down the ordinary roads, with the supporters hoping that they would arrive in time for the kick-off. They arrived at 7.30pm but the team had not arrived, so the Halesowen club had not opened the turnstiles. The Rovers team had set off at 1.45pm but had got so badly caught up in the traffic jam caused by the accidents that they had to cancel their pre-match meal and arrived at the Halesowen ground at 7.50pm, after spending six hours on the coach. The kick-off took place at 8.30pm but the match did not warm up until the second half. Five minutes in Duerden netted for the Rovers but Halesowen hit back 20 minutes later through Evran Wright. Although the Rovers piled on the pressure late in the game, the score was all square at one apiece when 90 minutes came. The home team scored first after 12 minutes of extra-time when Crisp blasted his shot through a crowded goalmouth into the net. Two minutes later Minett equalised for the Rovers, who got the decisive goal six minutes from time when Walling headed in off the bar. The match finished at just gone 10.45pm.

The late-night experience did not seem to affect the Rovers too much, because on the Saturday they completed the 'double' over Kingstonian at Belle Vue, when Maamria fired in after 29 minutes. However, they had the chances to run up a much bigger score. They stood at ninth in the table, with 35 points from 24 games but 11 points behind leaders Kidderminster Harriers.

Meanwhile, the club announced the signing of striker Gary Williams, aged 20, from Accrington Stanley of the Northern Premier League for a club record fee of £60,000, beating several League clubs to the punch. His scoring record for Accrington during the season stood at 24 goals in as many League and Cup games. The club also signed David Price, a former Bolton Wanderers midfielder who had been playing in the US, on a non-contract basis. Both Williams and Price were due to play in the McMillan Trophy quarter-final game against Scarborough on Tuesday 25 January at Scarborough but the match was called off on the morning because of a waterlogged pitch

The last Saturday in January brought another interesting match when the Rovers visited Hayes. On a bobbly, muddy pitch, with a blustery wind blowing, Maamria set the Rovers on their way with a goal after nine minutes. Hayes equalised through Moore nine minutes later but on 20 minutes Minett fired the Rovers back in front when he followed up his own penalty-kick, which Gothard had beaten out. Stevens equalised for the home team nine minutes from the interval. McIntyre put the Rovers back in front 12 minutes into the second half but again the home team equalised when Flynn glanced a header from a corner-kick into the Rovers net on 69 minutes. Ten minutes later another penalty to the Rovers was neatly put away by Minett for what turned out to be the winning goal, which took them up to seventh place. It was a hard-fought game, with Hayes picking up five bookings and the Rovers three.

The first evening of February took the Rovers to Scarborough for a quarter-final tie in the McMillan Trophy. Both teams turned out strong sides, with the Rovers coming out on top by two goals to one after being a goal down at half-time. Wright and Williams redressed the balance and took the Rovers through to the semi-final. Ian Snodin attended the game but had only arrived back in the country in the afternoon from Hong Kong, where he had been on a scouting mission. In the meantime, Mark Hume and the Rovers parted company by mutual agreement. He had been on loan at Barrow for the last three months and was continuing to play for them on a week-to-week basis.

Another Cup tie followed on the Saturday in the FA Trophy fourth round at Dover Athletic. The Rovers had entertained ideas of winning this trophy and were the better team on the day but it was the home team who got the vital goal when Vansittart scored after 57 minutes. Newell missed a sitter for the Rovers after 71 minutes when a low cross from Duerden beat the 'keeper. With an empty goal in front of him Newell hit the ball as it bobbled up and hit the bar from two yards.

Colin Sutherland, after trials with Airdrieonians and Queen of the South, finally made the move north of the border to Clydebank the following Tuesday, while Mike Newell transferred to Blackpool on Thursday. However, the Rovers fans were glad to hear that Kevin McIntyre had signed a new two-and-a-half-year contract with the club.

Hereford United were the next opponents in the League when they visited Belle Vue in the first of a vital three games for the Rovers that would confirm them as promotion challengers with three wins or condemn them to another campaign in the Conference with any other results. Hereford went away with a point from a 2–2 draw. McIntyre gave the Rovers an early lead in the fourth minute, which they held until the 65th when Fewings equalised. Maamria put the Rovers back in front seven minutes later but Leroy May levelled nine minutes from time.

The second in the trio of vital games was a rearranged game at Morecambe on Tuesday 15 February, which had the Rovers going all the way to the seaside resort, only to be met on their arrival with a continuous downpour of rain that had started around four o'clock. The referee, who had arrived at the ground at 5.30pm and found the pitch playable, inspected the pitch at seven o'clock – 45 minutes before the kick-off – and had no option but to postpone the game because of the waterlogged state of the pitch. The following day the Rovers shelled out £10,000 for Tristram Whitman from Arnold Town of the Northern Counties East League. A diminutive forward who had pace, he was one for the future according to Ian Snodin.

On the Saturday second-placed Rushden & Diamonds visited Belle Vue and went away with the full points when De Souza hit a superb strike past Warrington 10 minutes from time after a good run down the right. However, once again the Rovers outplayed one of the top teams but could not get any reward from the game. Rushden held on to their

Simon Marples against Sutton.

lead despite going down to 10 men after 85 minutes when Brady was sent off for receiving two cautions. Leaders Kidderminster Harriers lost their game, so Rushden & Diamonds took over top spot on goal difference, leaving the Rovers out in the cold in 10th place, 13 points behind and 15 games to play.

The game at Kettering Town on the last Saturday in February had to be postponed because of the Northamptonshire club's involvement in the FA Trophy. However, a behind-closed-doors match was arranged against Barrow from the Northern Premier League. Shaw had been out after rupturing ligaments in his knee in the first game of the season against Forest Green Rovers but had made good progress in his return to fitness. He was not risked in the friendly, though, after reporting a sore thigh. Glenn Kirkwood, Simon Marples, Scott Maxfield andy Watson, Lee Warren and Martin Foster were included to get some match practice after recent injuries, as were newcomers Gary Williams and Tris Whitman, together with a couple of trialists. Mark Hume returned to Belle Vue playing for Barrow, where he had reverted to the centre-half position. Tris Whitman, coming on as a substitute, scored the winning goal in the second half after an own-goal by a Barrow defender had given the Rovers the lead in the first half, with Mark Hume equalising just before half-time.

Simon Marples, having proved his fitness in the match against Barrow, made his international debut for the England semi-professional team against Italy Serie C Under-21s at Padova in a 1–1 draw on Wednesday 1 March. Ian Snodin was otherwise engaged that day, attending an FA disciplinary hearing at York to explain the club's disciplinary record, which had not shown any improvement from last season. Roger Furnandez, a Doncaster referee on the Football League list, had been brought in by the club to talk to the players in a bid to improve the discipline on the field and Snodin warned the players that any further serious infractions before the end of the season would result in a heavy fine for the club.

The Rovers' losing streak continued into March when they went down to defeat by the odd goal in three at Hednesford Town, with Penney squeezing a goal in between one either side of half-time for the home team. Apart from losing the match, the main gripe of the 305 Rovers fans who attended the game was that the home club increased the entrance price from £7, the normal price, to £10 for this one game. They showed their displeasure by verbally abusing some of the Hednesford officials but there was no trouble, which Hednesford admitted afterwards. The Hednesford club explained later that week that they had increased the price to pay for the increased police presence and the extra stewards that the police had advised were needed, which left them with a bill for £2,500. Ian Snodin missed the game, having gone to Scotland to check out a striker who had been recommended to him. He actually took in several League games while up there but came back empty handed. Having watched a video of the Hednesford game, the manager was unimpressed by what he saw from his team. A goalscorer was a desperate need, as the club's record showed, with just 33 goals scored from 28 games. Snodin tried to bring in a striker on loan from several Football League clubs in the couple of days before the Kidderminster Harriers game but did not get any joy.

So, on the evening of Tuesday 7 March the Rovers faced top team Kidderminster Harriers at home, with Duerden replacing Kirkwood to play alongside Maamria in attack. A much-improved performance saw the Rovers take the lead on the stroke of half-time when Penney drilled a low shot from the edge of the penalty area into the Harriers' net. However, two goals in the last four minutes took the points back to the West Midlands and Kidderminster widened the gap at the top of the table as the Rovers lost their third game in succession.

The following night the Rovers sent a second-string team to Frickley Athletic in the quarter-final of the Sheffield Senior Cup on a cold, wet, miserable night made worse by the fact that they were beaten once again in a Cup competition by the Northern Premier League club. Two clear goals scored by Thompson after 35 minutes and Hayward six minutes from time ensured the Rovers left empty-handed. However, one good thing to come out of the game was a first appearance for Simon Shaw after recovering from a cruciate knee ligament injury.

Remarkably, the Rovers then went to high-flying Yeovil Town on the following Saturday and, despite going down to a Tisdale goal after 45 seconds of the game, hit back through Penney after 26 minutes. Maamria added a goal eight minutes into the second half, while three minutes later Tonkin headed into his own goal to give the Rovers a 3–1 win. The Rovers had dominated the second half in particular and were worthy of their victory. They followed this three days later by visiting Telford United in the semi-final of the McMillan Trophy and took a 2–1 lead back to Belle Vue for the

Team and staff photo, 1990-2000.

second leg, courtesy of goals from Williams after six minutes and Walling on 21 minutes, with Edwards pulling one back for the home team two minutes later. It was a hard-fought game in which the Rovers showed their capacity to play good football and achieve a result. Glynn Snodin, in charge of the team because Ian was resting after a hernia operation the previous Sunday, expressed his disappointment at the team not scoring more goals, although he was happy with the lead and particularly with the performance.

The club turned down a reported six-figure sum from Sunderland for Simon Marples and also admitted that Wigan Athletic were very interested in Mattie Caudwell, although they had not received any concrete offer. Later in the week the Rovers signed yet another striker when Neil Campbell joined the club from Southend United for a fee of around £10,000. Ian Snodin knew the player from his Scarborough days and, with the added experience gained in the two years since then, he was expected to provide what had so far been missing this season – goals. The signing formality was duly completed on the pitch before the Yeovil Town game in the return at Belle Vue. After winning at Yeovil the previous week it was expected that the Rovers would triumph at home. But a different performance from the Rovers meant a different result, one that manager Ian Snodin was not happy about. No passion, no pride and the worst performance since he had been at the club were just some of the phrases used. Why? Because Yeovil rattled in three goals without reply. This prompted the fans to have a go at the players and management, whom they had backed until to this stage. The Rovers did have a penalty at the end of the first half but McIntyre put it wide. The Rovers now stood in 13th place.

In midweek a trip to relegation-threatened Southport proved fruitless once again when Guyett headed in six minutes from time. The Rovers were without the suspended Dave Penney, while Simon Marples and Kevin McIntyre were both with the England squad for a game against the Netherlands. The absence of Marples gave Simon Shaw a way back into the team after his long absence. The Rovers shaded the game and would probably have won if they had kept 11 men on the field. But the referee, inexperienced at this level, issued seven bookings to the Rovers, two of them to Minett, who was sent off in the first minute of the second half and four bookings to the home team. Officials from both clubs agreed on one thing: the performance of the referee left a lot to be desired, with the number of bookings not reflecting the type of game. Watching the video on the way back home only served to enhance the injustice of the result, because new signing Neil Campbell had a goal disallowed for offside after seven minutes, which the video showed was valid. However, the papers the next day said the Rovers had lost and the League table reflected this, with the three points throwing a lifeline to Southport and thrusting the Rovers, thinking of promotion only a few games ago, deeper into the bottom half of the table. The following day John Ryan sent a letter to the referees' committee at the FA, informing the head of referees of the views of the club with regard to the official in charge of the Southport match.

Wednesday 22 March saw Simon Marples start for England against the Netherlands at the Drill Field, Northwich, before being substituted by Kevin McIntyre. England won the friendly international 1–0. During the week a meeting between Doncaster Metropolitan Council, Doncaster Rovers and Doncaster Dragons, the Rugby League club, had been held to investigate the means by which a new stadium would be funded.

The following Saturday the Rovers took away a point from their visit to Nuneaton Borough by virtue of a goalless draw. A scrappy end-of-season-type game that would be soon forgotten gave Nuneaton a 10th home game without a win but the Rovers had at least halted their slide after suffering successive defeats prior to this game. The Rovers did win the cautions game by six bookings to three.

The midweek game at Belle Vue was the second leg of the McMillan Trophy semi-final against Telford United. Telford, who played a strong side despite having a semi-final game the following Saturday in the FA Trophy, dominated the first half as they tried to get the goal that would give them parity but a half-time pep talk roused the Rovers for the second half. They had the better of the game in the second period but the result rested on two penalties; the first by Maamria after 63 minutes hit a post and the second by Penney, eight minutes from time, gave the Rovers a single-goal win on the night and a 3–1 win on aggregate as they reached the Final of the trophy that they already held from the previous season.

The Rovers then had an 11-day break before their next game, at home to Morecambe on Saturday 8 April. Their League opponents for the April Fool's Day game should have been Telford United but their semi-final of the FA Trophy took precedence. This gave the Rovers an enforced break, which enabled their injured players – Glenn Kirkwood, Martin Foster and Mark Atkins – to regain fitness. However, despite having a full squad to choose his team from, the team that Ian Snodin sent out against Morecambe failed to justify the manager's confidence. The Rovers had the better of a poor first half and should have had the lead by half-time but a lacklustre Morecambe side managed to get a goal in the second half and take the points on offer. A through ball for Justin Jackson, the man whom Rovers wanted to sign for a record fee earlier in the season, to run on to and go through to score his 23rd goal of the season, gave Morecambe the win and dropped the Rovers to their lowest position of the season: 15th, with 43 points from 34 games, just six points above the relegation places. The fans were now getting at the manager from the terraces and many of the lowest League 'gate' of the season walked away long before the end.

The Rovers had gone four League matches without scoring but three days later they went to Kettering Town, two places below them and battled to a 2–2 draw after leading at half-time by an eighth-minute Kirkwood goal. The new pairing of Campbell and Kirkwood, who had not played for a month, up front showed up better than any previous duo. Four minutes into the second half a misunderstanding between Marples and Warrington let in Setchell for an equaliser and the home team took the lead through Carl Alford on the hour. It took a header by Atkins, 20 minutes from time, to salvage a point after the Rovers went down to 10 men when Walling was sent off after 64 minutes for a second booking.

On the Saturday the Rovers made the journey to Morecambe for the second time for their League fixture against the Seasiders. This time there was no problem with the pitch: the problems were on the field. Justin Jackson scored first from a penalty after 15 minutes and Eastwood added another for the home team halfway through the second half after McIntyre had been sent off following a second caution some minutes earlier. Williams did pull one back for the Rovers 10 minutes from time but it was too little, too late. Ironically, this was the Rovers' sixth game without a win but things might have been very different for the team and for the manager if they had played on the original date in February, called off because of the waterlogged pitch, when they were on a great run and Morecambe had gone nine games without a win.

As it was, because of other results on the Tuesday evening, the Rovers were pushed down to their lowest position of the season – 17th, seven points above the relegation zone. Thus, on Thursday 20 April the Snodin brothers were called to a board meeting and dismissed from their posts. The shock hit Ian Snodin hard. He was a fan of the club and had attended games during the Richardson era and been appalled at what he saw. He had been a player, passionate and committed to the game; these were the same sentiments that he brought with him as a manager. Very often such men cannot deal with other people that do not show that same passion and commitment to the cause, leaving them very frustrated in the quest for success. Unfortunately, by its very nature football can be a ruthless and unforgiving business, especially for managers, irrespective of their status as a player. The season had started with such bright prospects for the Snodin brothers once the new regime had bedded in. But it was not to be on the field of play, despite the hours put in watching match after match, two or three nights a week, in the hope of finding the right players to perform for them. Although a few fans had been calling for the manager's head the majority had backed him, so it was a sad day when such heroes were unceremoniously shown the door. Because of recent poor displays, the attendances had dropped to around the 2,000 mark and the prospect of dropping to the Northern Premier League must have seemed frightening to the men in charge of the club. The man who brought the players to the club was always the obvious man to go, especially when the top men had lost confidence in his ability to secure success. The board, having placed on record their appreciation of the efforts of the Snodin brothers, appointed Dave Penney as caretaker player-manager, with Mark Atkins as his assistant, to the end of the season.

The first game in charge for the new management team came two days later, with a home game against Dover Athletic. The team, selected from a full available squad, lost by a single goal, scored after 22 minutes by Le Bihan before a crowd of just under 2,000. The Rovers actually dominated the game but the same failing persisted; nobody could hit the back of the net despite the numerous chances on offer. Dover took their one real chance and that was the difference between the two sides. This took the club down to 18th place in the table, just four points away from the relegation places and another fight against the drop was in the offing.

Two days later, on Easter Monday, virtually the same team went to Altrincham and came away with a 2–1 win – their first victory at the eighth attempt – against a team in the same sort of trouble as themselves. While the Rovers had the better of the early exchanges, it was not until the 34th-minute dismissal of Maddox of Altrincham that the Rovers could exercise real dominance. They took immediate advantage of their numerical superiority and Campbell headed in to give them a half-time lead. They continued to press in the second half but when they took a breather just past the halfway mark the home team found an equaliser when Ellison headed in. Four minutes later Warren stabbed in from close range for his first goal of the season and the winning goal for the Rovers.

Another game on the Wednesday at Belle Vue against Telford United produced another win – their first at home since January – before the lowest League attendance of the season, 1,871. For both clubs it was their third game in five days and it showed in a drab first half of few incidents. The second half was more attacking and the Rovers

Andy Watson takes on a Welling defender in front of the main stand at Belle Vue.

claimed the points from this relegation battle, with goals from Atkins and Kirkwood late in the game. The win shot the Rovers up to 12th place, nine points above the relegation zone, with just three games to play.

With the end of the season nigh the Rovers had to get their games completed, so their fourth game in a week was a trip to Forest Green Rovers on the Saturday. Forest Green Rovers were second-from-bottom and in real danger of returning to the Southern League from whence they had come. The Rovers looked leg weary for most of the game, going down to a goal from Sykes seven minutes from time despite the home team being a man short from the 75th minute, when Adie Mings was sent off following a second booking. A late rally by the Rovers, who had not looked like scoring throughout the game, did not produce any alteration to the final score. For the Rovers of Forest Green the three points were a lifesaver, because they went on to keep their place in the Conference.

On May Day bank holiday in the penultimate League fixture at home to Northwich Victoria before a new low crowd of 1,865, a much-changed team scored a 2–0 victory over the Cheshire side. With the club safe from relegation and a number of players suffering from their exertions over the previous week, Dave Penney used the members of his squad to provide fresh legs. A brace of goals from Maamria late in the game gave the Rovers the three points and lifted them up to 11th place. Before the game, centre-half Colin Hawkins was introduced to the crowd as a signing for the new season from St Patrick's Athletic of the League of Ireland.

At a news conference held at the Grand St Leger Hotel on Wednesday morning, 3 May, the Rovers announced that Steve Wignall would be their new manager and former Telford United manager Alan Lewer would be his assistant. Dave Penney was appointed player-coach. Wignall had been chosen from over 100 applicants and would take over immediately. He had taken over as manager of Stevenage Borough in March but had been working on a non-contract basis.

Ian Duerden and Andy Watson in action against Welling.

The following Saturday, a goalless draw at second-placed Rushden & Diamonds was watched by the new management team of Wignall and Lewer, who saw their new charges look anything but a relegation team. The home team were presented with the League runners'-up Trophy before the start of the game but the Rovers had come to spoil the celebration party, not to join it. Dave Penney was in charge for this final match and his team had the home team hanging on at the end to get a draw to end the most successful season in their history. The result left the Rovers in 12th place for the season, with a record of: played 42, won 15, drawn 9, lost 18, goals for 46, goals against 48, points 54. Their average attendance figure for home games showed a 12 per cent drop from the previous season to 2,981, so they were second behind Rushden & Diamonds.

The very last match of a long season was the Final of the McMillan Trophy on Monday evening, 8 May, at Belle Vue. Because their opponents, Kingstonian, were in the Final of the FA Trophy on the following Saturday, it had been decided that a single match (usually it was over two legs) would determine the winners of the Conference Trophy. The Rovers won the choice of grounds and the match was won by two clear goals scored in the second half by Jason Minett and, perhaps fittingly, Dave Penney 10 minutes from time before a crowd of 3,837. Captain Dean Walling accepted the trophy, ensuring the Rovers ended the season with some more silverware to add to what they had won at the beginning. Before the match Beazer Homes, the Rovers' main sponsor, renewed their shirt sponsorship for another season by signing the documents on the pitch before the assembled crowd.

The first team had finished their season on a high, with a respectable 12th position in the table and some silverware for the boardroom. But the youth team still had games to play. On Sunday 14 May they beat Ossett Town Youth by five goals to four at High Melton College to be confirmed as champions of the Northern Academy League, with the trophy being awarded to them after the game. They still had one game to play three days later at Eccleshill United Youth, which ended in a goalless draw. The final record for the youth team in their League was as follows: played 24, won 16, drawn 7, lost 1, goals for 75, goals against 20, points 55. The main members of the youth team were Dennis Kindel in goal, Paul Robson, Kevin Leighton, Paul Robinson, Jamie Price, Michael Baker, Aaron Johnson, Paul Green, Duncan Milligan, Bryan Cox, Jim Lewis, Jonathan Greenland, Lee Snodin, Gary Lynch, Danny Martin, Matt Parker and Darren Fell. The man in charge was Mickey Walker, ably assisted by youth development officer Rob Smith.

The end-of-season presentation evening was held on Tuesday 10 May at the Earl of Doncaster Hotel. Kevin McIntyre was the chief recipient, winning two awards: the Young Player of the Year and the players' Player of the Year. Simon Marples was voted the *Doncaster Star* Player of the Year by their readers and the first award for a Youth Team Player of the Season went to Darren Fell, who had scored 14 goals in the League, two in the Youth Cup and nine in the many friendly matches played, including all three in a 3–0 win at Manchester United. The supporters' club Player of the Year was Dave Penney, who had beaten the previous holder for the last two seasons, Lee Warren, into second place.

The season had ended with a new man, Steve Wignall, in charge of the playing side of things. His brief was simple: get the club back into the Football League. The real work started the minute the final whistle blew on the season and he made his first signing two days later, with midfielder Jimmy Kelly joining from Hednesford Town for around £15,000. He was followed at the end of the month by striker Carl Alford from Stevenage Borough for a fee of £55,000 and Tim Ryan from Southport on a free transfer. Wignall also issued the retained list, keeping the players that were on contract, giving Mark Barnard and Martin Foster new contracts and releasing six players – Dino Maamria, Lee Warren, Scott Maxfield, Glenn Kirkwood, Jason Minett and Tommy Wright – who had come to the end of their contracts. Further good news for all Rovers supporters during the month of May came with the announcement by the Football Association that Ken Richardson had been banned from all involvement in football for life.

During the close season the dressing rooms and corridors in the Main Stand were refurbished with new flooring, which was suitable for studded boots. The club also agreed a 25-year lease with Case International Harvesters for the use of Cantley Park as a training ground and would spend around £75,000 on bringing it up to a suitable standard. The strip for the coming season was to be red shirts, navy blue shorts and white socks, with the away kit being white shirts with red collars, cuffs and piping.

The players reported back for pre-season training on 3 July, together with several trialists who would accompany them on their tour to Scotland. Manager Steve Wignall made some more signings as the preparations for the new season went ahead. Chris Newton, a midfield player released by Halifax Town, was signed after trials, Steve Halliday, a striker, joined the club on a free transfer from Motherwell and Jamie Paterson, who refused a new contract with Halifax Town, joined the Rovers on a two-year contract at the end of July. The question of a back-up goalkeeper to Andy Warrington was solved before the start of the League games when Barry Richardson was signed on a one-year contract.

A pre-season mini-tour to Scotland, where they played a St Mirren XI (2–3) and then a Motherwell XI (3–2), was followed by games against Football League sides Mansfield Town (2–2) and Hull City (1–2) at Belle Vue and a 1–1 draw at Ilkeston Town. A number of games behind closed doors also helped provide a stiff build-up to the new season.

In the first days of August it was reported that Mike Collett, who had already bought some shares in the club and Ken Chappell, who had assisted in preparing the new training ground at Cantley Park, would join the board of

An aerial shot of Belle Vue.

Photoshoot 2000.

directors. Meanwhile, the Rovers ran a reserve team in the Central League, a League for Football League clubs' reserve teams. Their season started on 16 August, three days before the Conference season opened, with a game against Hartlepool United at Belle Vue. Tris Whitman scored the Rovers' goal in a 1–1 draw. The youth team had also changed Leagues and would play in the Football League Youth Alliance North East Conference this season. Their first game on 19 August, against Bradford City Youth at Cantley Park on a rainy morning, ended all square at three goals each, with two goals from Darren Fell and the other from captain Jamie Price.

The first team opened their season at Belle Vue against Nuneaton Borough on Saturday 19 August as second favourites for promotion after Rushden & Diamonds. The Rovers started well and scored first through Paterson on 26 minutes but three minutes later a shot from Nuneaton's Taylor hit the bar then rebounded off the back of Warrington into the net for an equalising goal. Both teams had chances to win in the second half but the final score remained at one apiece.

The Rovers needed to get off to a good start because they would be playing two games a week for the first six weeks. However, the following Tuesday they visited newly relegated Chester City at the Deva Stadium and lost by three clear goals. The first goal, from Beesley, came after just 45 seconds and put the Rovers on the back foot for the rest of the game. A second goal from the same player on the hour was followed by Kelly, for the Rovers, receiving a straight red card for a tackle on Blackburn after 64 minutes. Three minutes later they had the chance to pull one back when they were awarded a penalty for 'hands'. Alford took it but Chester's 'keeper Greygoose smothered the ball. With 15 minutes left to play, Chester went down to 10 men when Carl Ruffer received a second booking but they still managed to score a third goal on 81 minutes through Paul Carden. On the same evening the Rovers' youth team entertained Chester City Youth in the first qualifying round of the FA Youth Cup at Belle Vue. Goals from Paul Green, just after half-time and Paul Robinson, a minute from time, earned a 2–2 draw and a replay at the Deva Stadium, Chester.

The next first-team game, on the Saturday, at Forest Green Rovers, started 15 minutes late to allow the Doncaster supporters into the ground after a series of accidents on the M5 had held them up. Another disappointing display at least brought a point from a 2–2 draw, with all the goals coming in an 18-minute spell in the second half. Twice the home team took the lead, with centre-back Barnard heading in from dead ball-kicks to keep the Rovers in with a chance each time.

The August bank holiday Monday fixture was a home game against Woking. In front of a disappointing attendance, under 2,500, the Rovers disappointed the faithful again by losing to a penalty goal from Steele, three-quarters of the way through the game. The frustrated fans had a go at Steve Wignall as the game ran to its close and even John Ryan was moved to call it a 'shocking display' after the game. The loss dropped them to 20th place, third from the bottom.

In the replay of the FA Youth Cup first qualifying round at Chester City on the evening of Wednesday 30 August, Mickey Walker was in a dilemma. The Rovers' 'keeper, Dennis Kindel, had broken his leg the week before in a friendly at Oldham Athletic but the Football Association insisted the match had to be played even though Rovers could not bring another 'keeper in because of the eligibility rules. Some obtuse thinking placed Irish lad Ciaran Kenna, a defender, in goal because he had played Gaelic football, which includes handling the ball. He acquitted himself well in the unaccustomed position but was also very well protected by a magnificent defence. The only time the ball passed him was from the penalty spot after 81 minutes but by then the Rovers had two goals on the board, scored either side of half-time by Jim Lewis and Darren Fell.

The first Saturday in September, the 2nd, was the day that the Rovers won their first game of the season when they beat Morecambe at Belle Vue with another headed goal from Barnard, following a Paterson free-kick after 62 minutes. The scoreline bore no relation to the game because the Rovers could have won by a hatful of goals. But at least the performance was what was required by the fans, who numbered just under 2,000.

Another point was picked up at Northwich Victoria in midweek after a hard-fought match, in which Campbell equalised for the Rovers after 77 minutes, eight minutes after going on as a substitute for Halliday, who had a great chance to score in the first minute. During the week the Rovers added to their squad, already hit by injuries, by signing Michael Stone, a defender released by Scottish club Rangers. Despite the injury to striker Carl Alford, the Rovers let Gary Williams, who had not fulfilled the potential he had shown the previous season, leave the club for Accrington Stanley for a fee of just £25,000. The club had also taken an Argentinian, Moriano, on trial but he did not impress Steve Wignall enough to want to sign him.

A visit to Kingstonian on the Saturday brought disappointment again when the Rovers could only take a point from a 1–1 draw. They could have won if they had taken only half of their chances. Caudwell put the Rovers in front after 24 minutes but in the 58th minute the home team equalised when a corner-kick skimmed off the top of Barnard's head into his own net. At last, on the Tuesday the Rovers beat Southport at home to record their second victory of the season and their first Conference win over the fourth-placed Lancashire side. While not playing at their best, the Rovers got the goal that mattered when Shaw bundled the ball over the line at the far post following a cross from Caudwell.

The following evening the Rovers youth team travelled to Workington to meet and beat their youth team by four goals to one in the second qualifying round of the FA Youth Cup. Early goals from Ryan Williams and Darren Fell were added to in the second half by Paul Green and Fell again to win the tie comfortably. The Rovers' first team got another win on the Saturday by 2–1 over second-placed Hereford United at Belle Vue, courtesy of two goals from Campbell, to extend their unbeaten run to five matches and move up to eighth in the table.

A week later the team travelled south on the Friday for an overnight stay before their match at Yeovil Town, who were second in the table, on the Saturday. Mattie Caudwell took ill overnight but the big news was that Jimmy Kelly and Jamie Paterson were told to make their own way home on Saturday morning after being caught ordering drinks to their hotel room in defiance of the club's ban on alcohol 48 hours before a game. This necessitated changes in the team, with Andy Watson replacing Paterson and Tim Ryan replacing Kelly. The not unexpected result was a defeat by two clear goals. Campbell scored again but this time it was for the opposition when a corner-kick went in off the top of his head. A Darren Way penalty sealed the points for the Somerset team.

All was forgiven in the midweek game when two goals from Paterson and one from Campbell sealed a 3–1 win at home to Hednesford Town. The visiting team arrived at the ground just 15 minutes before the scheduled kick-off because of an accident on the A38, with the kick-off delayed by 20 minutes. Paterson's second goal came when he followed up his own penalty-kick, which Gayle had pushed out. Two minutes later came the biggest cheer of the night when former Rovers player Mickey Norbury was sent off for something he said to the referee. It was his second sending off in two games, having received his marching orders on the previous Saturday at Dagenham.

The last day of September had the Rovers meeting Boston United at York Street for the first-ever competitive game between the two clubs. Unfortunately for the supporters, who attended in large numbers, the

Manager Steve Wignall and assistant Alan Lewer.

ineptness of the Rovers display prompted them to jeer their team off at half-time when they were two goals down and again at full-time when they had lost by three goals to one, the consolation goal coming five minutes from time from a penalty by Paterson. They also turned on the chairman, John Ryan, who was sat in the stand on the upper tier, above his own supporters. At least the Rovers kept a clean sheet on their visit to Kettering Town in midweek, buoyed by the presence of new signing Barry Miller at centre-half. The fact that they did not score was worrying, with Carl Alford yet to get on the first-team score sheet. Both sides had chances to score but the respective 'keepers, Steve Wilson for Kettering and Barry Richardson for the Rovers, were in fine form.

A goal after four minutes by Campbell gave the Rovers a fifth successive home win against Dagenham & Redbridge in the Friday evening game on 6 October. The change of date came about because England were playing Germany in the last game at Wembley the following day and it was live on television. Campbell could easily have had a hat-trick and put the game to bed long before the end, when Dagenham nearly got their hands on a point in the dying minutes. It was not to be for them and rightly so but the Rovers do like to keep their supporters hanging on.

The following afternoon the youth team played their FA Youth Cup third qualifying-round game at the Seamer Road ground, Scarborough. They went three goals up in the first 40 minutes through Darren Fell, Ciaran Kenna and Paul Robinson and even though Scarborough hit back in the second half they were restricted to just one goal.

On the next Saturday, the first team's journey home from Hayes was all the sweeter because they had not only come away with a three-goal win but it was also the Rovers' first victory of the season on their travels. An own-goal by Pluck after five minutes gave the Rovers a good start. Paterson put away a penalty on 54 minutes after full-back Ryan Spencer had turned goalkeeper to stop a Barnard header going in and got his marching orders. Then Turner, on loan from Barnsley, slammed in a third for the Rovers 10 minutes later.

The Rovers' interest in the newly named Variety Club Trophy, which they had won for the past two seasons, came to an end at the first hurdle in midweek at Southport, when former Rovers fans' favourite Dino Maamria fired in a minute before the half-time break. However, the gale-force winds and wet, slippery surface had already contributed to the Rovers' distress on 23 minutes when Andy Warrington slipped on the turf, collided with Simon Parke of Southport and broke his jaw. He was taken to hospital in Southport and moved to a Liverpool hospital, where he had an operation to set his jaw. The Rovers had made 11 changes from the starting line up at Hayes, only to find they were up against a full-strength Southport team. Alford did get the ball into the Southport net but it was chalked off by the referee for a foul on the 'keeper.

The Rovers returned to their old habits in another Friday evening game at Belle Vue against bottom-of-the-League Northwich Victoria, who came, saw and conquered by two goals, one in each half. One hardly needs to try and describe the fans' reaction to that result. After the match, chief executive Ian McMahon announced he was leaving the club to seek a new challenge, which was to be in the US.

The Rovers' youth team faced Hull City Youth in an FA Youth Cup first-round proper tie at Belle Vue on the evening of Wednesday 25 October. The Rovers youngsters went two goals down after just 11 minutes but battled away until the 83rd minute when Hull added a third. A minute later Paul Green received a cross, turned his defender and lashed in a shot from just outside the penalty area for a consolation goal, with Hull adding a fourth a minute from time. One Rovers player, Edward Tarsus, actually missed the Cup tie because he had played international football for Turkey Under-18s against Canada Under-18s the previous evening.

The last Saturday in October was FA Cup fourth qualifying-round day, with the Rovers meeting old foes Southport at Belle Vue. In driving rain, the Rovers scored first after 50 minutes through Marples but they were 2–1 down 24 minutes later after Marsh converted a penalty and Elam added a second. Only a strike two minutes from time by Paterson earned them a replay at Haig Avenue three days later, in which another Marsh penalty minutes before half-time put Southport into the first-round proper. Heavy rain over the previous 24 hours made for a difficult pitch to play on but the referee ruled the match should go ahead.

More rain faced the Rovers at Leigh RMI the following Saturday, 4 November and on a mudbath of a pitch they took the points with a 20th-minute penalty from Paterson, although they had to battle late on to keep the home team out as they tried to salvage their nine-match unbeaten record. Once again Alford had a 'goal' disallowed for offside, so he was still not off the mark for the first team. For the Rovers it meant a move up to seventh place. The continuous rain throughout the week had forced the Rovers players to use the indoor facilities at the Dome because Cantley Park was waterlogged. The Sheffield Senior Cup match against Sheffield Club scheduled for Wednesday 8 November at the Don Valley Stadium, home of the Sheffield side, was called off on the previous afternoon because it was waterlogged. Then, to compound matters, the ground at Belle Vue was broken into on Wednesday night and all the players' boots were taken, so new boots had to be obtained and broken in before Saturday's match against Rushden & Diamonds.

On the morning of the game at home to Rushden & Diamonds on Saturday 11 November a public meeting at the Earl of Doncaster Hotel was called by London-based fan Robert Woodmansey. Around 400 supporters attended, as did chairman John

Captain Mark Atkins leads out the team at Belle Vue.

Ryan, vice-chairman Peter Wetzel and manager Steve Wignall. An orderly meeting listened to what the three club officials had to say and appreciated their informative speeches. Steve Wignall stole the show when he proved that he was as passionate about the club that he used to play for as the supporters were, even if he did not show it like previous managers.

Second-placed Rushden & Diamonds visited Belle Vue in the afternoon to face a resurgent Rovers team, who had a new strike partnership in Mike Turner and Tris Whitman. The match took a dramatic turn after 14 minutes when Billy Turley, the Diamonds 'keeper, was sent off for upending Turner as he bore down on goal. Paterson put the penalty neatly past substitute goalkeeper Stuart Naylor for the opening goal. The visitors were still a force to be reckoned with and equalised after 28 minutes when Underwood fired in from a free-kick. It took just five minutes for the Rovers to regain the lead when Whitman headed in a Paterson cross and bang on half-time Penney blasted the ball through a crowded penalty area to send the Rovers in with a 3–1 lead at the break. The Rovers shaded the second half but it was the visitors who got a second goal a minute from time when Brady headed in a cross from Mustafa. An excellent game gave the 3,500 crowd what they wanted to see: a good football performance and a win that took the Rovers up to fifth place.

On the Monday, Simon Marples, Kevin McIntyre, Tim Ryan, Neil Campbell, who scored a goal and Barry Miller played some part for an FA XI at Lancaster City's ground against a Northern Premier League XI in a trial match for the England semi-professional side.

Two days later, on 15 November, the reserve match against Halifax Town was called off to enable the team to play a Sheffield Senior Cup first-round game against Sheffield Club at the Don Valley Stadium. The Northern Counties East club went ahead after just three minutes when Fox headed in a cross. However, Campbell rattled in an equaliser just two minutes later. The Rovers scored twice more before half-time through Sherwood from the youth team and Walling. Sheffield strove hard in the second half to get something out of the game but on loan 'keeper Elliott Morris was equal to the task of keeping them out. Campbell wrapped it up in the last minute when he broke clear and shot past the 'keeper.

On Wednesday 22 November club president and former player Alick Jeffrey died, aged 61, while on holiday in Benidorm, Spain. A great player, the best that pulled on a Rovers shirt in many people's view, was no longer with us. It was a stunning blow to his family, friends and fans of the club.

The Saturday game at Telford on the 25th was postponed after a pitch inspection at 12.15pm. This meant a wasted journey for the team and for the supporters, who had made the trek down to Shropshire. It also meant a second successive Saturday without a fixture because 18 November had been FA Cup first-round day and the Rovers were out of that competition.

The Rovers' next first-team match was on Tuesday evening, the 28th, at third-placed Southport in the Conference. John Ryan, the Rovers chairman and his fellow directors paid at the turnstiles and stood on the terrace behind one of the goals with the Rovers supporters. This boycott of the Southport boardroom came after John Ryan had been verbally abused at the FA Cup replay between the two clubs a month earlier. The Rovers played well but lost to a penalty slotted home by Marsh nine minutes from time, having played the second half with 10 men after Dave Penney received a second caution on the stroke of half-time.

The first Saturday in December brought Stevenage Borough, who were two points and two places behind the Rovers, to Belle Vue. A minute's silence before the start was held in memory of Alick Jeffrey. A goalless draw ensued as the home team failed to capitalise on their numerical advantage from the 73rd minute, when Chris Metcalfe was sent off for a second booking. Eleven minutes later Sam McMahon followed him for the same reason, leaving Stevenage to play the last six minutes with nine men. One unusual feature came in the second half when flying CDs started landing on the pitch, which prompted the referee to hold up play. However, they were not coming from the crowd, as first feared but were being thrown over the Popular Stand from the ASDA car park by children who were getting the free discs from the superstore. Action was quickly taken and the match resumed.

The following Tuesday the Rovers were one of the Conference teams invited to play in the Football League (LDV) Trophy. They drew Rochdale from Division Three at home in the Northern Section in a match played on a straight knock-out basis, with golden goal extra-time before penalties. In an entertaining, fast and furious game the visitors, in third place in their division, took the lead on 21 minutes with a Jones penalty that gave Richardson in the Rovers' goal no chance. Then, six minutes from the break, Rochdale hit the post twice but within seconds Turner headed in to equalise. The Rovers took the lead as the hour came up, with a penalty of their own after Whitman had been brought down. Penney drilled it into the net. The Rovers had the chances to put the result beyond doubt as time ran out but in the last minute of added time Campbell, back in defence for a free-kick, got his head to the ball only to see it nestle in his own goal and take the match into extra-time. He made amends in the second minute of extra-time when he chased a long ball and shot past Edwards at the second attempt to win the game on the golden-goal rule. It was a pity that only 1,453 spectators attended because it was probably the best match seen at Belle Vue all season.

Belle Vue has seen many great moments in its long history but none more poignant than the scene on Thursday afternoon, 7 December, when an estimated 750 people, including many of Alick's old teammates, attended a memorial service for Alick Jeffrey inside the stadium. His coffin was carried through the players' tunnel onto the pitch that he had graced on numerous occasions and it stayed there while *Abide With Me* was sung by the assembled throng. John Ryan spoke movingly, saying that it was one of his proudest moments when he was able to purchase the club and make Alick Jeffrey, his hero as a young man, the president. At the end his coffin was taken to Rose Hill Crematorium, accompanied by his family and later his ashes were scattered on the pitch at Belle Vue.

The Rovers played their Sheffield Senior Cup away game against Yorkshire Main at Brodsworth Welfare's ground on the evening after the funeral. As Yorkshire Main had no floodlights and the Rovers had no free Saturdays, the clubs were ordered by Sheffield and Hallamshire FA to play the match at Woodlands. On an atrocious night of continuous heavy rain the Rovers ran amok and ran in a record score for the club, 14–0. Ian Duerden scored six goals, Robert Gill two, Paul Green two (and he had a penalty saved) and Andy Watson, Colin Hawkins, Neil Campbell and Dean Walling all got one apiece.

Rovers legend Alick Jeffery's funeral on the pitch at Belle Vue – former teammates including Charlie Williams paid tribute.

Captain Dean Walling lines up against Scarborough.

Two days later the Rovers journeyed to Hereford United for a game brought forward from 3 March. It was to be a contest between fourth and fifth-placed clubs, although the Rovers were five points behind the Bulls. The Rovers contained the home team until the 71st minute when they were awarded a penalty after Miller brought player-coach Robinson down in the area. Robinson took the kick himself but fired wide. The Rovers, who had had their moments, showed how expensive that miss was by scoring a winning goal five minutes later with a header from Turner following a free-kick. This completed the Rovers' first 'double' of the season.

A reserve match at Hartlepool United in midweek was used to give Carl Alford a full 90 minutes of action following a knee operation. Mark Atkins, on his return from a long spell out with injury, also played 45 minutes, scoring one of the goals in a 2–0 win with Duerden getting the other. Unfortunately Dean Walling and youth-team player Ben Sherwood were sent off late in the second half. Walling would be unavailable to the first team for three matches. Later in the week former Leeds United goalkeeper Mark Beeney, who had been training with the Rovers, was signed on a non-contract basis as cover to Barry Richardson, because Elliott Morris had returned to West Bromwich Albion after his loan period expired.

The following Saturday the Rovers gained revenge on Chester City by beating them at Belle Vue through a goal from McIntyre after two minutes. This brought an end to Chester's 17-game unbeaten run in all competitions. A minute's silence was held before the game in memory of three Nuneaton Borough supporters who were killed in a car accident the previous weekend while returning home from an FA Cup match at Bournemouth.

After a 10-day lay-off, the first team returned to action on Boxing Day at Scarborough but came badly unstuck, going down to a 3–1 defeat. Fielding the same team that had beaten Chester City in the previous game, their performance was nowhere near as good. Perhaps they had too much Christmas pudding. All the goals came in the first half, with Scarborough registering the first one after 23 minutes when player-manager Thompson rifled in a free-kick. Two minutes from the break Diallo put in from close range after the Rovers' defence had been torn apart but Rovers' Whitman pulled one back within a minute. However, with the last kick of the half, in injury-time, Ingram scored a third for the 'Boro. Although nonplussed by his team's display, manager Steve Wignall responded by bringing the players in for training the next day.

The last week of December had brought snow and ice, which caused the last match of 2000 at Nuneaton Borough to be called off because of a frozen pitch. The return match with Scarborough on New Year's Day 2001 was one of the worst games seen at Belle Vue in the post-Richardson era. A below-strength Scarborough side won a poor match easily, with two goals from Ellender, just before half-time and Pounder, 12 minutes from time. After having an unbeaten run that took them to fifth place before Christmas, the Rovers had turned in two very poor performances over the Christmas and New Year period, losing both games to Scarborough while looking as though they had never played together. They were roundly booed off the pitch after the game and were closeted behind locked doors for over half an hour as the management tried to find out what had gone wrong. The team had a chance to put things right on the following Saturday when they visited Woking. A much better performance from the Rovers brought home a point and it could easily have been three but the Woking 'keeper, Vince Matassa, earned his title of Man of the Match. It was not until 11 minutes from time that Whitman got the goal that cancelled out Griffin's 16th-minute strike.

In midweek the second round of the Football League (LDV) Trophy meant a trip to Hartlepool United, where Rovers went down by three goals to one. In an entertaining game the Rovers went in at half-time a goal down but drew level five minutes into the second half when Campbell glanced a header into the net. Within a minute, though, Hartlepool went back in front when former Rovers player Ian Clark sent over a cross, he later admitted as much, which went into the Rovers' net. Then, on 55 minutes, the referee ruled that Marples had fouled Clark in the penalty area and Tommy Miller did the rest. The one good thing that came out of playing in the competition was that the Rovers, on their day, could compete with the Football League teams.

Later that week Dean Walling left the club after the remaining 18 months of his contract were cancelled by mutual consent. Despite starting the season in the team, he had been unable to regain his place following injury and the

Players get ready for a photoshoot.

acquisition of Barry Miller. Late on the Friday Steve Wignall signed Mike Turner, who had had a three-month loan spell at the club earlier in the season, from Barnsley on a contract to the end of the season. He was, however, ineligible for the Cup game the following day.

The 13th day of January proved unlucky for the Rovers when they went to the Deva Stadium to play Chester City in the FA Trophy third round. They lost by two Whitehall goals scored in the 33rd and 36th minutes. An unnamed Rovers player was punched in the tunnel after the game but the player concerned declined to press charges.

During the following week Martin Foster was made available for transfer, Carl Alford went on a month's loan to Kettering Town and Danny Williams was signed on loan from Wrexham. The treatment room was full, as physio Jon Bowden assessed the injuries of Barry Miller (ankle); Tim Ryan (thigh); Colin Hawkins and Michael Stone (torn muscle); Simon Marples (chest infection) and Simon Shaw (ankle injury suffered in training). Later in the week Ian Duerden finally signed for Kingstonian, having been on loan there in November. Another incident that received some publicity happened on Thursday 19 January when youth player Paul Green was driving along Melton Road at Sprotbrough and collided head on with a lorry. He suffered a fractured collarbone but still went to the aid of the trapped lorry driver.

The Rovers had little difficulty in beating Forest Green Rovers in their next match at Belle Vue to register their first win in six games. Shaw, Marples, Hawkins and Miller all passed fitness tests and took their places in the starting line up. Campbell put them in front after two minutes but it was well into the second half before Penney added a second on 65 minutes, with Whitman wrapping it up nine minutes later. However, some sad news came through shortly after the game when it was learned that Ken Avis, a former supporters' club secretary and a vice-president of the club, had died from a heart attack shortly after getting home from attending the game.

Only seven first-team players turned up for training on the Tuesday morning. Jamie Paterson, Kevin McIntyre and Tris Whitman were all suffering from a bug and had been told to stay away. Although Barry Miller and Colin Hawkins played against Forest Green Rovers on the Saturday, they both aggravated the original injuries they had. Tim Ryan, Mark Atkins and Michael Stone were not making much progress with their injuries and were ruled out of the Saturday game at Dover Athletic, as were Jamie Paterson and Neil Campbell, suspended after accumulating five bookings each. In the meantime there was a reserves game at Rochdale to play on Wednesday 24 January. This provided goalkeeper Andy Warrington with a chance to make his comeback after being out for three months with a broken jaw. While he did not have a lot to do, when he did he handled it confidently. The Rovers won 4–1, with a team containing two trialists and several youth players. It was also the last game in Rovers colours for Martin Foster, who joined Forest Green Rovers on loan at the end of the week, signing for them permanently later in the season.

Colin Hawkins, Kevin McIntyre and Tris Whitman were all passed fit for the trip to Dover Athletic and Barry Miller agreed to play despite not being fully fit. A well-earned draw was a good result. The Rovers went behind after 20 minutes but got a deserved equaliser only minutes after the introduction of Watson to the fray. Some clever footwork and a good cross gave Turner the chance to hit the net after 63 minutes.

The Rovers entered February in fifth place but a long way behind Yeovil Town and Rushden & Diamonds, who held the top two positions. In their game at Nuneaton Borough, on a heavily sanded pitch, they outplayed the home team in the first half but still went in at the break without a goal to their name, although they had enough chances to sew the match up. The home team shaded things in the second half on a pitch that, by then, resembled a ploughed field and they got the all-important goal on 63 minutes, which condemned the Rovers to defeat.

The same result came the Rovers' way on the following Tuesday at Telford United, when Martindale tapped in after 12 minutes. Former Rovers favourite Dean Williams in the Telford goal had little to do until the last few minutes but he kept a clean sheet to give his team the victory. The Rovers went down to a third successive defeat in a week when they entertained Kingstonian at Belle Vue. A minute's silence was held before the start in memory of the aforementioned Ken Avis, who had died on 20 January from a heart attack. The match turned out to be a triumph for Ian Duerden, who scored both goals in the second half against the club who had let him go just weeks before. While the visitors deserved their win, they were helped by the dismissal of Kevin McIntyre after 37 minutes for a two-footed tackle. A meagre attendance of 1,787, the lowest for a League game since the club joined the Conference, watched the game. A few of those fans vented their wrath after each goal with chants of 'Wignall out'. Afterwards, John Ryan wondered whether the Rovers' fans standing on the main terrace at the Town end, who barracked Steve Wignall and supported the visitors throughout the game, really wanted a club, because Wignall would think long and hard about his future if the fans carried on like that.

A week later Dover Athletic visited Belle Vue and went away with a point, watched by a record low crowd of 1,640. The Rovers included new on-loan signing Peter Smith from Crewe Alexandra, who had joined them on the Friday afternoon. The visitors took the lead against the run of play just before half-time when they cashed in on a defensive mistake. Then Caudwell levelled things up just before the hour. This result left the Rovers in sixth place but they had played five and in some cases six more matches than everybody below them.

Over the next two weeks the Yeovil Town fixture at Belle Vue on Saturday 24 February was called off because of Yeovil's involvement in the FA Trophy fifth round. A rearranged game at Morecambe three days later was also postponed because Morecambe had an FA Trophy replay and the Saturday fixture at home against Hereford United had been played on 9 December. This League inactivity left the Rovers in 11th place at the beginning of March as other clubs caught up with their fixtures.

However, on Saturday 3 March a friendly match was arranged at Northern Premier League Altrincham, which the Rovers won by five goals to two. The full first team played in a reserve game against Mansfield Town Reserves, which they won 3–1 and a Sheffield Senior Cup third-round game at home to Ecclesfield Red Rose, which they won by seven goals, thanks to an own-goal, three from Campbell and one each from Turner, Watson and Miller. To compound matters for the Rovers, their fixture at Dagenham & Redbridge was postponed because of a waterlogged pitch so a near-first team turned out against Rochdale Reserves. Their last League fixture had been on 17 February against Dover Athletic and their next would be at home to Boston United exactly a month later!

Meanwhile, Rovers had signed former Sheffield Wednesday and Rotherham United left-back Dean Barrick from Bury and Martin Foster's contract was cancelled by mutual consent so that he could join Forest Green Rovers, where he had been on loan. Carl Alford finished his loan spell at Kettering Town and reported back to the Rovers prepared to battle for his place in the team, while Peter Smith's loan from Crewe Alexandra was extended for another month because of the lack of games available to him as detailed above. Things had also changed behind the scenes and it was announced that Alan Lewer had left the club by mutual consent after agreeing a severance package.

The Boston United game was worth waiting a month for because it turned out to be a real blood-and-thunder game, with plenty of goals, before a faithful 2,296 crowd. The Rovers got off to a cracking start when Whitman scored on six minutes but Weatherstone levelled half an hour later as each side took it in turns to have a good spell. The Rovers went in front again three minutes into the second half through Atkins but six minutes later the visitors were awarded a penalty when the referee penalised Miller for a tackle on Nuttell. Charlery put the penalty away and the scores were level again. The Rovers got on top towards the end and with two minutes of normal time left they earned a penalty for 'hands', which Paterson converted to put the Rovers in the lead. In added time Paterson rifled in a fourth to settle the issue.

During the week that followed, the Rovers signed Francis Tierney, who had been released by Notts County early in the season and then had a few games for Exeter City before playing for Witton Albion in the Northern Premier League. They also allowed Mark Atkins to leave for Hull City on a free transfer, for a last hurrah in the Football League. Tim Ryan and Kevin McIntyre played for England in the Netherlands on Thursday 22 March, a game England won by three goals to nil.

Friday 20th October, 2000

Versus
NORTHWICH VICTORIA
Kick-off 7.45 p.m.

DONCASTER ROVERS

MATCH DAY MAGAZINE

PROGRAMME £2.00

AT LUNCH WITH THREE ROVERS PLAYERS

Official Club Sponsor
Beazer HOMES

Nationwide
NATIONWIDE CONFERENCE

LADIES PHOTO SHOOT ISSUE

Programme for Doncaster Rovers v Northwich Victoria.

Two days later Ryan was playing at Hednesford Town for the Rovers but McIntyre was suspended for this game. The match did not get going properly until Caudwell scored a brilliant individual goal after 23 minutes. Twenty minutes later Barrick added a second with a free-kick from 30 yards for the Rovers to go in at the break with a two-goal lead. Whatever happened to the League's bottom team at half-time livened them up for the second half because they came out fighting, rattling in two goals, from Norbury and Bradshaw, in the first 20 minutes. A draw seemed to be inevitable as added-on time at the end of the game came up. But Campbell shot in following a corner and, with the last kick of the match, Caudwell cashed in on a defensive error to send the Rovers fans merrily on their way back home. This lifted the team up to seventh in the table, a long way behind the leaders but at least in the top half.

The midweek game at Dagenham & Redbridge on Tuesday 27 March against a team third in the table after eight successive wins saw the Rovers make a determined effort to end that record. They took the lead immediately after half-time when Hawkins fired in but three minutes later the Daggers equalised when a shot from Cobb was palmed away by Richardson only to hit Barrick, who was getting back to cover and ricochet into the net. Both teams had chances before Goodwin headed in after 67 minutes to put the home team in the lead. In the end the Rovers could consider themselves unlucky to lose.

The only movement in the Rovers' camp on Conference transfer deadline day was from Peter Smith, who moved back to Crewe Alexandra, cutting short his loan period because of limited first-team opportunities. The lack of new players coming in was not for the want of trying because they had approached Paul Barnes of Bury but the player rejected the offer, along with approaches from at least two Football League clubs and went to Nuneaton Borough until the end of the season. In the days prior to the deadline, Tris Whitman, Simon Marples and Mattie Caudwell extended their contracts to 2003, with Dave Penney also signing a new two-year contract at the end of March.

Kettering Town, next to the bottom of the table, visited Belle Vue on the last day of March in a game that they would have won easily had the Rovers played to the standard they achieved at Dagenham. But it turned out to be a poor game, with neither side seemingly capable of scoring a goal, although the Rovers had plenty of chances late in the game. Goalless it started and that is how it finished.

In midweek Rovers travelled to Morecambe, only to be told, when they pulled into the car park, that it had been called off because of a waterlogged pitch. It had rained all day so there was no argument about that decision but it was the second successive season that the Rovers had travelled to Morecambe in midweek and found the match had been called off when they got there.

There was no game on the first Saturday in April but the Rovers had five games coming up in 12 days, starting on 10 April with a game at home to second-placed Yeovil Town, who had two games in hand over leaders Rushden & Diamonds and were five points behind. As was expected, the Rovers came up trumps in the big game and dominated the first half, scoring twice through Turner after 16 minutes and Tierney six minutes later. Although Yeovil rallied in the second half they could not break through and as tempers frayed Barrington Belgrave received his marching orders for kicking out at Ryan in the last minute. The Rovers' management had been expecting their best crowd of the season but only 2,111 decided to attend.

The following afternoon, the youth team played the Football League Youth Alliance Cup semi-final at Cantley Park against Bradford City Youth, with the winners playing the southern winners, Leyton Orient, at the Millennium Stadium in Cardiff on the day of the Football League Cup Final. The Rovers had most of the play and Robert Gill scored a first-half hat-trick and had another one chalked off for offside before Adam Hardy pulled one back for Bradford. The Rovers had lost influential centre-back Paul Robinson after just five minutes with an ankle injury and perhaps this told in the second half. The visitors hit back seven minutes into the second half when Scott Kerr fired in a penalty, given for 'hands' and scored again from open play after 76 minutes. Both sides tried hard to find a winning goal but extra-time came and went with the score remaining at three goals apiece. This meant penalties, with Bradford City starting first. They were successful with their five kicks and the Rovers scored their first four. Ryan Williams stepped up to take the fifth but the 'keeper dived to his right and saved. It was Bradford City who went to the Millennium Stadium.

The next game for the Rovers first team was at home to lowly Hayes on the Saturday. They had comfortably beaten high-flying Yeovil Town but could only manage a goalless draw against a team struggling to keep out of the relegation zone. This was no way to attract the fans back. The Rovers had a place in the top six to play for, which would give them a place in the Football League (LDV) Trophy next season but they were eighth and three points away as a result of this draw.

Irish Under-21 international Colin Hawkins heads away.

On Easter Monday the Rovers trekked to top-of-the-table Rushden & Diamonds and matched them to come away with another goalless draw. A great display from Barry Richardson in goal helped but it was a good team performance. Steve Wignall called the match 'a good advert for Conference football' and was pleased at the way his team had played.

Two days later the team headed north west to lowly Morecambe, who were not yet safe from the drop zone. A tired-looking Rovers side had two goals against them from Talbot and

Rigoglioso in the first half, with a penalty scored by Paterson for the Rovers in-between. That was the final scoreline and a first win in eight games for the Shrimps. Steve Wignall was in no mood to defend his team this time and threatened that players would be shown the door if they did not achieve greater consistency.

On the Saturday the Rovers faced fifth-placed Leigh RMI at Belle Vue and, in a one-sided first half, could only manage a penalty goal from Paterson two minutes from the interval. Paterson fired in again for a second goal three minutes into the second half and 10 minutes later it was 4–0 after Kelly and Tierney had added to the score. This was their best winning margin of the season but it was in front of the lowest attendance at Belle Vue, 1,532. Steve Wignall said himself that he never knew what to expect from one game to the next, despite always preparing the same way and playing the same way.

Later in the week, on Thursday, the semi-final of the Sheffield Senior Cup was played at Belle Vue when the Rovers, with virtually a reserve team, faced Worksop Town, who included former England

Ian Duerden – top striker during early Conference days, now a fireman in Doncaster.

international Chris Waddle in their team. This no doubt bumped the attendance up to 1,397, far more than in previous rounds. Worksop actually took the lead after just seven minutes when Varley shot in following a Waddle free-kick. Four minutes later and the Rovers levelled through Turner, with Alford netting six minutes before the break to put the Rovers in the lead. That was the final score in a hard-fought game and it was good enough to get the Rovers into the Final at Hillsborough, Sheffield, on 9 May against Emley.

Two days later, on the last Saturday of April, the Rovers went to Stevenage Borough and could only muster a goalless draw against the team in sixth place, who went down to 10 men after 25 minutes when Sam Sodje was sent off for headbutting Campbell. On 56 minutes Paterson's penalty-kick was saved by Wilkerson, Paterson's first failure from the spot all season. The fact that Wilkerson was named Man of the Match just about summed up the match.

The May Day match was the reserves' last match in Central League Division Two, in which they finished second to gain promotion to the First Division. This was a very creditable performance from Dave Penney's team. The following evening, at the Rovers' presentation night at the Earl of Doncaster Hotel, Barry Miller won a couple of awards – the players' Player of the Season and the *Doncaster Star* Readers' Trophy. Tristram Whitman won the Young Player of the Year award, while Robert Gill was named as the youth-team players' Player of the Season.

Before the Telford game the next season's kits were unveiled to the crowd by models Andy Watson – wearing the away kit of white-bodied shirt, with green sleeves and collar and green shorts – and Simon Marples – showing the red-and-white hooped shirt and red shorts bearing the name of the new shirt sponsors, One Call Insurance of Doncaster, who had replaced Beazer Homes. The building company had been sponsors for the last three years and still had a year to run but they had been taken over by Persimmon Homes and decided to withdraw from the sponsorship.

On the morning of Saturday 5 May the Rovers youth team travelled to play Tranmere Rovers Youth in the final match of the Football League Youth Alliance Northern Merit League Premier Division. The Rovers came up with a terrific victory by four goals to two to become champions of the North, a non-League club against Football League clubs. Ben Sherwood, an impromptu striker for the match, scored a hat-trick and Robert Gill got the other. This was a great achievement by Mickey Walker and his lads. The team had included, throughout the season: Richard Dell, Darren Fell, Robert Gill, Paul Green, Martin Kearney, Ciaran Kenna, Kevin Leighton, Jim Lewis, Duncan Milligan, Ryan Nelson, Jamie Price, Paul Robinson, Paul Robson, Ben Sherwood, Lee Snodin and Ryan Williams. On 19 June the successful youth team received a civic reception at the Mansion House from the Mayor, Councillor Beryl Roberts.

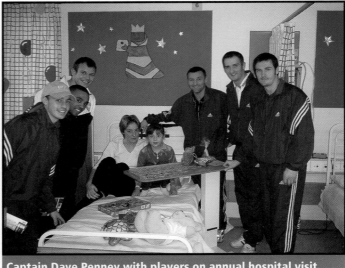

Captain Dave Penney with players on annual hospital visit.

The Rovers' last match at home to Telford United on Saturday 5 May ended in defeat, not that they deserved to lose. A fairly even game was brought to life straight after the start of the second half when Kelly put the Rovers in front but 10 minutes later the Telford leading scorer, Edwards, equalised and then shot them in front 10 minutes from time to complete the 'double' over the Rovers for the first time. The Rovers' record in the Conference read as follows: played 42, won 15, drawn 13, lost 14, goals for 47, goals against 43, points 58 and their position in the table was ninth.

The Rovers and Emley from the Northern Premier League contested the Sheffield Senior Challenge Cup Final at Sheffield Wednesday's Hillsborough ground on Wednesday 9 May. Barry Miller had to cry off with an ankle injury received against Telford United but otherwise the Rovers turned out a full team. Emley gave it a good go and took the lead after 17 minutes through Prendergast, keeping it until half-time but a roasting from manager Steve Wignall got the Rovers going and Whitman equalised after 69 minutes. Ten minutes later Whitman picked up a second booking and was sent to the dressing room. Turner came on for Campbell and headed in a fine cross from Tierney within four minutes of his entrance. The 10 men had gone in front and held out to win the Cup, which captain Dean Barrick duly received. The team that brought another piece of silverware home for the Rovers' cabinet was: Andy Warrington, Simon Marples, Dean Barrick, Jimmy Kelly, Colin Hawkins, Tim Ryan, Fran Tierney, Kevin McIntyre, Neil Campbell (Mike Turner, 81 minutes), Tris Whitman and Jamie Paterson (Mattie Caudwell, 59 minutes). Simon Shaw was an unused substitute. The last time that the Rovers had won this Cup was in 1912 when they were in the Midland League.

With the end of the season came the retained list. Not retained and released by the club were Simon Shaw, Michael Stone and Michael Turner. But four members of the successful youth team – Jamie Price, Robert Gill, Paul Green and Darren Fell – were given professional contracts for a year.

Steve Wignall moved immediately to sign Dean Barrick on a new two-year contract and Paul Barnes from Bury, also on a two-year contract. Days later he agreed a one-year contract with Mark Sale from Rushden & Diamonds and he also added Kevin Sandwith from Telford United on a two-year contract.

At the end of May, the club announced a rise on the price of a season ticket. If the tickets were purchased before 15 June they would be £200 for the Main Stand seats and £120 concessions, rising after that date to £215 and £135 respectively. Children under-16 prices were £66, rising to £76 after 15 June. The terrace prices were £160, concessions were £90 and under-16s were £33 until the June date, rising to £175, £115 and £43 respectively.

On 9 June, at the Football League AGM, the clubs voted on the principle of two up and two down between Division Three and the Conference. The result of 71 against and only one, Wycombe Wanderers, for the vote was a bitter disappointment for the Conference clubs. While the League clubs were not against the principle, they were not satisfied with the financial ramifications. This brought an immediate response from the Conference that, in future, if only one club was to be promoted, it would be decided by a Play-off. This was immediately banned by the FA.

Throughout July Steve Wignall continued his search for new players and signed Gareth Owen, who had been released by Wrexham. Wignall wanted an experienced midfielder to take over Dave Penney's role in the side and Owen fitted the bill. Penney would play less and be more involved with the coaching side of the game. Paul Carden, another midfield player, was also signed from Chester City. On the other side of the scale Wignall let Carl Alford, who had failed to score in the Conference for the Rovers, go to Yeovil Town for a cut-price fee.

Trevor Milton, owner of York-based Minster Carpets and chairman of Scarborough the previous season, joined the club's board of directors at the invitation of John Ryan, who had complained to the FA for failing to protect the club's youth system. The FA had been quick enough to ban the Conference from implementing their Play-off plans but the lack of support from the FA and Football League over the Robert Betts affair over the last three years had led to Mr Ryan warning that if the League teams were allowed to take their best young players without compensation, then he would have to abandon the club's youth policy, which would not do anybody any favours. After all, Coventry City had still not paid the fee set for Robert Betts by a tribunal and it was looking likely that the same could happen again over Lee Snodin, who had joined his father at Charlton Athletic.

The series of pre-season friendlies kicked-off with a game at Arnold Town from the Northern Counties East League

Manager Steve Wignall at Farnborough.

as part of the deal that had brought Tris Whitman to the Rovers. Kevin McIntyre, who had broken a bone in his foot while doing some running at home and Mark Sale, who had injured his back getting out of bed, missed the game. The Rovers, with the addition of some youth-team players, turned two separate teams out. The first-half XI – the probable first-team line up – put five in by half-time, while the second-half XI added three more, with Arnold getting one back late in the game. A game against a Manchester United reserve team followed at Belle Vue, in which the Rovers gave a good account of themselves and only a late goal gave United the draw of two goals apiece. Unfortunately the Rovers suffered some significant injuries, with Paul Barnes breaking a bone in his foot and Colin Hawkins picking up a thigh injury in the warm-up. The Rovers then moved on to play in a tournament at the International Stadium at Gateshead, sponsored by a local radio station and run by Gateshead Football Club. Dave Penney was in charge of the team, because Steve Wignall was at his wife's bedside after she had been rushed into hospital with a brain haemorrhage. After beating Bedlington Terriers of the Northern League by two clear goals in the semi-final, they went on to beat Hartlepool United – winners over hosts Gateshead in the other semi-final – to win the trophy in the Final the following day by the odd goal in five. Further friendlies followed against Scunthorpe United at Belle Vue (3–0) and then at Gainsborough Trinity (0–2).

The season proper opened at Farnborough Town on Saturday 18 August, with a 1–0 win courtesy of O'Shea putting the ball into his own net after 54 minutes. The Rovers were missing Paul Barnes, who had a foot injury but was also under suspension from the end of the previous season; Tris Whitman, also suspended from last season; Kevin McIntyre, with a foot injury; Andy Watson to a thigh injury and Jamie Paterson to an ankle injury. A total of 13 cautions were issued by the referee – six to Farnborough and seven to the Rovers. Steve Watson, captain of Farnborough and Neil Campbell of the Rovers both received two cautions each and were sent off three minutes into the second half.

As was the usual practice, two games a week were played well into October. A home win over Leigh RMI, with second-half goals from Whitman and Kelly (a penalty) gave the Rovers maximum points from their first two games. On the morning of Saturday 25 August, before the Yeovil game, a meeting was held at the Earl of Doncaster Hotel as the Viking Supporters' Co-operative held a secret ballot to elect a supporter/director as part of the Supporters' Direct Scheme. Andy Liney was elected to join the Rovers' board, who had been very supportive of the initiative. The co-operative pledged to raise £50,000 for the club by buying shares in exchange for a seat on the board. A cheque for £2,500 was handed over to the club at half-time of that afternoon's match against Yeovil Town, who snatched a winner through Giles in added time at the end of the game to gain their first victory of the season. Whitman had put the Rovers in front after 16 minutes and Way equalised eight minutes into the second half.

The last game in August, on bank holiday Monday, was played in front of the Sky Sports TV cameras at Stevenage Borough. While defences dominated, as a goalless scoreline suggests, the Rovers in particular had sufficient chances to win. To make it easier, Stevenage went down to 10 men on 69 minutes when Sam Sodje was sent off for a second yellow card but the Rovers failed to capitalise on their numerical advantage. Other bad news came when Kevin

Gareth Owen and Robert Gill attack Margate at Belle Vue.

Sandwith, deputising for Barrick, suffered a broken foot; it was the third such injury at the club and the season was only four games old. Their position in the League at the end of August was fifth, with seven points from four games.

The Rovers started September with a win over Dover Athletic at Belle Vue on a warm afternoon, with just over 2,000 spectators in attendance. Sale put the Rovers in front in the second minute, Scott equalised just after the half hour and Paterson put the Rovers back in front a minute before the break. No more goals were scored as Dover suffered their fifth consecutive defeat and stayed rooted at the

Kitman Dave Richards puts the kit out for the game against Nuneaton.

bottom of the League, while the Rovers moved up to third.

Early the following week the club signed defender Jamie Squires, released by Carlisle United in the summer. The following day they forked out £100,000 to Rushden & Diamonds for Justin Jackson, the player they could not sign from Morecambe two seasons earlier. He had cost the Diamonds £175,000. The midweek game was at leaders Boston United and if the Rovers won they would go top. Boston had gone full-time and spent a lot of money so they meant business. But so did the Rovers, going two goals up from Kelly after 64 minutes and an Owen penalty 20 minutes later. In between these goals Jimmy Kelly was sent off after a second booking. The Rovers held out until the last minute of normal time when Clare finally beat Richardson. Then, with 94 minutes on the clock, Boston were awarded a controversial penalty that came about following a free-kick to Boston when the referee overruled the linesman, who was flagging for a free-kick to the Rovers for a foul on Hawkins. Clare converted the penalty to gain a point for the Pilgrims, which kept them on top.

A 1–1 draw at home to lowly Woking cost the Rovers three places when they dropped to sixth. It was Justin Jackson's home debut in front of 2,500 people – the top attendance of the day in the Conference – but he failed to make it a scoring debut by missing a couple of chances. Carden got the goal after 22 minutes, scoring direct from a corner by Roddis to equalise a 10th-minute goal for the Cardinals. Another draw followed in midweek at Telford United when the Rovers had the bulk of the play but could only score once, through Paterson after 23 minutes. They were then caught out by a ball over the top of their back line for Quayle to fire in on the half hour. A second booking for Tim Ryan six minutes from the end meant he took an early bath, followed by a suspension.

The following Saturday the Rovers finally found their goal touch, despite having eight players out with injury, including strikers Paul Barnes, Mark Sale and Justin Jackson. Playing at Hayes, the Rovers raced into a three-goal lead after 22 minutes through Owen, Caudwell and Whitman. Paterson rattled in two more in the second half, with Hayes managing one in between.

Once again, in midweek, the Rovers could only draw at home to Nuneaton Borough. In a one-sided first half, which had the Rovers in full flow, they actually lost the first goal after 26 minutes before Campbell brought them level seven minutes later. In a more even second half the Borough took the lead again after 56 minutes through the same player, Sykes. This time it took the Rovers until the 78th minute to equalise, when Owen hit a scorcher from 25 yards into the net. In a terrific finale the Rovers just could not find the winning goal. The following evening the youth team entered the FA Youth Cup at the second-round stage and in an exciting and entertaining game they beat Emley Youth by four goals to three after extra-time. Emley took an early lead but two goals late in the first half from Jon Maloney and Liam Slack gave the Rovers a half-time lead. Emley again took the lead in the second half with two well-taken goals but a goal in the last minute by Slack forced extra-time. Three minutes into the extra half-hour Liam Slack completed his hat-trick for the Rovers to run out the winners.

For the third successive home game the Rovers' first team were held to a draw, this time by Morecambe. The visitors took the lead on 14 minutes through Drummond but five minutes later Owen levelled. Campbell put the Rovers in front on the stroke of half-time but six minutes into the second half Gouck equalised with a penalty and 13 minutes later Black put the Shrimps in front. Campbell levelled the score 14 minutes from time as Morecambe finished with 10 men after Lee Colkin was sent off 10 minutes from time for a professional foul on Campbell. The resulting penalty by Paterson was saved by Craig Mawson.

The last game in September was at Haig Avenue, Southport, where the Rovers met defeat again at the hands of their bogey team, when a 30-yard shot from Jones went in off the underside of the bar in added time, although the Rovers claimed it had not gone over the goalline when it bounced down. The Rovers slipped down to 10th in the table.

Monday evening, 1 October and the Rovers Youth played Scarborough Youth in the FA Youth Cup third qualifying round at Belle Vue. Two goals by Scarborough in the first seven minutes took them through to the next round. The next evening the first team went to Northwich Victoria and came away with a win by the odd goal in five – a scoreline that did not do justice to the Rovers' display. The Rovers were two goals up in the first 40 minutes through Whitman and Campbell but Talbot pulled one back in the dying seconds of the first half. Barry Miller got a third for the Rovers 25 minutes into the second half but was sent off two minutes from time for headbutting Jimmy Quinn, the Northwich player-manager, in retaliation after being punched. As usual the original offence went unseen by the officials, who had failed to give a blatant penalty to the Rovers in the very first minute. Devlin scored from the penalty spot following Miller's dismissal.

The next game, on a Friday evening against Forest Green Rovers at Belle Vue, provided little indication in the first half of what was to come. Paterson had sent the Rovers in at the break a goal in front but Ward equalised seven minutes into the second half. Five minutes later Campbell put the home team ahead and in the following 22 minutes Whitman, Miller and Caudwell got on the score sheet to seal a convincing win and move the Rovers up to fourth in the table.

On Monday 8 October Tim Ryan was named as the England Semi-Professional Player of the Year for 2000–01 by the *Non-League Directory*, an official FA publication. Another home game came the following day against Barnet, who had been relegated from the Football League at the end of the previous season. Before the Rovers' biggest crowd of the season, just under 3,000, the home team went two goals down in the first seven minutes to strikes from Flynn and Purser, before pulling one back three minutes before half-time through Whitman. Flynn added another in the second half but Owen added a second for the Rovers 12 minutes from time. Although the Rovers pushed for an equaliser, the Barnet defence kept them out and the three points went south.

A first-time trip to the Kent resort of Margate, second in the table, followed on the Saturday. Despite the attempts of the officials on the pitch to sabotage the game, it was a game of full commitment by both teams, a real blood-and-thunder encounter that ended all square at one goal apiece. The goals came from Collins, on the stroke of half-time and Jackson for the Rovers, three minutes from the end. Margate's Lee Williams was sent off on the hour after his second caution. The referee and his assistants had to be escorted off the pitch at the end as players, club management and fans from both sides approached them about the handling of the game.

Jamie Squires, with Rovers on a non-contract basis, signed a contract to the end of the season. Injuries and suspensions were now taking their toll as the next midweek game came up in the Football League (LDV) Trophy first round against Kidderminster Harriers at Belle Vue. Despite this, they only lost out to a goal from Larkins after 73 minutes and generally gave as good as they received.

Dave Penney and Steve Wignall with Paul Green at a photoshoot in 2001 – Dave Penney would take over when Wignall was sacked.

Before the Saturday game, at lowly Chester City, manager Steve Wignall had to check on who was available to play before he could announce a team. However, the team that did turn out, with some of the players not fully recovered from injury or illness, earned a draw, with Neil Campbell putting the Rovers in front after 15 minutes and then being sent off for use of an elbow on Rose after 27 minutes. The referee evened the numbers up a minute later by giving a red card to Dean Spink for stamping on Ryan in retaliation for being fouled, with Ryan booked for the foul. Just before the hour, Ruscoe drew Chester level against the run of play when he seized on a defensive mistake. The Rovers were fifth in the League, 14 points behind leaders Dagenham & Redbridge.

The last game of the month was played on Sunday 28 October in the fourth qualifying round of the FA Cup against Northern Premier League side Emley, after some discussion about the day it was to be played. The tie could not be played on the Saturday because of racing on Town Moor and Emley refused to play on Friday. Tim Ryan, Jimmy Kelly and Barry Miller were all suspended for this game. The Rovers went two goals up in the first 15 minutes through a Paterson penalty and Jackson but on 23 minutes Emley got one back when former Rovers youth player Gary Hatto converted a penalty. Squires scored his first goal for the club and Rovers' third after 66 minutes, before Day scored a second for Emley with six minutes left. It was an entertaining and hard-fought game, which Emley could have levelled in added time at the end but former Rover Mickey Norbury hit the post from two yards.

A four-match ban on Neil Campbell came into effect for the Stalybridge Celtic match on Saturday 3 November at Belle Vue. Also banned were Tim Ryan, his last match and Gareth Owen, for this match, after accumulating five cautions. Stalybridge, second from bottom of the Conference, made their first-ever visit to Belle Vue and provided the shock of the day when they went home with a single-goal victory, Courtney scoring in added time in the first half. The

Fans get ready for the game against Scarborough, which would prove to be Steve Wignall's last game in charge.

Rovers played badly and the fans let Steve Wignall know this in no uncertain terms at the end of the match. The manager actually sympathised with them and understood their frustration.

However, on the following Tuesday, for the match against Dinnington Town from the Central Midlands League in the Sheffield Senior Cup at Belle Vue, he called all his first-team squad in and chose the team from them despite having previously played fringe players and youth players in this competition. The manager denied that it was a punishment by saying some of the players were short on confidence and needed games. This game was actually drawn out as an away game but Dinnington had asked for it to be played at Doncaster. Six of the team from the previous Saturday were included in the Rovers' starting line up and they went four up in the first half before adding another two in the second half. Tierney started the rout after just two minutes, then Hawkins, Penney with two, Barnes and Watson added the rest.

On Thursday 8 November came a bombshell when the local evening paper came out with 'I QUIT' splashed across the front page. This related to John Ryan resigning his post as chairman on the evening of the Dinnington game after meeting with the Doncaster Council chief executive David Marlow, regarding the plans for a new stadium. Despite hearing that there would be a decision before the end of the year, he carried out his threat to resign his official post because he felt let down by the council and other people, having been given assurances when he took over the club that a new stadium would be built. Mr Marlow had told him that he could not uphold previous regimes' promises. Mr Ryan stated that he had come in and put his money, about £1.5 million, into the club as a fan but he doubted that the club would be allowed back into the Football League with the current stadium at Belle Vue, even if they won the Conference. If football and rugby were to be sacrificed for the Holy Grail of the Racecourse, for which the council had recently approved a £50-million investment, then so be it. He went on to say off the record that he 'would not like to be a councillor in Doncaster at present, there are 62 of them and we know where they all live. The people are disgusted with the council over their prevarication and there could be blood on the streets over it. It could be a bloody riot but I bet we get our stadium'. This was printed in a national Sunday football paper and caused a furore. Ryan would remain as a director and continue to assist the club financially in the short term but not at the previous level of assistance.

The council acknowledged the meeting with Doncaster Rovers and Doncaster Dragons and said an agreement to establish a project team to move the stadium proposals forward had been made. Having already spent money on a feasibility study, it was difficult to see what a project team could find out that they did not already know from the feasibility study. This situation immediately set the alarm bells ringing among the supporters and indeed Westferry, as talk of cuts in finance emerged. In the meantime Trevor Milton took over as interim chairman. His first act was to meet with David Marlow, thoroughly shaken by Ryan's tirade, who stated that if anything should happen it would put the stadium project back 100 years. Mr Milton promised him there would be no trouble and used the media to communicate the message that fans should not do anything that would hinder the stadium project. As various groups of fans were making plans to protest to the council about its position in regard to the stadium, they were urged not to proceed before a supporters' meeting at the Earl of Doncaster Hotel on 24 November. Consequently all demonstrations were called off. An interested party was the FA in London, who wrote to the club for an explanation of the comments, which Mr Ryan said were metaphorical and designed to indicate his level of disgust with the council and not to foment trouble. The FA later fined Mr Ryan £10,000 plus costs, £8,000 of which was suspended, for bringing the game into disrepute. Some time later Trevor Milton met again with David Marlow, who thanked him for keeping his promise of no trouble and went on to tell the chairman that the council had earmarked £1 million for feasibility work on a 10,000-capacity complex in the Lakeside area. The club hoped that the stadium would be ready for 2004–05.

The following Saturday the Rovers visited Hereford United and came away with a point from a goalless draw in a hard, competitive match. It was only goalless for the Rovers because of the failure to put away good chances in a game that they had the better of. An emergency board meeting on the Monday appointed Trevor Milton as chairman but received the resignation of Peter Wetzel from his post as deputy chairman. Both John Ryan and Peter Wetzel would continue as directors in the short term but Mr Ryan announced that he would not put any more money into the club

A rainy day at Belle Vue.

Goalmouth action against Hereford United at Belle Vue.

until the picture regarding the stadium became clearer. With none of the other directors in a position to increase their financial input, it was left to Denis O'Brien and Kevin Phelan, the major shareholders of Westferry, to put money into the club over the next few months to avert a financial crisis and protect their original investment. The following day Trevor Milton met David Marlow of the council, who told the chairman that a decision as to whether the council would proceed with the building of a new stadium could be made in the next month. Even so, the result of Mr Ryan's withdrawal of funds meant there would have to be some cost-cutting measures and already clubs had been notified about the availability of some players.

The next game was at home to Scunthorpe United in the FA Cup first round at Belle Vue in front of a crowd of over 6,000. A hard-fought, entertaining contest showed that the Rovers could compete at Football League level. They took the lead on 20 minutes through Tierney and it took another 21 minutes before the Iron equalised with a long-distance rasping shot from Hodges. Just before the whistle went for half-time, Carruthers gave the visitors the lead. Watson levelled for the Rovers four minutes into the second half but Calvo-Garcia scored a third after 62 minutes and, although the home team tried hard, that proved to be the winning goal. There was one incident of trouble in the town centre, when fans from both teams met at Yates' Wine Lodge and beer glasses were thrown around but good work by the police sorted it out and the Scunthorpe fans were escorted to Belle Vue.

The Rovers followed this excellent showing by facing Conference leaders Dagenham & Redbridge at Belle Vue. Unfortunately for them, they had left their shooting boots at home because they failed to score for the third successive League match at home. Fortunately the only four defenders who were available stopped the opposition from scoring but Dagenham did play the second half with 10 men after Lee Goodwin was sent off on the stroke of half-time for a second booking.

In midweek the prospect of facing cuts in expenditure was already being addressed, with Paul Carden, who had been kept out of the first team by the form of Owen and Kelly, going back to Chester City for a small fee. Colin Hawkins followed him out at the end of the week, moving to League of Ireland club, Bohemians, for a £20,000 fee. Andy Mutch, a full-time scout for the Rovers, also left the club to join Morecambe as assistant manager. John Ryan called upon all fans to support the club over the next month, because they only had one home game in that period, meaning income would be small but wages still had to be paid.

At a board meeting held before the game against Farnborough Town on Saturday 1 December a new budget was agreed and it was also decided that no extra funding would be put in towards a promotion bid for the current season. Following the meeting the club issued a statement, in which it was stressed that any delay in the provision of a new stadium on the Lakeside development could spell the end of the club. With an affirmative answer there was potential new investment but a negative decision could well jeopardise the continuing support of existing backers.

In the match against Farnborough Town the Rovers finally scored a goal at home. Paterson got it after 71 minutes but the visitors levelled five minutes from time following a defensive error, despite having been down to 10 men since the 47th minute when Tom O'Shea was sent off after a second booking. However, there were only 1,800 hardcore fans there to see the match, so John Ryan's call for support from the fans had gone unheeded. There were even fewer fans the following Tuesday when only 378 saw a young Rovers team play a Sheffield Senior Cup game against Northern Counties East League club Hallam, which ended in a win for the Rovers, with goals from Jackson in the first half, a minute after Richardson had saved a penalty and Whitman in the second half. Hallam played the last 10 minutes with 10 men after Craig Worsfold was sent off for collecting a second booking.

An away trip to Yeovil Town followed, in a match brought forward from 29 December and resulted in another draw, 1–1. Paterson put the Rovers in front after 56 minutes but McIndoe got an equaliser at the fourth attempt, after Warrington and his defenders had blocked three strikes at goal, just three minutes from time. However, at the ninth attempt Rovers got back on the winning trail at Hilton Park in a game against lowly Leigh RMI before 546 spectators. The Rovers played as well as at Yeovil but this time they put the chances away. Even so it took the home team to go down to 10 men before the Rovers got their first goal. Gerry Harrison of Leigh was sent off for a second booking on 26 minutes and two minutes later Sale buried a header in the Leigh net. Paterson then scored twice in the first 20 minutes of the second half before Twiss pulled one back for the home team two minutes later. Watson fittingly sealed the win on 75 minutes, having had a fine match. This win gave the Rovers their first 'double' of the season.

The Rovers now had an 11-day break before their next match on Boxing Day. During this time Peter Wetzel resigned from the board of directors and Barry Richardson moved to Halifax Town just before Christmas, leaving the Rovers with only one goalkeeper for the first team. The Boxing Day match at Belle Vue against bottom-of-the-table Scarborough was played on a bitterly cold afternoon on an icy pitch that got worse as the match went on, causing players to slip and lose their footing on regular occasions. That may well have contributed to the goal feast that followed. The visitors scored first after three minutes when Warrington dropped a cross and Rennison tapped in but Rennison then blotted his copybook by giving the Rovers a penalty five minutes later, which Paterson duly despatched. That was it for the first half but the excitement came in the second period. Scarborough again went in front when a corner-kick glanced off Barrick's head into his own net after 52 minutes. Then just past the hour Watson fired in after a good run, followed on 70 minutes by Owen hitting a terrific 25-yarder into the top corner of the net. Seven minutes later a fine individual goal from Whitman apparently sealed the win but the Seasiders thought otherwise and pulled one back two minutes from time when Blunt fired home, causing the Rovers some anxious moments as they hung on to their one-goal lead. This win lifted them to sixth place, two points behind third-placed Yeovil Town but 13 points behind the leaders, Dagenham & Redbridge.

The New Year's Day game at Scarborough was frozen off, which gave the Rovers time to bring in a back-up goalkeeper for Andy Warrington. Michael Jones, the 16-year-old goalkeeper from the youth team, had been on the bench on Boxing Day but Steve Wignall brought in Andy Walker, aged 21, whom he knew from their time together at Colchester United. The team had another week off after their home game against Boston United was called off because of adverse weather. What the players did not know was that they had played their last game under Steve Wignall, because on Thursday 10 January he was dismissed from his post as manager with immediate effect, along with chief executive Joe Hoggins. Trevor Milton issued a statement saying that they had been axed as part of a cost-cutting exercise brought about by the club's deepening financial crisis after they had only played one game at home since 1 December. No doubt the loss of the Boston United game, which would have drawn a decent crowd, to the weather played some part in the timing, because the Rovers had gone six League games undefeated.

With Dave Penney put in charge of team affairs, the first game they played in January, on the 12th, was an FA Trophy match at home to Northern Premier League side Harrogate Town. The Rovers made hard work of winning but two goals from Campbell, just before the interval and Watson, in the last minute of the game, sent them through to the fourth round. In midweek they played a rearranged game at Scarborough and went behind to a stunning drive from 25 yards by Blunt. The Rovers had most of the midfield play but both Woods in the Scarborough goal and Warrington in the Rovers goal had only one save to make and were virtually unemployed. A win would have put the Rovers into fourth place but the loss dropped them to 10th.

The next match was a visit to another club in the bottom three and also fighting for their lives on and off the pitch, Dover Athletic. Tim Ryan played his first match for two months, having been out with ankle and knee injuries. The Rovers accepted their first real chance after 12 minutes when Barnes headed in a free-kick from Tierney. They went on to either spurn further chances or find goalkeeper Paul Hyde in their way. Their second 'double' of the season took them up to fifth place.

Andy Warrington suffered a thigh injury at Dover and, although Andy Walker was still at the club, Rovers moved to sign Matthew Ghent from Barnsley on loan and also signed midfielder Ricky Ravenhill from Barnsley on a non-contract basis. In the latest cost-cutting measure, physiotherapist Jon Bowden had left the club 'by mutual consent'. His workload was taken on by youth team physio Barry Windle, who now had to handle all the injuries at the club.

The last match in January took place on a wet and windy evening at Belle Vue on Friday 25 January against Stevenage Borough. Two goals from Paterson and Campbell in the second half gave the Rovers the points after an even and hard-fought first half. Matthew Ghent was due to play for the Rovers in goal but was injured in training at Barnsley on the Thursday. Lee Butler, who had recently joined the club as a goalkeeping coach on a part-time basis, was registered as a player by the club and given the task of stopping Stevenage scoring. He had retired from full-time professional football at Halifax Town before Christmas because of injury, with Barry Richardson from the Rovers succeeding him. The Rovers ended the month in fourth place, 12 points behind the leaders, Boston United.

The first Saturday in February, the 2nd, was FA Trophy fourth-round day and Rovers were due to meet third-placed Yeovil Town in that competition but heavy rain in the south west put paid to that, as it did for the rearranged game on the following Tuesday. The Rovers' next game was at Forest Green Rovers, where they had never won but that record was changed when Paterson (in the first half) and Sale (a minute from time) claimed a two-goal victory on a rain-sodden pitch. The following Tuesday, having postponed a rearranged game against Boston United, the trophy game at Yeovil was called off again because of waterlogging. On the Saturday the Rovers were at home to Margate but they nearly had to send out for players when Barnes, Sale, Gill and Whitman were late arriving because of an accident on the M1. As it was, the referee put back the kick-off. Margate probably wished he had not because they lost to a penalty from Paterson after 74 minutes.

At the fourth time of asking, the FA Trophy tie at Yeovil went ahead on the evening of Tuesday 19 February, with a rearranged League game against Northwich Victoria having to be postponed. As befitted the two form teams in the Conference, an even game with both sides having a number of chances ended equal at 1–1. Barnes had given the Rovers the lead after 15 minutes but Stansfield back-headed a free-kick into the Rovers' net 11 minutes from time.

The replay was at Belle Vue on the following Saturday, FA Trophy fifth-round day and it turned out to be a nine-goal thriller. The Rovers, with a fine display in the first half, went three goals up after 49 minutes. A penalty put away by Paterson after six minutes set the tone. Gill then scored twice after 22 and 49 minutes. Whether the Rovers relaxed will probably never be known but Yeovil, with a stiff blustery wind behind them, hit back after 57 minutes when Pluck netted. Fifteen minutes from the end, Alford did what he never did when he was with the Rovers – he scored. That was the first of five goals to go in before the end of the 90 minutes. Stansfield scored twice after 79 and 86 minutes to give Yeovil a 4–3 lead but Owen rifled in two minutes later to level the score. At this point Jamie Price was bundled to the floor by Adam Lockwood, suffered a dislocated elbow and left the Rovers with 10 men for the last two minutes because they had used all their substitutes. And in that last minute Skiverton scored a fifth and decisive goal to the disbelief of most of the 2,178 crowd. Yeovil Town went on to beat Stevenage Borough 2–0 in the Final at Villa Park.

In fact the Rovers added further to their injury list in that match. Jamie Paterson dislocated his shoulder just before half-time and Paul Barnes received an ankle injury. With Jamie Price and Simon Marples out, the right-back position was a problem. Andy Watson pulled out of the Yeovil match on the morning of the game with a stomach strain, Neil Campbell was out with a back problem, Kevin McIntyre had not played all season because of a broken foot and Tim Ryan, just back from two months out with injury, was banned for four games after being sent off in a reserve game.

However, on Saturday 2 March the Rovers returned to the League and to winning ways when they went to Nuneaton Borough and came away with the points from a 3–2 win. Tim Ryan was back from his suspension, Paul Barnes was fit and Justin Jackson got off his sick bed on Saturday morning, having had food poisoning for 48 hours. He lasted the course, won a penalty, assisted in the second goal and scored the third. Barnes scored with a penalty after 10 minutes but Love equalised to send the teams in at the break at 1–1. Gill put the Rovers in front five minutes into the second half and Nuneaton hit back with a penalty from Peyton 15 minutes later. Jackson got the winning goal seven minutes from time after getting the better of Weaver and firing in.

In midweek Kevin McIntyre should have had a pin removed that had been inserted in his broken foot before Christmas but an infection delayed the operation to remove it. This effectively put him out for the rest of the season. The Rovers played away at Parkgate in the quarter-final of the Sheffield Senior Cup on the Tuesday evening and made their way into the semi-final with two goals from Campbell (in each half) and a penalty from Penney in the first half. The Rovers won their sixth successive League game the following Saturday at home, with a goal from Jackson a minute after Telford's Mark Albrighton had been sent off for elbowing Owen on 70 minutes.

At a meeting of the board on Monday 11 March Dave Penney was confirmed as manager, with Mickey Walker as his assistant, each signing new contracts for two years to the end of 2003–04. The Rovers went into the midweek game against third-placed Boston United at Belle Vue knowing that a win would put them level on points with the Lincolnshire side. But alas, the best-laid plans can go awry and Clare put the top hat on Rovers' promotion prospects when he scored from a penalty in the second half to give Boston the points from a very good game, watched by a crowd of 4,027.

The Rovers lost more ground on the Saturday when they went down at Woking by a 3–1 margin. In a full-blooded game, with Woking needing the points to stay above the relegation zone, the Rovers were up against it from the 25th minute when Justin Jackson was sent off for shoving Steele for something that was said. Woking went ahead on the stroke of half-time and got a second four minutes into the second half. Campbell pulled one back six minutes from the end but Woking wrapped it up with a third goal two minutes later.

A midweek rearranged game at home to Northwich Victoria was only five minutes away from another defeat for the Rovers. Blundell, for Northwich, scored inside the first minute and they held the lead until the 49th when Barnes drew the home team level. The Rovers were awarded a penalty just before the half hour but Gibson saved Paterson's kick. Garvey gave Northwich the lead again on 74 minutes but five minutes from time Tierney hit a free-kick from 25 yards in off the underside of the bar to rescue a point for the Rovers. Tim Ryan missed the game because he was playing for the England National Game XI against the US at Stevenage. He scored the winner in a 2–1 win from the penalty spot late in the game.

Three days later, on the Friday evening, another home game saw Paul Green make his starting debut in a League game against Hayes at Belle Vue. Terry Brown was the manager of Hayes until Friday morning but moved to Aldershot Town as manager that very day, so it was without a manager that they arrived in Doncaster. Due to work commitments Hayes could only field three substitutes. They certainly had their troubles at this time, because they were also in danger of going down and desperately needed points. In their three previous games at Belle Vue they had kept clean sheets but this night was to see the Rovers make amends for that in what was an entertaining game. Paterson set the Rovers on their way with a 12th-minute goal but Charles equalised nine minutes before the break. Squires restored the Rovers lead just before half-time and Gill increased the Rovers lead 12 minutes into the second half. Goals from Green and Barnes in the next 12 minutes took the tally to five. Molesley got another one 11 minutes from time for Hayes, who had battled gamely against all the odds stacked against them. This win took the Rovers to their highest position yet in the League, third.

The following Tuesday the destination was Westfield Lane at South Elmsall for the semi-final of the Sheffield Senior Cup against Frickley Athletic. Having lost out to Frickley in Cup competitions in recent times, the Rovers made no mistake this time and a full first team gained a 3–1 victory. It was only after Rob Hanby had been sent off for swearing at the referee two minutes before the break that the goals came. Frickley manager Gary Marrow, upset by the dismissal, harangued the official and was sent to the stand. Two goals at the end of the first half – an own-goal from former Rover Mark Place in the last minute of normal time and the second from Ravenhill in added time – gave the Rovers a half-time lead but Evans got Frickley back in the game two minutes into the second half. A third goal two minutes from time by Barnes settled the issue. At the end of the game came a very strange incident. The referee, Gary Mellor, refused to leave the pitch until all the spectators had left the ground, claiming that he had been

Rovers reserves win the Avon Insurance Cup at Oakwell by defeating Barnsley.

repeatedly spat upon at half-time when he left the pitch. He was still on the pitch with his linesmen when the lights were switched off but 20 minutes after the end of the game, with spectators still around the tunnel, they made a dash for the safety of the dressing room. Frickley Athletic were later fined by Sheffield and Hallamshire FA.

On Conference transfer deadline day, Thursday 28 March, the Rovers signed giant defender Ben Futcher, who had been released by Stalybridge Celtic, the Rovers' next opponents. It was also announced by the Conference that the FA and the Football League had come to an agreement to implement a two up, two down system from 2002–03.

In the Press box for the match against Scarborough.

Chester City visited Belle Vue on Saturday 30 March in a bid to get some points to keep them away from relegation. They hardly gave the Rovers a game as they went down by two goals, scored by Gill and Barnes in the first half. Easter Monday on 1 April saw a first-ever visit to Bower Fold, home of Stalybridge Celtic, third from the bottom and in dire need of points. Playing in a manner that belied their position in the table, the home team scored on 10 minutes through Ayorinde and saw off the Rovers, who scarcely offered any resistance. However, a week later Rovers hammered four goals past the Hereford United goalkeeper without reply, despite being without several first-team regulars because of injuries. Watson, with two goals in the first half and Green, with a goal in added time at the end of the game, together with a second-half goal from Squires, secured the victory that kept them in a distant third place behind Boston United and Dagenham & Redbridge.

A televised match on Sky Sports at Dagenham on the following Friday evening gave the Rovers the chance to put on a show for the watching fans but two questionable decisions by the referee left a bad taste in the mouth. The first came a minute before half-time when Whitman received a straight red for a nothing tackle and the second two minutes from the end of normal time when Price tackled Stein at the corner flag and was stamped on in front of the linesman, who apparently saw nothing. Price was also shown a straight red. Danny Hill scored after 70 minutes to put the Daggers on top of the pile but even their manager, Garry Hill, admitted they had been lucky, particularly with the first sending off. The club appealed against both dismissals.

The following Saturday was the first of four games in a week that would take the Rovers to the end of the season. This was at Belle Vue, where a goal from Barnes halfway through the second half was sufficient to take the points off Southport. Two days later, Dave Penney made a number of changes for the visit to Barnet but they were sent away pointless after losing by two goals, which dropped them to fourth place behind Yeovil Town. On the Thursday the team comprised of Lee Butler, Jamie Price, Kevin Sandwith, Ricky Ravenhill, Barry Miller, Ben Futcher andy Watson (Jamie Paterson, 69 minutes), Paul Green (Gareth Owen, 80 minutes), Paul Barnes, Robert Gill and Tris Whitman (Fran Tierney, 80 minutes) beat Emley in the Sheffield Senior Cup Final by three clear goals, scored in the second half by Barnes with two and Gill. In the meantime Price's appeal against his sending off at Dagenham was rejected, which meant him missing the game at Morecambe but Whitman's appeal was upheld, leaving him free to play in that game.

Rovers win the Sheffield Senior Cup, beating Emley at Hillsborough.

It was the last game of the season and the Rovers suffered another defeat (1–2) at the seaside to early goals for Morecambe in the first and second halves, with Whitman scoring just past the half hour. This left the Rovers in fourth place on goal difference over Barnet, their best position to date, with a record of: played 42, won 18, drawn 13, lost 11, goals for 68, goals against 46, points 67. However, there was still one match to come, on Monday 30 April at Oakwell, where the reserves met Barnsley Reserves in the Final of the Central League Cup. The Rovers scored after just four minutes through Paterson and Gill scored in the second half to wrap the game up and take away the silverware, which captain Mark Sale was able to collect in his last game in a Rovers shirt. The reserves had finished second in Central League Division Two and won promotion to Division One for the following season, while the youth team had also finished as winners of the Football League Northern Youth Alliance Merit League Division Three. So, despite the disappointment of failing to gain promotion to the Football League and the troubles that had afflicted Rovers in mid-season, the season had been more successful than previously.

On 1 May the retained list was released and, as usual, it was the players who had been released that caused most discussion. Neil Campbell, Jimmy Kelly, Jamie Squires, Matt Caudwell, Ben Futcher and Mark Sale were released, while Tim Ryan, Jamie Paterson, Ricky Ravenhill and Kevin McIntyre, who had missed the entire season with injury, were offered new contracts. The first three signed up again but Kevin McIntyre opted to move on to Chester City. At the club's awards presentation evening at the Earl of Doncaster Hotel a couple of days later Gareth Owen was named players' Player of the Year, Jamie Paterson won the *Doncaster Star* Readers' Player of the Year award, the first team's Young Player of the Season went to Robert Gill and Liam Slack was awarded the youth-team players' Player of the Year. The chairman, Trevor Milton, praised the work of Dave Penney and his backroom staff in obtaining the results they got with all their teams, considering the financial restraints they were under. He also said it was an exciting time to be chairman and confirmed his belief that they would be playing in a new stadium by 2004, thanks to the backing of Doncaster Council.

The Rovers' commercial department came up with a novel idea to determine their shirt sponsors for the coming season. About two dozen firms from the Doncaster area entered a raffle, for which the top prize was the sponsorship of the shirts worn by the club's teams. This brought in about £20,000 and all the entrants were awarded a prize and treated to a gala evening at the Earl of Doncaster Hotel. The top prize was won by Ledger Mobility, a firm who provided vehicles for the infirm.

Dave Penney and Mickey Walker now had the task of plotting the way forward for the Rovers as they began their first full season in charge of the club. The aim was to build a team to reach the promised land of the Football League now that their chances had doubled with the acceptance by the Football League of the two up, two down idea. The first incoming players were Mark Albrighton from Telford United and Dave Morley from Oxford United, both centre-halves. The players reported back for pre-season training on 5 July, together with a number of trialists. Paul Barnes was appointed player-coach and would look after the reserve team and Barry Richardson, released by Halifax Town, was back at the club as the goalkeeping coach.

The first four friendlies were against League clubs at Belle Vue and Trevor Milton called for the supporters to turn up in force because, while the team needed their support, the club needed the finance. But already injuries precluded Mark Albrighton, with a knee problem and Jamie Paterson, Barry Miller and Tris Whitman with strains, from playing in the first match against Sunderland. However, the games went well for the Rovers, with a 1–1 draw against Premier League Sunderland (Reserves), a 1–2 loss in a competitive match against Division One side Rotherham United, a goalless draw against Division Two side Oldham Athletic and a 4–0 win over Northern Premier League side Bradford Park Avenue, who had stepped in at 48 hours' notice when Mansfield Town pulled out. Further friendlies were played at Worksop Town (5–2) and Gainsborough Trinity (2–0), who had Barry Richardson in goal. Midfielder Alan Morgan, released by Tranmere Rovers, was signed on a two-year contract after impressing in the pre-season games, while Barry Miller missed the start of the Conference games after undergoing a knee operation at the end of July. So, in the week before the opening game, the Rovers signed Steve Foster, a centre-half, who had been released by Bristol Rovers.

Whereas in their previous seasons the Rovers had been favourites for promotion, this season they were only fourth favourites behind Yeovil Town, Dagenham & Redbridge and Chester City. New regulations in the Conference allowed teams to have squad numbers and names on the back of their shirts to bring them into line with the Football League. The season proper started on Saturday 17 August when Barnet visited Belle Vue to play in front of a crowd of 3,000. The Bees went in at half-time leading by a goal from Strevens after 32 minutes but the Rovers came out in the second half determined not to repeat the previous season when Barnet had done the 'double' over them. Green equalised after 69 minutes and eight minutes from time the ball came down off the crossbar, hit the Barnet 'keeper, Harrison, on the back of the head and rebounded into the net to give the Rovers a winning start. Three days later they went to Hilton Park, Leigh, where two late goals by Barnes and Jackson gave them maximum points and third place after their first two games.

The game on the following Saturday at Telford United had to be seen to be believed. The Rovers, helped by some clinical finishing, ran up a half-time lead of four goals from Morley (11), Tierney (22, 32) and Barrick (27) but whatever was said or done during the interval in the Telford dressing room left the Rovers shell-shocked at the end, as the home team plundered four goals through Moore (50), Foran (61), Smith (84) and Brown (90). The last two of Telford's goals came after they had gone down to 10 men after second-half substitute Jordan King was sent off in the 84th minute. Dave Brown's goal actually came in the seventh minute of added time, which caused some measure of controversy.

The bank holiday Monday encounter at home to Farnborough Town was won with a header from Tierney on 63 minutes after Barnes had hit a post with a penalty-kick in the first half. Despite their great start to the season, the Rovers – apart from the first half against Telford – were not yet at their best, especially over the full 90 minutes. This game was designated as Ladies' Day and attracted about 700 women, more than usual, who were charged £1 to stand and £6 to sit, with various other promotions to go with it.

The last day of August brought a visit to Northwich Victoria, where the Rovers picked up another three points from goals by Watson (26) and Jackson (59), which looked likely to give them a comfortable win, although a goal from Allan 19 minutes from time set up a tense finish as the home team battled to get some points out of the game. The Rovers hung on to take top spot in the table, two points clear of their nearest challengers. To round off a successful month, Dave Penney won the August Manager of the Month award for the Conference.

On Sunday 1 September the youth team began their quest for the FA Youth Cup at Workington Youth in the first preliminary round by winning handsomely 7–2, with Michael Rankine netting five times and Bryan Craig and Richard Gregory getting the others. Two days later the Rovers first team entertained lowly Kettering Town in front of their best crowd of the season (3,764) but only a tremendous strike by Owen from 25 yards after 62 minutes separated the teams at the finish, although Owen had a penalty saved by Ian Bowling in added time at the end.

Then came Saturday 7 September, when the Sky Sports Television cameras came to Belle Vue to broadcast a live game for the first time from the venerable venue. The opposition for the 12.15pm kick-off were Dagenham & Redbridge, who must have wished they were anywhere but Belle Vue at 2 o'clock that afternoon as the final whistle went. The Rovers were in scintillating form, running up a three-goal lead by the interval, with some cracking goals from Watson (16), Gill (30) and a Vickers own-goal a minute before the break when he diverted in a shot from Paterson that was going wide. Carrying on in the second half, Paterson put away a penalty after 66 minutes before Shipp registered one for the visitors three minutes later. The revival was brief because Barnes wrapped it up on 73 minutes with a terrific strike from 25 yards. Dave Penney was pleased with the performance, having seen what he had been wanting: a consistent performance of high quality over 90 minutes. An attendance of 4,294 was the best so far, particularly as the match was live on television. Before the match Rovers groundsman Pete White was presented with the non-League Groundsman of the Year trophy. The Rovers were leading the table with six wins and a draw out of seven games, in which they had scored 17 goals.

Because of a plethora of injuries, the Rovers could only muster 16 players for the match against Halifax Town on the following Tuesday at the Shay. They were brought down to earth when they lost by the odd goal in three after a cracking game, rather unluckily because they had the better chances but found Lee Butler in the Halifax goal in terrific form. All three goals came in a 17-minute spell either side of half-time, with Clarkson putting the home team in front on 40 minutes then Barnes equalising on the stroke of half-time. The winning goal came after 56 minutes when Ryan, trying to clear his lines, put the ball into his own net. The Rovers' injury list was extended by

Rovers top scorer Paul Barnes with young mascots at Chester.

one more when Ricky Ravenhill suffered a broken collarbone during the second half.

Although the Rovers were without a game until the following Tuesday, Dave Penney moved quickly to bring in a couple of loanees to augment his available playing staff. Dene Shields, a striker, was brought in from Sunderland and Erdem Artun, a midfielder, from Ipswich Town. A near 4,000 crowd at Belle Vue witnessed a goalless draw against fourth-placed Southport in a match that was played with 10 against 10 for 83 minutes. Jamie Paterson (Rovers) was sent off for retaliating against Steve Soley, who was red-carded for a two-footed tackle after just seven minutes.

Steve Foster in action against Burton Albion with Tim Ryan in the background.

The following evening the Rovers Youth entertained Prudhoe Town Youth team in the second qualifying round of the FA Youth Cup and had an easy time of it following Richard Gregory's goal after 27 seconds, eventually running out winners by five goals to one, even though Chris Dickman hit a post with a penalty after six minutes. Gregory scored four of the goals for Rovers.

The next first-team game against Margate was played at Dover Athletic's ground, as Margate's ground was being upgraded. Margate took a two-goal lead in the first half but Rovers could only manage one in reply, from Green eight minutes from time. This meant they lost top spot in the table to Chester City and dropped to third place behind Yeovil Town. Another midweek game followed and again the Rovers made a long trip to Kent to play Gravesend & Northfleet. This time they salvaged a point in the last minute when Barnes swept a cross from Green into the net for a 2–2 draw. Paterson had opened the scoring halfway through the first half but the home team went in at the break with a 2–1 lead.

The last Saturday in September brought leaders Chester City and a crowd of 4,867 to Belle Vue. Unbeaten and yet to concede a goal on their travels, Chester retained that record when they went away with a point from a goalless draw. It was also Kevin McIntyre's first time back at Belle Vue and he received a hot reception from the Rovers fans, including shouts of 'Judas', following his defection from the Rovers camp during the summer. Jimmy Kelly, also with Chester, was received in a much friendlier manner. The Rovers finished the month in fourth place, five points behind new leaders Yeovil Town.

On Tuesday evening, 1 October, the Rovers Youth visited the Shay to take on Halifax Town Youth in the third qualifying round of the FA Youth Cup. The Rovers won a good, hard-fought contest by a couple of goals from Richard Gregory, the first after four minutes and the last in added time at the end. On the Saturday the first team visited Nuneaton Borough, looking for their first win in six matches. They achieved this aim with three goals – two from Barnes, of which one was a penalty and the other from Watson – without reply from the home team.

In midweek they were at home to Stevenage Borough and yet again found the defensive tactics of the opposition hard to break down. The result was another match without any goals and one point for each side. Rovers included non-contract signing (on trial) Jon McCarthy, a Northern Ireland international released by Birmingham City in the summer. He played for an hour before coming off with tight hamstrings.

The following Friday evening, the 11th, was another home game brought forward from Saturday because of England playing Slovakia in a televised European Championship qualifying match. The Rovers' opponents were Forest Green Rovers and due to Tierney (ankle) and McCarthy (hamstring) being incapacitated a Doncaster lad, Ben Muirhead, was brought in on loan from Manchester United. Injuries were an ongoing problem for the Rovers, especially in midfield, with Paterson suspended and Morgan, Ravenhill, Tierney, McCarthy and Owen all injured. For this game the middle line read Muirhead, Price, Albrighton and Watson. A goal from Barnes in added time at the end – the first goal at home since the Dagenham game – gave the Rovers the points.

During the following week Dave Penney brought in midfielder Danny Hudson on loan from Rotherham United. Barry Miller learned that he would have to have another operation on his troublesome knee and this would keep him out for the rest of the season. In the meantime the youth team were making further progress in the FA Youth Cup, with victory over Stockport County in the first round proper. In an exciting match that went to extra-time, Jon Maloney put the Rovers in front with a terrific strike in the 65th minute but 20 minutes later the home team levelled. Extra-time did not decide anything so a penalty shoot-out ensued and the Rovers won 3–1 after their 'keeper, Joe Freeman, saved the first two penalties.

For the first team the next match, away against leaders Yeovil Town, was all important. Before 6,674 fans – the biggest Conference crowd of the season – the Rovers took the lead after two minutes when Hudson, with his first touch of the ball, picked up the ball just inside the Yeovil half and ran to the edge of the penalty area before driving the ball low into the net. Not willing to give up their 13-match unbeaten run, the home team responded and equalised after 15 minutes through Williams, with a shot from 30 yards. A battle royal followed but the score remained the same at the end. This point put the Rovers up to second place on goal difference from Chester City but five points behind the leaders.

In midweek the Rovers went to Scarborough for a Football League (LDV) Trophy first-round game with eight changes to the team that started at Yeovil. Scott put Scarborough in front just before the interval but Hudson levelled it for the Rovers 12 minutes from time. Hudson went on to score in extra-time to win the match on the golden-goal rule.

The last Sunday in October, the 27th, was FA Cup fourth qualifying-round day for the Rovers, with a visit to Telford United. Gale-force winds put the match in doubt but they had lessened by kick-off time and with an early penalty from Barnes followed by another goal in the second half from the same player the Rovers progressed to the first round proper.

The Conference-winning team.

November started with Dave Penney winning the Conference Manager of the Month award for October. The first game of November was a visit to Belle Vue from Hereford United, who had won six of their eight away games but they were no match for the Rovers, who scored early through Albrighton and then added to their score after 20 minutes when Barnes converted a penalty.

Yet another Cup game came up in midweek when the Rovers entertained Yorkshire Main at Belle Vue in a Sheffield senior cup tie originally drawn to be played at Yorkshire Main's ground at Edlington. A reserve team rattled in 10 goals, with centre-half Steve Foster getting three, Gill, Whitman and Green getting two apiece and Bent one. Further good news came when all three graduates from the youth team, Jamie Price, Robert Gill and Paul Green, signed two-year extensions to their existing contracts.

The first team took over for the visit to Morecambe on the following Saturday and went down to their first defeat in eight League games by three clear goals but three days later they travelled to Wigan Athletic (top of Division Two) in the Football League (LDV) Trophy second round and came away with a win courtesy of a second-half goal from Albrighton. Around this time, club owner John Ryan sold his shares in the Transform Medical Group that he had set up in the late 1970s. The sale brought in around £20 million and although he had other business interests he was hoping to spend more time on his work at the club. Also, finance would be available if the manager wanted a player to complete the push for promotion. Mr Ryan was not only keen to get the club back into the Football League but he also wanted them to reach Division One, the second tier of English football, which the Rovers had graced when he first attended Rovers games. Meanwhile andy Watson turned down an offer of a new contract and was placed on the open-to-offers list because his existing contract finished at the end of the season.

The following Saturday a visit to third-placed Third Division side Bournemouth in the FA Cup first round ended in a 2–1 defeat. Played on a pitch that turned into a bog, with heavy rain falling throughout the second half, the Rovers were one goal down, scored by Thomas, at half-time. Nine minutes into the second half Justin Jackson was sent off for kicking out at Carl Fletcher. Gill equalised on 70 minutes but two minutes later Elliott scored the winner for the home team. The Rovers' disappointment turned to sadness when it was learned after the match that Chas Walker, the supporters' club chairman, had been rushed to a Bournemouth hospital after a heart attack.

In midweek Barry Richardson, the part-time goalkeeping coach who continued to play for Gainsborough Trinity, was appointed full-time to the post of youth-team coach, taking over from Ronnie Branson, who had found it difficult to devote time to the job because of his college commitments.

The Rovers returned to Conference games on Saturday 23 November at home to Nuneaton Borough but they could only manage a 1–1 draw, with a penalty by Barnes 10 minutes after Quayle had put the Borough in front. Five minutes from time Quayle had a chance to win the game for Nuneaton with a penalty but Warrington made a fine save.

Sunday 1 December saw the Rovers back on Sky Sports television in a match against Woking, shown live from Belle Vue. The home team were without three players, Jackson, Albrighton and Ryan, all suspended. But this did not stop them again putting on a show for the TV audience with a well-deserved win by 3–1. Although goalless at the break, the Rovers scored twice in the first five minutes of the second half through Morley and Gill, although Patmore hit back on 53 minutes for Woking. A goal from Paterson on the hour settled the scoreline, even though Rovers went down to 10 men after 76 minutes when Ricky Ravenhill was sent off following a second caution. This result lifted the Rovers back to third place and further good news came over the weekend when Chas Walker was transferred to Doncaster Royal Infirmary, despite being unconscious and in a critical condition.

The following Friday evening the Rovers went to Eton Park, Burton, to meet Burton Albion for the first time in a competitive match and dominated the game more than the scoreline of 2–1 suggested. Goals from Barnes (13) and Gill (46) put the Rovers in command but a penalty on 81 minutes, converted by Kavanagh, gave the Rovers some anxious moments at the end. The Rovers were now level with Chester City on 30 points, just three points behind leaders Yeovil Town, who lost at Scarborough.

Riding on a high, the Rovers went to promotion-seeking Division Two side Crewe Alexandra in the quarter-final of the Football League (LDV) Trophy Northern Section, with new signing Chris Beech making his debut for the club. However, the Rovers were completely derailed on the night by a classy Crewe side that proved to be unstoppable. Crewe went in at the break three goals up, scored in the first 24 minutes. They made it four 10 minutes into the second half and added four more at regular intervals before the end of the match came to the Rovers' aid. Crewe's scorers in Rovers' worst defeat since 1997–98 were David Vaughan, Dean Ashton (3), Rodney Jack (2), Steve Jones and Kenny Lunt. The following day midfielder Warren Peyton was signed on a free transfer from Nuneaton Borough as cover for the second half of the season.

The next match was back to the Conference at middle-of-the-table Dagenham & Redbridge. A tough, hard-fought match, in which the Rovers twice held the lead, was finally settled as a 3–3 draw. Barnes gave the Rovers an early lead, which they held until a minute from the break when McGrath equalised for the Daggers. Seven minutes into the second half Barnes put the Rovers in front again but only two minutes later the home team were level through West, who then put the Daggers in front 20 minutes from time. Five minutes elapsed before Gill equalised to give the Rovers a point.

Unfortunately for the Rovers, Marples received a badly gashed calf that would keep him out for a number of weeks and, with Price also out with an ankle injury, the Rovers were short of cover in the right-back position. However, a loan signing from Rushden & Diamonds, Tarkan Mustafa, was completed in time for him to turn out against Halifax Town on the Friday evening before the Christmas period. This match ended in a goalless draw as once again Lee Butler performed well in goal for the Shaymen, who had been reduced to 10 men just before the half-hour mark when Scott Guyett was sent off for a bad tackle on Paterson.

On Boxing Day came the Yorkshire derby game against Scarborough at Seamer Road. The teams were level on points, with the Rovers one goal better off in goal difference, putting them in third place and Scarborough in fourth.

Dave Penney and Mickey Walker take a training session at Cantley Park. Players include John Doolan, Tim Ryan, Chris Beech, Simon Marples and Jason Blunt.

But that was where the similarities ended, as the Rovers treated both sets of fans in a near 3,000 capacity crowd – Scarborough's biggest for two years – to a feast of football and goals in a 5–2 victory. Two goals up at the interval through Barnes and Gill set the Rovers on their way but Shepherd converted a penalty for the homesters just before the hour. However, the Rovers poured forward and two efforts from Paterson made the game safe, despite Henry pulling another goal back on 84 minutes. Former Rovers player Neil Campbell was sent off after 80 minutes following a second booking. The Rovers' three-goal lead was restored a minute from time by Gill. Chester City drew at Northwich Victoria and Yeovil Town lost at Forest Green Rovers, which left the Rovers in second place, four points behind Yeovil and one in front of Chester.

Meanwhile, Alan Morgan's contract was terminated by mutual consent due to insufficient opportunities to gain a regular first-team place. Two days later the Rovers signed off the old year with a single-goal victory over Leigh RMI at Belle Vue, thanks to Paterson's goal after 75 minutes. Yeovil's draw at home to Barnet left the Rovers in second place, just two points behind as the old year faded out.

Ricky Ravenhill, Paul Green and Tim Ryan celebrate getting to the Play-off final by beating Chester in the semi-final.

The Rovers started the new year disappointed that the New Year's Day game at home to Scarborough had to be called off because of a waterlogged pitch. This extended rest until Saturday 4 January probably worked in their favour, because their visit to Barnet resulted in a win by the best of three goals, with Paterson and Gill registering on the score sheet in the first 18 minutes. Although Hendon pulled one back early in the second half, it was not enough to stop the Rovers taking the points from their first-ever win at Barnet.

On the following Saturday, the FA Trophy third-round match against Halifax Town was called off because of the frozen state of the pitch at the Shay. The match did go ahead three days later but, despite Dave Penney insisting that he wanted to win the competition, the team's performance was possibly the worst so far. Green, a second-half substitute, got the Rovers' only goal late in the game as they slipped to a 4–1 defeat. Danny Hudson returned to Rotherham United after his loan spell before the next game at home to Telford United.

The Rovers had gone eight League games without defeat and Telford had gone six games without a win in the same competition but they came to Belle Vue and rammed in three goals when the Rovers had only conceded four all season at home in the League. A consolation goal from Barnes six minutes from time was all the Rovers achieved. It should have been four goals against them but a fierce drive from Moore on 67 minutes hit a stanchion at the back of the net and rebounded into play. Several Telford players ran to the dugout to celebrate, while the Rovers went upfield and nearly scored because the referee had not blown for the goal.

Tarkan Mustafa, who had impressed with his performances, returned to Rushden & Diamonds after refusing to extend his loan spell and also refusing the offer of a contract to sign for the club. The Rovers then had a three-week break from competitive football because their scheduled opponents were involved in various Cup competitions. So at the end of the month they found themselves in fourth position, having played 27 games for 51 points, nine points behind leaders Yeovil Town, who had played two games more. Chester City and Halifax Town, sandwiched between Yeovil and the Rovers, had also played more games.

Robert Gill was selected for the England National Game XI to play against a Belgium XI at Ostend on 11 February. The squad, all selected from Conference teams, were then all withdrawn, with the exception of the Yeovil Town contingent, by the Conference clubs because of the prospect of injuries that could affect clubs' chances of reaching the Play-offs. To save any resentment among the Conference clubs, the FA decided to scrap the original squad and select another from the feeder leagues.

The Rovers returned from their enforced rest on 8 February ready to pick up where they had left off, which is exactly what they did. At home to mid-table Northwich Victoria, they took a one-goal lead into the interval after Barnes scored just past the half hour but a penalty by McNiven and a good header from Blundell either side of the hour mark gave the visitors the points. This was definitely not promotion-winning form but the one good thing to come from the game was the return of Simon Marples, who had had 30 stitches put in the calf wound he received in a game two months earlier. Meanwhile, the club had taken forward Steve Burton, from Wadworth and a third-year trainee from Ipswich Town on trial and then signed midfielder Jason Blunt, a former Leeds United trainee, from Scarborough on a contract to the end of the season.

The Rovers hit the winning trail on Saturday 15 February after Dave Penney made changes, bringing in Warren Peyton for his first start and giving a debut to Jason Blunt. Two first-half goals from Barnes provided a win at bottom club Kettering Town, who had Murphy sent off after 62 minutes following a second booking. In midweek the manager signed full-back Keith Foy (after trials with the second team), released by Nottingham Forest, until the end of the season.

The following Saturday Burton Albion visited Belle Vue and went away beaten by a single goal from Barnes. Chester City lost at Dagenham & Redbridge and Halifax Town played in the FA Trophy, allowing the Rovers to move back into second place. However, the loss of two points in a goalless draw at lowly Farnborough Town on the following Tuesday, even if it was an entertaining game, did not help the Rovers in their quest to catch Yeovil Town. They did not have the help of Dean Barrick either, as he and the club parted company by 'mutual consent' because he would not be offered a new contract at the end of the season. He finished the season at Nuneaton Borough.

The first day of March brought a trip to Southport but it was anything but sunny at the seaside. Rain, thunder, lightning and hailstones could not stop the Rovers gaining their first win over Southport in the Conference at Haig Avenue and by the considerable margin of four clear goals, scored by Green (25 and 85), Gill (52) and Barnes (79). Even the Rovers fans on the uncovered terracing did not mind the weather with a scoreline like that.

Fran Tierney, who had such an impressive game at Southport after his long absence with an achilles tendon injury, signed a new two-year contract a couple of days later. On Tuesday a reserve team took on Mexborough Main Street from the County Senior League in the Sheffield Senior Cup quarter-final and scored seven times without reply. Jon Maloney from the youth team scored twice, along with Tris Whitman, with a hat-trick, Bryan Craig from the youth team and Warren Peyton.

Another four-goal blast by the Rovers on the Saturday, when they beat Gravesend & Northfleet 4–1, consolidated their second place in the table, three points in front of their nearest challengers, Dagenham & Redbridge, who had won their last 10 League games. But the Rovers were still nine points behind the leaders, with only one game in hand. Blunt scored two of the goals, with Morley and Barnes getting the others and only a superb display by Paul Wilkerson in the Gravesend goal stopped the score getting to double figures.

Meanwhile, 36-year-old Don Goodman joined the club on loan from Exeter City to add experience to the side in their pursuit of promotion. The game on the Saturday away at Chester City was put back to Monday 17 February and shown live on Sky Sports television. Chester had slipped up of late and were in fifth place, six points behind the Rovers, with Hereford United and Halifax Town breathing down their necks for that last Play-off place. A poor, scrappy game was settled around the half-time break. Dave Morley, of the Rovers, was sent off on the stroke of half-time after receiving a second booking and Jason Blunt followed him for the same reason just two minutes into the second half. This left the Rovers to battle on with nine men. They did such a good job that the home team, with a two-man advantage, only got through once, just past the hour when Twiss shot in from the edge of the penalty area. The Rovers were now 12 points behind Yeovil Town, with a game in hand.

Nationwide Conference Play-Off Final squad 2003.

In midweek the Rovers spent £25,000 bringing John Doolan to the club from Barnet. He went straight into the team on the Saturday against relegation-haunted Woking, along with Goodman, who was also making his first start. The Rovers did not play up to their normal standard but went in at the break leading by 2–1 from a goal by Steve Foster and an own-goal by Campbell after the home team had taken a seventh-minute lead. The Rovers were second best in the second half but only conceded one goal, thereby going home with a point from a 2–2 draw. While it was still mathematically possible for the Rovers to beat Yeovil Town to the title, it was getting more improbable as the distance between them was now 14 points. In fact, to qualify for the Play-offs in the most advantageous position they now had a struggle between second or third, because Dagenham & Redbridge were level on 65 points with them, Chester City were one point behind and Morecambe had 62 points.

The midweek game on 25 February was at home to Margate and was comfortably won, with a goal from Blunt and two from Barnes, although the visitors did give the fans a scare when they pulled one back. Barnes settled the issue with his second goal minutes later. Then, on transfer deadline day, the club signed striker Gregg Blundell from Northwich Victoria for an undisclosed fee and midfielder Tyrone Thompson on loan from Sheffield United. Having provided the money for these acquisitions, John Ryan warned the fans that the gate of 2,800 for the game against Margate was way below expectations for a club in second place and bound for the Play-offs and he asked the question as to whether the town wanted a League side at all. He also asked the fans to share his ambition of getting the club back into the second tier of English football and come out and support the team, otherwise he would have to consider whether to continue to support the club with the sort of money that he had done over the last five years.

The Rovers were without a game on the last Saturday of March because their scheduled match against Burton Albion had been played earlier in the season. Their next match, therefore, was the semi-final of the Sheffield Senior Cup on the last day of March at Belle Vue against Maltby Main. A young Rovers side struggled to beat the Northern Counties East team, managed by Shaun Goodwin and it was only after Maltby went down to 10 men on 80 minutes when Nicky Brown broke a leg that the Rovers managed to get the winning goal five minutes from time through Steve Burton. Liam Slack had opened the scoring on 12 minutes but Maltby equalised before half-time through Peter Owen.

The following evening, Tuesday 1 April, Scarborough came to Belle Vue and played the biggest April fool of all by taking all three points back to Scarborough. The fans heeded John Ryan's call as the attendance of 4,155 suggests but the players did not and a scrappy game was won by the visitors, with a 53rd-minute goal from Mohammed Sillah. The fans were not pleased, Mr Ryan was not pleased and the manager was not pleased as the players found out over the half hour that they spent in the dressing room after the game.

Was the strain of achieving the dream getting to Dave Penney? One wondered this at the time when it emerged that he had complained to Radio Sheffield about the use of former Barnsley manager Steve Parkin as the expert

The three Play-Off Final goalscorers.

summariser when broadcasting the Rovers games live. Although he had no personal gripe against Mr Parkin, Dave was superstitious to the point that the Rovers had lost on the four occasions Mr Parkin had been summariser, the last one being the Scarborough game.

The next game, on Saturday 5 April, was at Forest Green Rovers and the Rovers got back on the winning trail when Barnes shot past Perrin two minutes from time. It was perhaps a somewhat fortuitous victory, because it was against the run of play that they had scored the first goal through Morley a minute before half-time and Forest Green equalised in added time when former Rovers player Neil Grayson put the ball past Warrington. The Rovers played better in the second half, eventually getting a winning goal.

Injuries were again to the fore as the run down to the Play-offs went on. Recent new faces Gregg Blundell and Tyrone Thompson had been out since their first training sessions with the Rovers because of hamstring and ankle injuries sustained in that time. Tim Ryan (hamstring), Jamie Paterson (knee), Justin Jackson (groin), Barry Miller (knee) andy Watson and Jamie Price (ankle) and Keith Foy were all out.

Saturday 12 April saw champions elect Yeovil Town in town to play at Belle Vue in a live broadcast on Sky Sports television at tea time. But once again, before the biggest attendance of the season (5,344) at Belle Vue, the Rovers failed to turn up and were turned into cannon fodder for the team who knew they were champions before they kicked-off, because the only team who could mathematically catch them, Chester City, had only drawn earlier that afternoon. The Rovers also knew before a ball was kicked in their game that their place in the Play-offs was safe because Hereford United had lost. Had all this information affected either side psychologically? Because Yeovil played like the champions they were and the Rovers seemed to accept their place as secondary to them. The men from Somerset were three goals up at half-time through Way, a penalty from McIndoe and Johnson and they added a fourth four minutes into the second half through Gall. Yeovil had come from three goals down on their last visit to Belle Vue but there was no way that the Rovers would emulate that. They did have a perfect chance to get on the score sheet after 91 minutes but Barnes had a penalty-kick saved by Weale. It was especially embarrassing for Dave Penney after receiving the Conference award as Manager of the Month for March before the game; for the fans it was…well, choose your own adjective.

In midweek the reserves went to Prenton Park and beat Tranmere Rovers Reserves handsomely by four clear goals in the Central League Cup semi-final. Watson, Maloney (twice) and Burton scored the goals. This put them in the Final to play Hull City Reserves but owing to fixture congestion this match did not take place until August 2003. But all was not good because Mark Albrighton was sent off for retaliation after being struck by Andy Robinson of Tranmere. This would mean him missing the two legs of the Play-off semi-final and the Sheffield Senior Cup Final.

With their place in the Play-offs secured, it was no longer necessary for the Rovers to fight for the best position, because whatever position they finished up in they would have to play the second leg away because of an agreement with the Racecourse in 1965 relating to the use of the car park on race days. The team finishing in second or third place had the choice of playing home or away in the first leg and Dave Penney's choice was to play away, as it was for most managers. But that choice was taken away from him by the stipulations of the above agreement, because the first match was due to be played on a race day. However, Mickey Walker said they had their pride to play for and wanted to finish in second spot so they would tackle the remaining games like all other games.

This was put to the test on 19 April with a visit to Stevenage Borough, who had pulled away from the relegation zone with six successive victories under their new manager, Graham Westley. Because the Rovers had a game two days later on Easter Monday, the manager made a number of changes, which included giving Stuart Nelson his debut in goal. Dino Maamria, a former Rover, put the home team in front after two minutes and, with the Rovers not showing up too well in the first half, Stevenage went in at the break two goals to the good, with Wormull adding the second. The second half was a different story as the Rovers dominated the game and goals from Tierney, Whitman and Barnes in the last minute gave the Rovers their first goals and first victory at Stevenage in five seasons of trying.

Only Nelson and Marples from Saturday started the game at Belle Vue against second-placed Morecambe, who only made one change to their team on Easter Monday. A 1–1 result kept both teams locked on 75 points, with one game to play but Morecambe stayed second on goal difference. Burton, making his League debut for the Rovers, scored their goal just past the half hour to equalise the score. Before the game Paul Barnes was presented with the supporters' club Player of the Season Trophy. After the match a meeting was held in regard to a complaint from Barnes that Andy Liney, supporters' director, had breached boardroom confidentiality by revealing to supporters the pay package offered to him for a new one-year contract. The meeting was attended by chairman Trevor Milton, director Stuart Highfield, Mr Liney, the management and Paul Barnes. Liney tended his resignation from the board and in a statement afterwards he admitted that he had inadvertently mentioned some figures to supporters on the coach to the Stevenage game while defending the club and manager over the reasons for not offering a longer contract. He apologised to Paul Barnes and went on to say that he had experienced difficulty in balancing the need for secrecy and the thirst for information from the fans. But at a board meeting on the Thursday the directors refused to accept his resignation and urged him to reconsider. Mr Liney apologised for the events and explained that he would gladly continue in his role as a director and learn from the incident so that nothing like it would occur in the future.

Another matter that had all the different media outlets talking was John Ryan's decision to make an appearance on the field as a player in the last match at Hereford. He had registered as a player at the beginning of the season and, with all the relevant issues settled, he wanted to make a substitute appearance in the final minutes of the final game. The pros and cons of this were discussed on nationwide television, radio and newspapers, with the general opinion being that, as the owner of the club and the financial provider of around £4 million since 1998, there was no harm in a few minutes' appearance at the end of a match that did not have anything riding on it. John Ryan had spoken to the Hereford United chairman-manager, Graham Turner and received the okay before deciding to go ahead with the plan.

Saturday 26 April arrived, as did the Rovers team and their newest member, John Ryan, at Hereford United for the last match of the regular season. On the other side of the coin, however, for one member of the team it meant the start of a long process to get back to fitness in time for the following season. Justin Jackson, the most expensive player that

Doncaster Rovers had ever brought to the club, went into hospital for an operation on his troublesome groin injury, which had kept him out of action for the previous two months. In the meantime his teammates were locking horns with Hereford United at Edgar Street. The home team took the lead on 38 minutes through Williams and generally had the better of the first half but the second half belonged to the Rovers even though the Bulls took the lead through Correia for a second time after Watson had equalised just past the hour. Eleven minutes from time Whitman equalised then Barnes put the Rovers in front five minutes before the end of normal time, with substitute Blundell adding a fourth goal three minutes later. It was then time for John Ryan's entry to the gladiatorial arena to tumultuous acclaim from the Rovers fans as he replaced the main gladiator, Paul Barnes. Even though he did not touch the ball in his three minutes of glory, for John Ryan it was the culmination of a lifelong ambition to wear the Rovers shirt on the field of play. At the age of 52 years 11 months and 360 days he achieved that ambition and became the oldest player to have played for a senior professional club. For Paul Barnes the season had been exceptional because he finished up as the leading scorer in the Conference to win the Golden Boot.

The final League table showed the Rovers finishing third on 78 points, with an inferior goal difference to second-placed Morecambe. Chester City were fourth on 75 points, while Dagenham & Redbridge were fifth with 72 points. The Rovers record was: played 42, won 22, drawn 12, lost 8, goals for 73, goals against 47, points 78. Their average home 'gate' was 3,540, second to Yeovil Town's 4,741.

The Play-off semi-finals were Dagenham & Redbridge versus Morecambe and Doncaster Rovers versus Chester City. Thursday 1 May was John Ryan's 53rd birthday and what better way to celebrate than the first leg of a Play-off game televised live on Sky Sports and played before a crowd of 6,857. This took place at Belle Vue against Chester City, who had the best defensive record in the Conference during the regular season, having only conceded 10 goals in 21 games on their travels. They succeeded in stifling the Rovers' attempts to play their brand of football and took the lead after 36 minutes when former Rover Kevin McIntyre fired in from 12 yards. The Rovers huffed and puffed but could not find a way through until the 93rd minute, when a terrific low drive from 20 yards by Whitman zipped into the net for an equalising goal. The one sour note on the night was the sending off of Chester's Mark Quayle, who put Ravenhill into the dugout from the touchline in the 85th minute, just three minutes after he had come on as a substitute.

Meanwhile, on the same evening Dagenham & Redbridge were at home to Morecambe and were able to take a 2–1 win into the second leg. The return leg was played on bank holiday Monday, 5 May, at the Deva Stadium in front of 5,702 spectators, with many thousands more watching it live on Sky Sports. The Rovers made three changes to their starting line up as Morley, Green and Tierney replaced Marples, who had a groin injury and Doolan and Watson both dropped to the bench, while Chester were unchanged. Chester again took the lead, on 31 minutes, when Foster headed a free-kick off the line and against a post for Hatswell to meet the rebound and fire in. However, the Rovers defence stemmed the tide as the home team sought to wrap the game up. In the second half the Rovers got their game going to level on 57 minutes through a Barnes header from a rebound off the bar. The match developed into an end-to-end struggle as each side sought to get the advantage, with Warrington pulling off two great saves late in the game to keep the Rovers in it. Extra-time came and went without altering the scoreline. Penalties! It was Rovers to have first try. Paterson stepped up and Brown saved. Clare took the first one for Chester and Warrington saved. Blundell, Blunt, Morley and Ryan scored for the Rovers, while Quayle, Davies and McIntyre scored for Chester to leave the score at 4–3 to the Rovers. Cameron stepped up to take the fifth penalty for Chester. He had to score to take it to sudden death but Warrington produced a terrific save and the Rovers were through to the Final.

Their opponents would be Dagenham & Redbridge, who were one minute away from losing the tie on aggregate. Morecambe were leading 2–0 until the 89th minute when Terry scored the goal that equalised the scores on aggregate. Extra-time did not solve things so it went to a penalty shoot-out. With the score 3–2 to Dagenham, their 'keeper, Roberts, saved Murphy's kick and the Daggers were through.

Fran Tierney scores a golden goal at Stoke.

A day later the Rovers had another Cup Final to play, at Hillsborough against Worksop Town in the Sheffield Senior Cup. Having won the trophy for the previous two seasons, the Rovers were anxious to make it a third in what could well be the last time they would enter. Of course the timing was wrong but the date had been set in stone from the beginning of the season. The Rovers team was: Stuart Nelson; Adam Frazer, Jon Maloney, Callum Selby, Keith Foy; Andy Watson, Gareth Owen, Warren Peyton, Steve Burton, Don Goodman (Brian Craig, 68 minutes) and Robert Gill (Rob O'Brien, 58 minutes). Watson put the Rovers in front after 22 minutes but former Rovers man, Mark Barnard, equalised three minutes later. A disputed penalty, awarded to Worksop four minutes from time, was put away by Ludlam and the Nottinghamshire side took the Trophy 2–1.

The inaugural Final of the Play-off to decide who was to go into the Football League took place at the Britannia Stadium, Stoke City's ground, on Saturday 10 May. Dave Penney had already won two issues over his counterpart Garry Hill by winning the toss to decide who had to change colours – both teams' usual colours were red and white – and then winning another toss to decide who used the home dressing room. The atmosphere from around 10,000 Rovers supporters, out of the 13,092 who attended the match, was electric and expectant as the match kicked off in front of the Sky Sports cameras, which were showing it live. The Rovers controlled the game for the first hour and only some brilliant saves by Roberts in the Daggers goal, plus some timely defending, prevented the Rovers repeating their early season scoreline. They finally took the lead after 39 minutes when Green headed in a cross from Ryan, followed by Foster's header being cleared off the Dagenham goalline two minutes later. Ten minutes after half-time Morley bulleted a header into the net from a corner and minutes later Tierney should have made it three with a free header on goal but he put wide. Having ridden their luck, the Daggers got on the scoresheet on 63 minutes when Stein slotted in and drew level 15 minutes later after Mustafa cut in from the right, took a pass and fired across Warrington into the far corner. The Daggers were now in the ascendancy and held it to the end of 90 minutes. Extra-time followed, with the golden-goal rule being applied. The Rovers got back into the game and started to move forward in extra-time. Five minutes into the second period Blundell put Barnes away down the left. Getting into the penalty area, he pulled the ball back for Tierney in the middle to rifle in and end the game. The Rovers were back in the Football League. John Ryan had seen his first ambition come to fruition and was a very proud man. Jubilant supporters piled on to the pitch, despite the entreaties of the stadium announcer to keep off and swamped their favourites in celebration. It was a scene to behold.

The players who took the Rovers into the Football League were: Andy Warrington; Simon Marples, Steve Foster, Dave Morley, Tim Ryan; Jamie Paterson (Jason Blunt, 83 minutes), Paul Green, Ricky Ravenhill, Fran Tierney; Paul Barnes and Tris Whitman (Gregg Blundell, 83 minutes). Unused substitutes were John Doolan, Mark Albrighton and Stuart Nelson.

John Ryan's reward to players and staff was to send them to Spain for a four-day celebration, of which there are many tales that could be told. The same could no doubt be said about the supporters on their return to Doncaster. On Sunday 18 May the team paraded through the town in an open-top bus and were received at the Mansion House for a civic reception.

After the euphoria of winning promotion to the Football League had subsided, the task of reshaping the playing squad was uppermost in Dave Penney's mind. Five first-team players were released – Gareth Owen, Barry Miller, Warren Peyton, Keith Foy and Stuart Nelson – and five more, who were out of contract, were offered new terms, Paul Barnes, Tristram Whitman, Steve Foster, Jason Blunt and Andy Watson. Barnes, Blunt and Foster signed new contracts, Whitman and Watson turned down the offer, with Watson leaving the club altogether, while Whitman signed on a week-to-week basis. Meanwhile, Dave Penney was busy identifying and signing players to begin a new era for the club in the Football League. Leo Fortune-West, a giant striker, was signed from Cardiff City on a free transfer, John McGrath joined from Aston Villa after being released and Michael McIndoe left Yeovil Town to sign for the Rovers for a £50,000 fee. Several bids were made for Adriano Rigoglioso at Morecambe but they were turned down. There were numerous trialists but none measured up at the end of the day. The one sad factor was that there would be no youth team for this season, due to there being no grants forthcoming and it would have to be funded entirely by the club. Brian Craig, Chris Dickman, Rob O'Brien and Jon Maloney of the previous season's youth team had been retained but they would assist the reserves. The one big change in the Football League from this season was the introduction of a wage limit because of the concern over clubs hitting financial trouble. The limit placed on players' wages in Division Three was 60 per cent of turnover at the club.

The repercussions of the pitch invasion at Stoke were also being felt. Sixteen Rovers fans who admitted running on to the pitch at the Britannia Stadium were fined a collective total of £3,800 and six of them were also given banning orders totalling 22 years. The FA held an inquiry and left the threat of a heavy fine and deduction of points hanging over the club at the first hint of any further infractions. Trevor Milton, the club chairman, issued a warning to fans through the local media that anyone running on to the pitch would be banned from Belle Vue for life.

There was activity in the boardroom, too, at the end of June, with John Ryan taking over as chairman and Trevor Milton moving upstairs as president of the club. Stuart Highfield became vice-chairman, with a brief to handle the day-to-day business of the club, and two new directors Andrew Smithson, the club's solicitor and Paul May, a local businessman, were appointed.

Work was done during July to increase the capacity of Belle Vue by extending the terracing at the Town and Rossington ends, which raised the capacity to 9,500. A movable tunnel cover was also installed in the away tunnel to comply with the requirements of the League.

The players reported back on 1 July and a succession of public pre-season games were played against Sheffield Wednesday (0–2) at Belle Vue, at Bradford Park Avenue (0–1), at home to Chesterfield (2–1), at Nuneaton Borough (0–3), at Belper Town (5–0), at Belle

John Ryan launches the new strip for the first season back in league.

Vue against Livingston from Scotland (2–4) and at home to Rotherham United (2–0). Michael McIndoe missed all these games because he did not sign for the club until 2 August, the day of the Rotherham game. So his first outing in a Rovers shirt came the following Tuesday when the Reserves Cup Final, left over from the previous season, was played at North Ferriby's ground against Hull City reserves. He played for the first hour in a good match that went to extra-time before Hull got the goal in the last minute that won the Cup for them.

Saturday 9 August signalled the start of the competitive season. The Rovers' first match in Division Three was at Leyton Orient and the first line up in the Football League for five years was: Andy Warrington; Simon Marples, Steve Foster, Tim

Dave Penney signs Michael McIndoe from Yeovil on the pitch at Belle Vue.

Ryan, Chris Beech; Jamie Paterson (Fran Tierney 85), Paul Green (Ricky Ravenhill 79), John Doolan (Dave Morley 90), Michael McIndoe, Leo Fortune-West, Gregg Blundell. The unused substitutes were Paul Barnes and Barry Richardson. The last time the Rovers had visited Brisbane Road they had shipped eight goals but this time a goal from Blundell on the stroke of half-time and two from Fortune-West in the first 20 minutes after the break gave them a winning lead of three goals. The Orient did pull one back on 77 minutes with a penalty from Matt Lockwood but the Rovers had done enough to start the season with a good win in a match played in exceptionally hot weather, reported to be 38 degrees. The Carling League Cup was next, in mid week, against Division Two Grimsby Town at Belle Vue. In a hard-fought game the Mariners took a two-goal lead with an own-goal by Ryan and a penalty from Anderson after 65 minutes. However, three minutes earlier they had gone down to 10 men when Des Hamilton was sent off for punching Blundell. Fifteen minutes from time Fortune-West put the Rovers on the scoresheet and four minutes later Marcel Cas was sent off for a professional foul on Barnes. Barnes took the resulting penalty and levelled the score. Two minutes into added time Blundell got a winner in front of a 6,000 crowd that augured well for the club's finances. On the playing front Jamie Price, who had an injury-ravaged season in 2002–03, was now back playing, so he was loaned out to Halifax Town in the Conference to regain his match fitness, while Robert Gill was sent out on loan to Chester City to keep his match fitness up to scratch. The first League match at home was attended by 5,500 fans to witness the reopening of the Town end by Charlie Williams and they then watched as the Rovers put a couple of goals, courtesy of Foster and Green, in Southend United's net to give them a 100 per cent record for the first two games. It was also Steve Wignall's first return to Belle Vue as manager of Southend United. Two draws followed: a goalless game at Lincoln City on the Saturday, which the Rovers did enough to win, and 1–1 at Belle Vue against Huddersfield Town on bank holiday Monday, in front of a crowd of 7,367, with Fortune-West scoring straight after half-time to equalise a Booth goal early in the game. Doncaster-born Danny Schofield received his marching orders in added time at the end for a foul on Doolan. The last Saturday in August and a visit to Sixfields left the Rovers pointless, unluckily so, as Northampton Town took the points with a goal by Dudfield 14 minutes from time.

During the first week in September Tris Whitman, on a week-to-week contract with the Rovers, was sent on loan to Tamworth in the Conference to keep his match fitness up. Although the Rovers ran a reserve team, the fixtures were few and far between. The first game in September against Hull City at Belle Vue was put back from Saturday to Monday 8 September for live broadcasting on Sky Sports. Even so there was the biggest crowd of the season in attendance, 7,132, for what turned out to be a bit of a damp squib, with the game ending as it began, goalless. Five days later came a trip to Darlington to play them for the first time in their new Arena. After eight games, seven in the League and one in the League Cup, the Rovers made their first change of personnel in the team. The Rovers scored first when Paterson converted a penalty after 53 minutes but five minutes later Darlington brought on substitute Wainwright. Within 60 seconds he had levelled the scores and eight minutes later he put the Quakers in front, a position they held to the final whistle. In midweek Yeovil Town came to Belle Vue for the first clash of the promoted teams and went away with the points as usual after Williams scored on 34 minutes. It did not help the Rovers' cause when Fortune-West was sent off 12 minutes from time for elbowing Lockwood. The Rovers slid to 18th in the table, having gone six games without a win, while Yeovil were in fourth spot. Oxford United, second in the table, were

John Ryan on a bus travelling round town.

the next visitors to Belle Vue but they were sent away having been beaten by goals from Tim Ryan just before half-time and Green eight minutes from time to give the Rovers their first win in seven games. Oxford lost their leading scorer Julian Alsop on 47 minutes when he was despatched to the dressing room for use of his elbow on Foster. In midweek the Rovers went to First Division Crystal Palace in the second round of the Carling League Cup but after an excellent showing that brought a standing ovation from both sets of supporters they lost out to two penalties scored in the first quarter of the match by Andy Johnson. Blundell pulled one back two minutes into the second half and showed the second-tier team that the Rovers could play but they were unable to get a second goal. In midweek Rob O'Brien, from the previous season's youth team, was sent out to Gainsborough Trinity on loan to get some matches under his belt. The last Saturday in September took the Rovers to Gigg Lane to capture a 3–1 victory after a great display of football shook the Shakers of Bury. Their player-manager Andy Preece, who had scored Bury's lone goal from the penalty spot to level the scores in the first half, was dismissed from his post after the game. Fortune-West, Blundell and McIndoe were the Rovers' sharpshooters. There was much activity at Belle Vue during the last week of September, with new signs appearing that announced the signing of a sponsorship deal with Earth Mortgages that included renaming the Belle Vue Stadium the Earth Stadium.

The successive wins in the League had shoved the Rovers up the table to ninth place but a midweek visit to Cambridge United pegged them back a bit. Tudor and Kitson put the home team in front in the first half, while Kitson made it 3–0 after 56 minutes. Then the Rovers hit back within a minute when Tierney took a pass from Barnes and slammed the ball into the net. Albrighton made it two seven minutes later, with a header from a corner and Ryan levelled the scores with a stunning 30-yard drive 15 minutes from time. With three minutes left they were awarded a penalty but Barnes had his kick saved by Marshall.

Later in the week Jamie Paterson was put on the transfer list at his own request. The return to the Football League was bringing in sponsorship from a number of sources. On the Wednesday the Main Stand was renamed the Earth

Finance Main Stand following a sponsorship deal with Earth Finance, who were based in Rotherham and four sponsored cars were presented to the club by Hayseldens, a local Skoda dealer. On Friday, because of injuries to Paul Barnes and Gregg Blundell and Leo Fortune-West being suspended, the manager was short of firepower up front so he signed Chris Brown, aged 18, from Sunderland on a month's loan. On Saturday 4 October the Rovers went to town on their visitors Bristol Rovers. Tierney scored after 11 minutes but the turning point came on 23 minutes when Doncaster-born Graham Hyde was sent off after receiving a second yellow card. Brown added a second goal five minutes before the break. In the first minute of the second half, Miller in Bristol's goal tried to clear a back pass but it cannoned off the challenging McIndoe into the net. Ten minutes later McIndoe added another but Haldane pulled one back just past the hour. Nine minutes from time McIndoe put away a penalty to complete his hat-trick and the rout of the Pirates.

On the Monday Tris Whitman extended his loan at Tamworth and was joined a day later by Jason Blunt, who transferred his allegiance from the Rovers after finding himself down the pecking order at the club. Two days later Justin Jackson also left the club by 'mutual consent' and was signed by Accrington Stanley later in the week. In the meantime Paul Green signed an extension to his contract that would keep him at the club until 2007.

The following Saturday, lowly Macclesfield Town suffered their first defeat on their own ground in a match that had kicked-off at one o'clock on the advice of the police. Carruthers scored early for the home team and Blundell equalised in added time in the first half. Green and a penalty from McIndoe completed the job of giving the Rovers a 3–1 win. A following of over 1,200 Rovers fans gave Macclesfield their biggest crowd of the season, 2,831. This win put the Rovers into fifth place, five points behind the leaders Hull City.

Rovers returned to Cheshire three days later, to the Deva Stadium, where they met old friends Chester City and put them out of the League (LDV) Trophy with a goal from Tierney after 61 minutes. To compound matters for the Cestrians, Peter Dogun was sent off after 88 minutes, just six minutes after coming on, for a two-footed tackle on Jon Maloney.

Returning to the League on the following Saturday, the Rovers kept on the winning trail with a 4–2 demolition of third-placed Mansfield Town at Belle Vue, even though the visitors scored first on 21 minutes through Lawrence. The Rovers scored four times through Blundell, Green, a McIndoe penalty and Brown before Corden got a consolation second goal for Mansfield. A crowd of 8,500 was the Rovers' biggest since 1988. The game of football paled into insignificance after the match for Kevin Pilkington, the Mansfield goalkeeper, when he was informed that his father had died of a heart attack earlier in the day.

The success story continued on the Tuesday at Belle Vue when Rochdale went down to the odd goal in three. Tierney opened the scoring on two minutes but Townson levelled almost immediately. After that, only brilliant goalkeeping by Neil Edwards kept the Rovers at bay. He was eventually beaten after 74 minutes when Brown netted the winning goal.

The last Saturday of October brought the sixth successive win, five in the League, for the Rovers when they went to Kidderminster Harriers. Blundell after 15 minutes and Brown on the hour sealed the points. With wide men Tierney and Paterson out with injury, Rob O'Brien was called back from his loan at Gainsborough Trinity and given his debut on the right side of midfield in place of the injured Tierney. He gave a good account of himself before being substituted late in the game. The Rovers finished the month in second place, four points behind Hull City.

On Wednesday 29 October came news from Doncaster Council that at a Cabinet Ratification Committee meeting unanimous approval was recorded for the £20 million Community Stadium project to go ahead, with a projected opening in time for the 2005–06 season. Such joyous news was added to at the end of the month when Dave Penney was made Division Three Manager of the Month for October, followed by Michael McIndoe being voted the PFA Player of the Month in Division Three for October. McIndoe also received two further Player of the Month awards for October from Umbro Isotonic and Radio Sheffield.

On Saturday 1 November it was getting cold but the Rovers just went on winning, this time turning over Torquay United at Belle Vue, albeit only by a single goal scored by Green but the three points garnered kept them in second place.

Rob O'Brien had been involved in a car accident and was injured, so John McGrath was brought into the team on the right for his first start of the season.

The night before Bonfire Night needed a fire to warm everybody up at Blackpool as the Rovers went out of the League (LDV) Trophy to a late goal from Sheron, despite holding their own with a much-changed team against the Second Division team. The following day Adriano Rigoglioso was signed from Morecambe for a £20,000 fee with a further £10,000 if the Rovers were promoted.

Saturday brought a visit to Scarborough in the FA Cup first round. The Rovers struggled to get their game going against a lively Scarborough team, who scored 11 minutes from the end through Rose to win the game and progress to the next round. The Rovers were now out of all the Cup competitions and could concentrate on the League.

During the week, Robert Gill, who had recovered from an injury received while on loan at Chester City, was sent out on loan again, to Dagenham & Redbridge in the Conference, together with Tris Whitman, who joined the Daggers on a free transfer.

A week later the Rovers' run of six successive League wins came to an end at York City when they went down to a disputed Dunning penalty on the hour but it was possibly their worst performance of the season so far, causing them to drop down to fourth place.

On the Monday the Rovers brought in midfielder John Melligan, known as JJ, from Wolverhampton Wanderers on a month's loan as cover for Fran Tierney. Later in the week Andy Warrington and Michael McIndoe extended their contracts to June 2006, while John Doolan signed a one-year extension to his contract until June 2005. The management team of Dave Penney and Mickey Walker also signed new contracts until June 2006. Shirt sponsors Streetwise extended their contract for another three years.

The Rovers returned to winning ways on Saturday 22 November in the home game against Boston United, who fielded two former Rovers, Graeme Jones and Neil Redfearn. Brown put the Rovers in front just past the half hour and goals from Melligan (53) and Brown (54) settled the game in the Rovers' favour. Brown was substituted later and found to have a broken toe. The last Saturday in November brought the first away win in four games for the Rovers, at Carlisle United in a match played in hurricane-force winds and driving rain. A goal from Fortune-West after 67 minutes brought the points back to Doncaster after a hard-fought game. They finished the month in second place, one point behind Oxford United.

During the following week Dave Penney persuaded Sunderland to extend Chris Brown's loan until the end of the season, such was the impact he had made on the goalscoring front. Paul Barnes was transfer-listed at his own request. He had failed to hold down a regular place in the first team and was uncertain about his role with the club in the future as a coach. A few days later he left the Rovers and joined Tamworth, which was much nearer home for him. Tim Ryan signed a two-year extension to his contract to run to 2006 and Rob O'Brien went out on loan again to Gainsborough Trinity. Work started on replacing the wooden seats in the Main Stand, which had been there since time immemorial, with modern red plastic seating.

Dave Penney and John Ryan hold aloft the trophy.

The first Saturday in December was FA Cup second-round day but the Rovers were out of that competition so it was a blank date. Wednesday 10 December was a red letter day for Michael McIndoe when he made his debut for the Scotland Futures XI, the 'B' team, against Turkey 'B' at Tannadice Park, Dundee. The following day Dave Penney brought in a forward from Aston Villa, Peter Hynes, to cover for Chris Brown, who had broken a toe.

Saturday 13 December held no terrors for the Rovers, who went to struggling Cheltenham Town and collected another three points on the road by virtue of a 3–1 win, with McIndoe setting them on their way with a penalty after 12 minutes. Former Rovers player Mark Yates equalised for Cheltenham seven minutes later but Morley restored the Rovers' lead on 24 minutes. A third from Melligan six minutes into the second half sealed the win and put them back into second place, one point behind Oxford United.

On the Friday evening before Christmas the Rovers entertained sixth-placed Swansea City at Belle Vue. A McIndoe penalty after nine minutes set them on their way, with Green adding another goal 10 minutes later. Robinson pulled one back for the Swans 17 minutes from time but Blundell confirmed a hard-earned win in added time. This put the Rovers on top of the table, which position they kept for the Christmas break because Oxford United could only draw on the following afternoon, which left them a point adrift. During the week before Christmas JJ Melligan's loan was extended for another month and 10 days later it was extended to the end of the season.

Boxing Day fell on a Friday, with the Rovers being at home to local rivals Scunthorpe United before an attendance of 8,961, the best for 19 years. Only slack finishing by the Scunthorpe forwards prevented them from getting some reward from the game, which the Rovers won with a goal from Blundell on 67 minutes. Two days later they went to the new KC Stadium, the home of fourth-placed Hull City and lost out to a hat-trick by Jason Price. A goal by Fortune-West just before half-time equalised the fourth-minute goal from Price but the Hull player added two more in the later stages of the second half before the biggest crowd of the season in Division Three, 23,006, to knock the Rovers off the top place. Oxford United replaced them, with the Rovers second, two points behind.

Huddersfield Town were next on the list in the first away match of 2004 on Saturday 3 January and the same scoreline prevailed in favour of the home team. Stead opened the scoring for the home team three minutes from the break and added another halfway through the second half. Blundell pulled one back a few minutes later but Worthington settled things eight minutes from time. This pushed the Rovers down to third place behind Oxford United and Hull City but brought Huddersfield Town up to seventh, the last Play-off place. During the week it was decided by the Board to go ahead with the club's youth policy next season but despite receiving funding John Ryan stated that there would be a large shortfall and appealed to supporters and businessmen to get behind the youth team.

The Rovers had lost two successive games so the critics were to the fore. Crisis, what crisis? A week later, on 10 January, the Rovers faced Leyton Orient at Belle Vue, with the kick-off at 3 o'clock. By 18 minutes past Fortune-West had planted the ball into the Orient net three times. Goals from Blundell and Hynes in the second half added up to five unanswered goals. During the week Peter Hynes returned to Aston Villa at the end of his loan. The following Saturday the Rovers went to Roots Hall and scored twice in the first seven minutes through Fortune-West and Melligan, before letting Southend United get into the game in the second half, although they did not allow them to get on the scoresheet. In the following week a second offer was made to Exeter City for James Coppinger, who was showing good form for the south-coast club but they were rebuffed.

On the evening of Friday 23 January old rivals Lincoln City paid a visit to Belle Vue and put the brakes on the Rovers' winning ways. An own-goal from Ryan on 11 minutes was added to in the second half by Fletcher and the Imps went home knowing they had been the better team on the night. An all-ticket crowd of 8,774 turned up, with the majority going away disappointed.

A week later there was another Friday evening game at Belle Vue, with Northampton Town as the visitors on a very wet night. The Rovers took the lead with a goal from Green after seven minutes, which proved to be sufficient in a game dominated by both defences. Steve Foster extended his contract until June 2006 and the Rovers were in second place at the end of the month, a point behind Hull City.

The first game of February on Saturday the 7th was a remarkable one at Scunthorpe United. Scunthorpe had gone two goals up in the first hour, through Torpey and Butler, against a somewhat disjointed Rovers team. But on 71 minutes Jamie Price was sent off for a two-footed lunge on Kevin Sharp, leaving the Rovers with 10 men. Ten minutes later McIndoe scored from the penalty spot and in added time Fortune-West rescued a point after a terrific fightback.

The following week the Rovers made hard work of beating next-to-bottom Macclesfield Town at Belle Vue by a goal from Blundell in added time in the first half. Ten minutes earlier they had been awarded a penalty from which McIndoe 'scored' but the referee decreed there had been encroachment and ordered a retake. McIndoe put the ball in the same place and 'keeper Wilson saved. During the week Dave Mulligan, a New Zealand international and former Barnsley player, was signed until the end of the season as cover for the full-back positions after impressing in trials. Another trialist from Rushden & Diamonds, Adebayo Akinfenwa, a forward, was signed on a contract to the end of the season.

Dave Mulligan went straight into the team for the visit to Mansfield Town, replacing the suspended Jamie Price. The Rovers completed the 'double' over the fourth-placed team with a 2–1 victory. Lawrence put the home team in front on 14 minutes with a penalty but two goals in seven minutes by Blundell around the halfway mark in the second half gave the Rovers the points and a return to the top position, two points in front of Hull City.

Imagine the scene on Friday evening, 27 February, at Belle Vue. It was cold and frosty and 7,000 fans turned out to watch the game against Kidderminster Harriers, who were struggling to keep clear of the relegation places. A goal from Albrighton took some of the cold away and one from Blundell in added time in the first half fair warmed the cockles but during the interval it started to snow and sleet. Two minutes into the second half Scott Stamps of Kidderminster was yellow-carded for the second time and headed for the warmth of the dressing room he had just left. Ten minutes in, Ravenhill added a third goal. Then, on 70 minutes, a curtain of snow came down that must have blotted the view of the Harriers defence as Blundell made it four. In added time a terrific drive from full-back Mulligan from 20 yards zipped into the net, with the Harriers glad to hear the final whistle. Hull City lost at Lincoln the

Michael McIndoe in action against Leyton Orient.

following afternoon, so the Rovers led the table by five clear points.

The Tuesday evening match on 2 March against Rochdale at Spotland was postponed because of a frozen pitch. The next match, at Swansea City's Vetch Field, was another Friday evening game. A hard game was characterised halfway through the second half when a challenge by Iriekpen on Foster brought the Swansea man a booking. Foster retaliated and got booked, while Albrighton and Fortune-West 'discussed' the matter with Iriekpen and also got booked. A hard-fought game ended in a 1–1 draw, with a Roberts goal for Swansea before half-time being pulled back in the second half by Brown. Further good news came the following afternoon when Hull City lost at Mansfield and fell six points behind the Rovers.

Robert Gill was sent on his travels again, this time to Burton Albion for a month on loan. Another 7,500 spectators turned up at Belle Vue on Saturday 13 March to witness the Rovers salvage a draw from the game against Cheltenham Town, when Brown scored in added time at the end to cancel out the goal from Devaney five minutes after half-time. A visit to Yeovil Town on the Tuesday night resulted in the Rovers collecting three points, courtesy of a goal from Ravenhill on 72 minutes, so it was a happy coach on the long trip back to Doncaster. But it was McIndoe's return that caused the Yeovil supporters to get all excited

Gregg Blundell goes in on goal against Orient.

as they unfurled banners with the word 'Judas' and hurled foul-mouthed abuse at him, as well as booing him every time he touched the ball. The Rovers appeared to be struggling a bit at this stage of the season, particularly at home where the pitch didn't exactly help their game. They again left it late to snatch a draw from their home game against lowly Darlington. With a blustery wind getting stronger as the match went on, Convery put Darlington in front just before the hour but substitute Akinfenwa equalised five minutes from time. During the week Barry Richardson, who had acted as backup 'keeper to Andy Warrington, left the club for Nottingham Forest, where he accepted the position of goalkeeping coach. Nineteen-year-old 'keeper Adam Collin was brought in on loan from Newcastle United as cover, along with Mike Williamson from Southampton as cover for the central-defensive positions. After a successful trial in the reserves, Chris Black, a wide-right player, was signed from Sunderland on a contract to the end of the season. The last Saturday in March brought a goalless draw from a visit to Oxford United's new Kassam Stadium. With Tierney and Melligan out with injury, Chris Black came in for his debut on the right of midfield and showed up well, with his pace in particular proving a big asset. Amazingly he went home after the game and was not seen at the club again. Former Rovers Manager Ian Atkins, then at Oxford, had been suspended for applying for the job at Bristol Rovers and Doncaster-born Graham Rix was placed in charge of the club, who were in fifth place. He gave young goalkeeper Simon Cox his debut for the club and he played an absolute blinder to keep his team in the match. The following Tuesday a 1–1 draw at third-from-bottom Rochdale was again snatched in the dying seconds of added time at the end when Albrighton equalised McEvilly's goal, scored after 73 minutes. Foster was missing because of suspension for accumulating 10 points and Morley replaced him. Despite the run of five draws in the last six games, the Rovers ended the month in first place but Hull City were just one point adrift with a match in hand. The Championship would be won by one of the two teams.

The run of draws ended on Saturday 3 April at Belle Vue when a brace of goals from Blundell and one from Akinfenwa in the second half gave the Rovers a comfortable win, leaving Bury to go home with just the consolation of Singh scoring two minutes from time. The Rovers campaign against unruly fans following complaints from fans on the Popular side saw 10 fans ejected from the stadium and they were handed notices banning them from attending matches at Belle Vue for life. The following week the Rovers went to the Memorial Ground at Bristol, where three goals early in the second half settled the match. Ravenhill (51) and Akinfenwa (61) scored for the Rovers, with a goal from Agogo (59) sandwiched in between for Bristol Rovers. However, Adebayo Akinfenwa blotted his copybook on 67 minutes when he and Kevin Austin of Bristol Rovers were singled out by the referee and sent off after a general fracas among some of the players. Hull City lost, so the Rovers moved six points clear of them.

Two days later, on Easter Monday, lowly Cambridge United turned up at Belle Vue and proved to be the sacrificial lambs, which confirmed the Rovers' promotion to Division Two before a sell-out attendance of 9,644. The U's succumbed to two goals, scored by Akinfenwa (60) and Green (65), which gave the Rovers the necessary three points. The Championship of the Division was the next step. Rovers, with three games to play, were six points in front of Hull City, who had four games to play. Five days later the Rovers made the long trip to Torquay United, who were in the mix for a top-three place that would bring them automatic promotion. The Rovers, who were missing McIndoe for the first time in a League game, rode their luck because Torquay could have scored from the kick-off through Graham, who missed another chance two minutes later. However, their luck was out after 17 minutes when Dave Mulligan was dismissed for a tackle on Kevin Hill, who proceeded to go on and score against the 10 men after 38 minutes to put the home team into third place. In the next match two goals in the first eight minutes by Blundell and Brown set the Rovers on course to beat York City at Belle Vue. Four minutes into the second half Dunning gave York, who were next-to-bottom, some hope but on 57 minutes Brown scored a third for the Rovers that relegated York City to the Conference. There were two games left for everybody to play and the only contenders for the Championship were the Rovers and Hull City, who were six points behind.

May Day brought a visit to Boston United, where one point would be enough to crown the Rovers as the Champions of Division Three. Although the Boston players provided a guard of honour to applaud the Rovers on to the pitch before the start, they were not going to give the Rovers an easy game. But with 2,096 Rovers fans making up nearly half of the attendance and backing their favourites, a hard-fought game ended goalless. The one point gained was sufficient to confirm the Rovers as the Champions of Division Three. It was a double celebration for John Ryan because it was his 54th birthday and he had made another step towards the second tier.

9,720 fans turned up for the final game to celebrate the winning of the Championship. Before the match, Dave Penney was presented with the Manager of the Month award for April and Michael McIndoe was presented with the Third Division 'Player of the Year' award and Hallam FM Radio's Golden Boot award. With the permission of the

Centre circle line up for first game back in the League.

Football League, Mr David Pugh was presented with a memento by the Rovers at the end of the game, as this was his last match before he retired from refereeing at professional level. The Rovers players were introduced to the crowd individually as they took to the field. Their opponents were Carlisle United, who would be playing in the Conference in the following season. No doubt Dave Penney had assured Paul Simpson, the Carlisle manager, that it was not the end of the world to fall into the Conference. The Carlisle supporters evidently knew this too, because they chanted incessantly that 'they would be back' and so it proved. The Rovers were made to fight hard to win the game, which they duly

Ricky Ravenhill, John McGrath, Paul Green and Dave Morley celebrate the Championship.

did but not before Glennon had saved a penalty from Blundell after 65 minutes. However, three minutes later Blundell atoned for that blunder and scored with a header so that the Rovers could leave Division Three on a winning note. Rovers captain Steve Foster was then presented with the Championship Cup to much acclaim, with the players receiving their medals.

With the end of the season came the retained list. The players not retained and released were: Jamie Paterson, Rob O'Brien, Steve Burton and Barry Richardson. Robert Gill and Chris Beech were placed on the open-to-offers list. Jon Maloney signed a one-year contract to stay at the club and Dave Mulligan and Adebayo Akinfenwa were offered two-year contracts. Mulligan signed his but Akinfenwa did not fancy moving to Doncaster from London as the club wanted him to do, so he left and joined Torquay United.

On Sunday 9 May the Rovers were once again present at a civic reception after a tour of the town in an open-top bus. The following evening, at the end-of-season dinner at the Earl of Doncaster Hotel, the awards were distributed as follows: *Doncaster Star* readers' Player of the Year – Michael McIndoe; *Doncaster Star* Fan of the Year – John Ryan; Rovers Players' Player of the Year – Steve Foster; Rovers Players' Young Player of the Year – Chris Brown; Top Goalscorer – Gregg Blundell. A special award was made to Andy Warrington for keeping a record 19 clean sheets throughout the season. The awards kept rolling in. Dave Penney was named as Manager of the Year for Division Three, Michael McIndoe came third in the voting by fans for the PFA Player of the Year but became BBC Radio Sheffield's 'Football Heaven Player of the Season'. Michael McIndoe and Mark Albrighton were named in the Football League Division Three Team of the Season. Dave Penney came sixth in the Tissot League, a scheme that measures the performance of the 92 Premier and Football League managers, backed by the League Management Association and Sky Sports. The winner was Arsène Wenger of Arsenal.

In early May Gary Brazil was appointed as the youth-team coach for the coming season. He had been released by Notts County, where he had been for the last six years as youth-team coach and had two spells as caretaker manager of the first team. He inducted the first youth players into the club and held trial matches to find further talent. But early in July he asked for his release after being offered a coaching job with the FA. The Rovers acquiesced and former Barnsley manager Eric Winstanley was appointed to replace him.

Before May was out Mark Albrighton and Ricky Ravenhill signed one-year extensions to their contracts. Dave Mulligan accepted a two-year contract and Dave Penney signed a contract to the summer of 2008.

The club were now in the third tier of English football for the first time since 1988, following their rapid rise from the Conference. But while success had come on the pitch, they were still at Belle Vue in an antiquated stadium that could hold barely 10,000 spectators. For this season in Division Two, now renamed by the Football League as League One, there were more local teams that would bring a lot of supporters with them, with Sheffield Wednesday, Barnsley and Chesterfield added to Huddersfield Town and Hull City, who had accompanied the Rovers into the higher Division. With the new stadium not yet on the horizon, the club used portacabins to build some executive boxes at the rear of the Town End to increase the income stream and extended the Popular side towards the Rossington End. An office block was also built outside the ground at the Town End to do away with the portacabins that had been used as offices for a number of years.

The first new signings were two wide midfielders, James Coppinger from Exeter City for £30,000 and Jermaine McSporran from Wycombe Wanderers. Nick Fenton, a defender, was then signed after being released by Notts County, who were having serious financial problems. Gregg Blundell signed an extended contract to the summer of 2006 and Michael McIndoe also signed to 2007. Chris Beardsley, a 20-year-old forward, was signed from Mansfield Town as one for the future, Frenchman Nicolas Priet, a defender, who began his career at Olympique Marseille and Olympique Lyonnais, was signed after his release from Leicester City and Guy Ipoua, a forward, joined after playing in Dubai for Al Shaab. A second goalkeeper was also required, so Stuart Jones, who had left Brighton & Hove Albion, was added to the payroll. But the signing that caught most people's eye was Ian Snodin junior, who joined the youth team on a YTS.

As usual, a number of pre-season friendlies were played at Bradford Park Avenue (2–1), York City (2–0), at home to Preston North End (1–1) and Manchester City (1–1), away at Stocksbridge Park Steels (4–0), a testimonial for Gary Hatto at Frickley Athletic (5–2) and at home to Sunderland (1–3) to give Dave Penney some idea of what talent he had to work with.

For the first match, at home to Blackpool on 7 August, the new hospitality boxes were in use behind the Town End terrace. James Coppinger was suspended for the first two games, Jermaine McSporran had cartilage trouble and Guy Ipoua had work permit problems, so only one of the summer signings started the first game, Nick Fenton at centre-back in preference to Mark Albrighton and Dave Morley. A cracker from 30 yards by Ryan after eight minutes and a goal from Fortune-West nine minutes from time gave the Rovers a great start in League One in front of 7,082 fans. There were six more games to play in the remaining 24 days of August, so the squad would certainly be tested. A cracking game at Brentford was lost by the odd goal in seven after the Rovers had gone in at half-time with a 2–1 lead through two goals, one a penalty, from McIndoe. Green got a late goal to narrow the gap. Matt Somner of Brentford had only been on the pitch for seven minutes when he was dismissed on 88 minutes for a two-footed tackle on Rigoglioso. A visit to Valley Parade ended in a two-goal defeat at the hands of Bradford City, the Rovers having Adriano Rigoglioso sent off a minute from time for a foul but the next home game against Tranmere Rovers produced a goalless draw. After beating Port Vale in the Carling League Cup first round at home by coming from behind, with goals from Fortune-West, Doolan and McIndoe, the Rovers ended August by taking a pasting at Colchester United (1–4), losing three goals in 11 first-half minutes before Doolan pulled one back just before the break. Rovers then managed a win over Huddersfield Town at Belle Vue on Bank Holiday Monday, Fortune-West and Green doing the needful before Worthington scored late in the game for Town. John Ryan was not happy about the level of support, however, although there had been two games, Blackpool and Huddersfield Town, with 7,000 in attendance and he urged the stayaways to come along and support the team. Because of the form of Michael McIndoe, John McGrath was loaned out to Shrewsbury Town to keep in match trim. The Rovers were in 18th place in the table at the end of the month.

There had been some disquiet, now that the Rovers had moved up in the world, about the proposed new stadium only having a capacity of 10,000 but this was dispelled when the council announced that a revised plan would be accepted for a 15,000-capacity stadium.

At the beginning of September Mark Wilson, a former Manchester United player, was brought in on loan from Middlesbrough but returned after a month because he had only managed one start. Jamie Price went out to Burton Albion to play first-team football in the Conference and regain match fitness after his injury problems but refused a second month because he wanted to fight for his place in the Rovers first team. The month began with two League wins, the first at home to Walsall comfortably by 3–1, with goals from Fenton, McIndoe and Blundell. McIndoe had a penalty saved in added time in the first half, with the Walsall coach Iffy Onuora sent to the stand for his prolonged protests about the validity of the penalty. Just over 6,000 turned up to watch, so John Ryan's appeal for more support had not been heeded. At the weekend a visit to Milton Keynes Dons brought the Rovers their first away win when Albrighton headed in following a corner on 65 minutes. Good defensive work earned them the win, as well as some profligate shooting from the Dons. A 1–1 draw followed the next week when Oldham Athletic visited Belle Vue, with a McIndoe penalty just before half-time equalising the score after a scrappy and niggly game that brought six bookings, two for the Rovers and four for Oldham. However, three days later, the Rovers really turned it on when Ipswich Town, third in the Championship, the new designation for Division One, came to Belle Vue in the second round of the Carling League Cup. Rovers outplayed their illustrious visitors and went through, with two goals from Ravenhill and McSporran. The next League game on the Saturday at Bournemouth brought them down to earth with a loud thump. A home side containing Spicer, Stock and Hayter tore the Rovers to shreds in the first half, with four goals at regular intervals as they exploited the unfortunate Priet at left-back, who had injured his ankle in the first 30 seconds. He was not replaced until the Rovers were three down after 21 minutes but the home team gave their visitors a footballing lesson and a 5–0 drubbing. The last match of the month was at Lincoln City in the League (LDV) Trophy, where Steve Foster, the Rovers captain, suffered ankle ligament damage that kept him out until Christmas. The Rovers still won by a single goal from Beardsley, set up by debutant Ben Jackson from the youth team, where he was a prolific scorer. At the end of the month Rovers were 13th in League One.

The first Saturday in October brought a goalless draw at home to Wrexham before a gathering of the players who were the 1965 Division Four Champions and 7,500 fans. The occasion was to celebrate the 125th anniversary of the club's foundation but the game was disappointing, with the crowd getting fractious over the Rovers' inability to break through. On the Monday Dave Penney added to his strike force by signing Neil Roberts from the Championship leaders Wigan Athletic for a £65,000 fee after attempts to sign Doncaster-born Darius Henderson from Gillingham failed. The Rovers went to Port Vale on the Friday night because England's World Cup Qualifier against

Dave Penney and Mickey Walker look on from the Belle Vue dugout against Hull City.

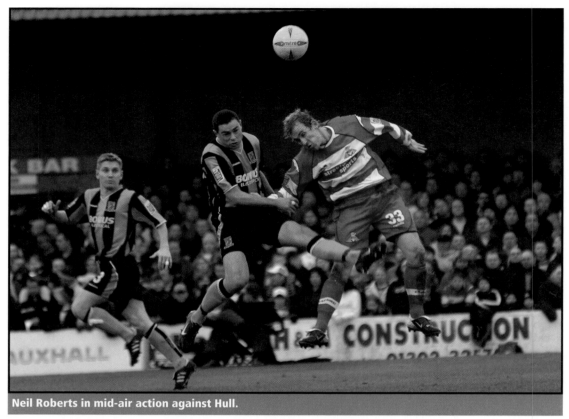

Neil Roberts in mid-air action against Hull.

Wales was shown live on television on the Saturday afternoon. Although it was a relatively equal match, the Valiants scored twice in the first half hour and it remained that way to the end. The Rovers had now lost five of their six away games. Striker Guy Ipoua went to Mansfield Town on a month's loan to get match practice. The following Saturday Rovers were held to a 2–2 draw at home to Torquay United, who took an early lead through Akinfenwa, branded a 'Judas' by the Rovers fans, who booed his every touch. But two goals from McIndoe put the Rovers in front at the break and it stayed that way until added time at the end when Kuffour levelled it for the visitors. However, that elusive second away win was just round the corner, at Barnsley in midweek when the Rovers profited from an excellent showing, with two own-goals together with one from Blundell giving them a deserved 3–1 win. Barnsley had Jacob Burns sent off on 77 minutes after two bookings, then former Barnsley man Ricky Ravenhill was dismissed four minutes later for retaliation after being fouled by Chopra. A goalless draw followed at Chesterfield at the weekend after a terrific game played in steady rain. But in midweek Rovers faced relegation-haunted Championship side Nottingham Forest at Belle Vue in the Carling Cup third round in front of over 9,000 spectators and crashed out of the competition with a two-goal defeat. However, they proved to be good enough to beat lowly Peterborough United on the last Saturday of the month, when an early goal by McIndoe and a late goal from Green proved to be better than the one goal from the Posh, even though the Rovers had gone down to 10 men after 40 minutes when Doolan was sent off on the say-so of the female assistant referee following an off-the-ball incident with Burton. The team were in 11th place at the end of the month.

John McGrath returned to the club after two months on loan at Shrewsbury Town. Goalkeeper Michael Ingham was brought in on a month's loan from Sunderland because Stuart Jones was injured and replaced Andy Warrington for the visit to Hereford United in the Northern Section of the League (LDV) Trophy on 2 November. The Rovers made eight changes for this match but it was still a strong line-up. Nothing much happened until the 59th minute when Rigoglioso met a McIndoe cross on the edge of the penalty area and volleyed an unstoppable shot past Mawson in the Hereford goal. The lead lasted 13 minutes before Danny Williams, who had once had a loan spell at Belle Vue, equalised for the home team. On 81 minutes McIndoe had the chance to win the game but put a penalty-kick straight into Mawson's hands. Extra-time came and the Rovers pulverised Hereford in the second period but Mawson was in fine form. So, on to the lottery of penalty-kicks. Hereford took first shot and scored, followed by McIndoe scoring for the Rovers. The next two penalties from each side were saved, the Rovers penalty-takers being Morley and Fenton. Hereford took the lead with their next kick but Rigoglioso shot wide. Hereford scored and won the tie 3–1 on penalties. Ingham kept his place for the visit to Hartlepool United, who were level pegging with the Rovers in mid-table. Roberts put the Rovers in front on 32 minutes and the team had an excellent first half. They did a good job in protecting that lead in the second half and should have had the opportunity to go further ahead early in the second half, when Barron brought down Blundell in the penalty area. The referee gave a free-kick on the edge of the area and then compounded his mistake by booking the wrong player, Westwood, for the foul! A substitution by the home team, with Porter on after 70 minutes, made all the difference. In the last 13 minutes he scored twice to give his team the win. In midweek the youth team were knocked out of the FA Youth Cup by Sheffield Wednesday youth by virtue of a single goal at Belle Vue. The FA Cup first round was next up for the first team, with a long trip to new territory at Tiverton Town of the Western League. A small but tidy ground welcomed the Rovers team and their fans but the Rovers were not over-extended as they scored twice in the first half through McIndoe and Fenton and then six minutes from time through Blundell before the home team got on the scoresheet in added time from a penalty. The Rovers carried on with their success at home when they beat Stockport County by 3–1. Blundell scored early for the Rovers in the first half and Stockport equalised early in the second but a deadly drive from 30 yards by Ryan and a close-range effort from Blundell within two minutes, halfway through the half, put paid to the County's challenge. The shock news in midweek was that Dave Mulligan, Fran Tierney and John McGrath had been placed on the transfer list because they wanted first-team football, which they were not getting at the time. The last Saturday of the month was a big challenge for the Rovers, who met leaders Luton Town at Kenilworth Road. The Rovers matched the top team for most of the game but Luton took the lead on 62 minutes through Nicholls with a free-kick from 20 yards. It was another 20 minutes before Roberts levelled for the Rovers to go home with a well-earned point. The Rovers were 12th, with 27 points from 19 games, just three points off the Play-off places.

The FA Cup second-round day kicked off the month of December but it kicked the Rovers in the teeth. They were drawn away to Conference side Exeter City, James Coppinger's old team, the second successive game down in the south west. To cut the travel time to a minimum the Rovers flew down to Exeter from Yeadon Airport on a chartered plane. It did not help, because they went down to the Conference side, who went into a two-goal lead before Blundell got one back very late in the game. Exeter, in dire financial trouble, drew Manchester

Michael McIndoe celebrates a goal against Hull.

Gregg Blundell takes on Barnsley players at a foggy Oakwell in the LDV Vans Trophy.

United in the third round and held them to a draw at Old Trafford before losing in the replay and solved all their financial problems with the revenue generated from those games. The Rovers got back to League business in midweek at Belle Vue against Bristol City and included new loan signing Simon Johnson from Leeds United for the injured Coppinger but they were held to a 1–1 draw despite Roberts putting them in front after 35 minutes, the City equalising in added time in the first half. Dave Penney was awarded the Coach of the Year award by BBC *Look North* and Chris Beardsley moved to Kidderminster Harriers on a free transfer. The following Saturday the Rovers went to Swindon Town and took the lead in the first half through Blundell but were pegged back by a goal in the second half from a battling Swindon side, who were level in mid-table with the Rovers. On Tuesday 14 December came an announcement from Fran Tierney that he had decided to retire from the professional game on advice from his surgeon because of persistent knee injury problems, which had so far required three operations in 12 months. He will never be forgotten by the fans, because it was his goal at the Britannia Stadium that set the Rovers on the promotion trail. On the Sunday before Christmas, the Rovers were engaged in a long-awaited 12-noon shoot-out with Sheffield Wednesday at Belle Vue. A capacity crowd of 10,151 witnessed the Wednesday stroll to a four-goal hammering of a Rovers team that simply did not perform. However, they got back to winning ways and back in the fans' good books on Boxing Day by handing out a beating to relegation-haunted Milton Keynes Dons by three clear goals – an own-goal and two from on-loan Johnson. However, the midweek game at top-of-the-table Hull City ended in a 2–1 defeat, with Hull's former England man Nick Barmby and Rovers' Jermaine McSporran sent off following an altercation between them. The Rovers goal came from Mulligan on the stroke of half-time. Thus the end of the year found the Rovers in 14th position.

The Rovers started the New Year of 2005 with a couple of 1–1 draws, away at Walsall on New Year's Day, in a match they could have won after going in front from an early own-goal and at home to Bournemouth on the bank holiday Monday, with a goal from Green after 67 minutes to level the score after Spicer had scored a minute before the break. Brian Stock of Bournemouth was sent off a minute after the equaliser for a poor tackle on Doolan. Meanwhile Jon Maloney went to York City for first-team experience on an initial month's loan. Rovers' first win of the new year came at Belle Vue on the following Saturday when, despite a good showing by Port Vale in the first half, goals from Ryan a minute before the break and one from Green in added time at the end gave the Rovers the points. In midweek defender Dave Morley moved to Macclesfield Town for a five-figure fee and John McGrath left to join Kidderminster Harriers on a free transfer. Both players had been kept out of a regular spot in the first team by the good form of others. The Rovers followed the win over Port Vale with one the following week at Oldham Athletic by the odd goal in three, with Blundell getting on the end of a McIndoe cross just two minutes after the start. Despite the best efforts of Oldham, the Rovers added to their lead through McSporran after 80 minutes, although the home team got one back four minutes from time. Hull City, second in the table on goal difference to Luton Town, were the next visitors to Belle Vue and a goal from McIndoe after 59 minutes sent them away empty handed. Ian Ashbee of Hull was sent off on 77 minutes after receiving a second booking. Hull had an equal share of the game until then but the Rovers had chances to add to their score in the last 13 minutes. After Christmas Andy Campbell, a striker, was signed from Cardiff City on a month's loan, as was Ross Flitney, a 20-year-old goalkeeper from Fulham, also on loan because Stuart Jones was injured. The next game took the Rovers to Wrexham, who were in the relegation zone after having 10 points deducted for going into administration and came away with a point from a goalless draw. This game rounded off an unbeaten first month of the year for the Rovers, which ended with them having 44 points from 30 games and sitting in eighth place, just three points outside the Play-off places.

The first game in February was at Torquay United, who were just outside the relegation zone. The Rovers included their midweek loan signing Andy Campbell from Cardiff City but it was former Rovers player Akinfenwa who starred. Torquay went a goal up on seven minutes and Akinfenwa added another shortly after to go in at the break two up. The Rovers, with the wind at their backs, tried hard to get something from the game but found Phil Barnes in excellent form in the home goal. Johnson did put one past him three minutes from time, just a minute after going on as a substitute but that was all the Rovers achieved. Johnson then went back to Leeds United at the end of his loan period and Guy Ipoua went to Lincoln City on a month's loan. For the second Saturday in succession the Rovers lost, this time in a derby game at home to Chesterfield by a single goal three minutes from time by N'Toya. For the visit to Peterborough United, next to bottom in League One, the Rovers had just 17 fit players, including on-loan 'keeper Ross Flitney. With the backing of over 1,600 fans the Rovers took the game to the opposition but it was the second half before they got the goals from Roberts and Foster to confirm their superiority. The following Saturday the visit of Barnsley to Belle Vue got off on the wrong foot before the start when the Barnsley players got off their coach already stripped, having changed at Oakwell and word soon spread. Although there had been some snow early in the day, the evening was fine but cold and over 7,000 turned up for this South Yorkshire derby. The Rovers did not mess about, they simply played them off the park and the goals flowed from Blundell, with two in the first half, Doolan and Green in the second. Of course it made it easier, although they were already two down, when Barnsley captain Tony Vaughan was sent off by Uriah Rennie after 39 minutes for a complete demolition job on Coppinger that instantly led to a general mêlée in which more players could have walked if the officials had seen what went on. There is nothing like a derby game to get everybody excited! The Rovers crowd certainly let Paul Hart, the Barnsley manager, know what they thought of him as he stalked away at the end. After the match John Ryan expressed his disappointment at the size of the crowd to see the Rovers in such scintillating form. The final match of the month, at home to Swindon Town, who were just outside the Play-off zone together with Bristol City and the Rovers, ended in a stalemate at one goal each. Swindon took the lead after five minutes but Roberts equalised on the half hour. The Rovers were ninth, with 51 points from 35 games.

March began with a Sunday trip to Hillsborough, with the express desire to atone for their drubbing in the home game. Sheffield Wednesday were in fourth place and going well but the Rovers had the better of the first half without hitting the net. The Wednesday got on top in the second half and two goals wrapped up the points for them and their chances of promotion before an attendance just short of 29,000. After scoring twice in a reserve game, Lewis Guy was signed after being released by Newcastle United and made his debut at Hillsborough as a substitute three days later. Chris Beech left the club in midweek by 'mutual consent' and joined Carlisle United for the rest of the season. Guy made his full debut for the club six days later at home to Brentford, who were one place outside the Play-off positions. A goalless draw suited them rather than the Rovers. A day at the seaside brought another point in a 1–1 draw at Blackpool. The Rovers included new loan signing from Everton, goalkeeper Iain Turner, in goal. A tremendous 25-yarder from Ryan gave the Rovers a half-time lead but the home team levelled things up shortly after the break, despite being a man down from the 15th minute when Richie Wellens was sent off for punching Ryan. The Rovers had made a £150,000 bid for striker Warren Feeney from Stockport County, to which County had initially agreed but after scoring a hat-trick at Huddersfield the price went up, so that ended the dialogue. With England playing Northern Ireland in a World Cup qualifying match shown live on TV on Saturday 26 March, the Rovers played Bradford City on the previous evening at Belle Vue. A good start by City saw Bridge-Wilkinson score after nine minutes but the Rovers equalised on 20 minutes through an own-goal by Bower. An excellent match was soured on the hour when McSporran, who had run the Bradford defence ragged, went down after putting over a cross on the run. It took five minutes to splint his legs and carry him off the pitch to a standing ovation but the injury turned out to be very severe. He had torn his patella (kneecap) tendon and dislocated his kneecap and needed surgery, which kept him out of the game for the next 12 months. The teams were locked together in mid-table and a draw did not do either team any good with regard to challenging for the Play-offs. In fact both managers, after the game, agreed that the Play-offs were out of reach. Three days later, on Easter Monday, the Rovers travelled to Tranmere Rovers, third in the table and came away with a brilliant win by 4–2. McIndoe and Blundell put them two up in the first four minutes before sealing the win in the second half with goals from Ravenhill and Roberts. Eugene Dadi had been sent off in the 33rd minute, leaving Tranmere with 10 men. This put the Rovers in ninth place with 57 points from 40 games, three points adrift of the last Play-off place.

Because of horse racing on the Saturday on Town Moor, the Rovers met Colchester United at Belle Vue on the Friday evening, April Fools' Day. With the win at Tranmere giving them an outside chance of a Play-off, they needed to win this game against a lower-half team. But Colchester took the lead on 14 minutes and chose to defend after that. It was the 75th minute before Guy, a half-time substitute for Coppinger, levelled matters and try as they might Rovers could not pierce the Colchester defence again. A week later they crashed at Huddersfield Town 3–1. Huddersfield went in front in the first minute through Abbott but Fortune-West equalised after quarter of an hour. Just before the break Booth sent the home team in at half-time with the lead, with Brandon adding to the score in the second half. With their Play-off chances all but extinguished, the Rovers journeyed to relegated Stockport County with two young players in the squad, as Dave Penney looked at his options for the next season. Twenty-year-old Jon Maloney, who had had a three-month loan spell at York City earlier in the year, made his full League debut for the Rovers at right-back, having come off the bench at Huddersfield for the last half-hour and Adam Brown, 17, from the youth team. Ravenhill set the Rovers on their way with a first-minute goal but Stockport went in at half-time with a one-goal lead. They held it until the 72nd minute when Green equalised and 10 minutes later McIndoe put them in the lead, with Brown, on the field from the 28th minute after replacing the injured Mulligan, settling the match three minutes from time on his debut. In midweek a meeting of supporters was held at the Dome in which a new call for support for a promotion push next season under the banner of 'Going4 it' was issued. Hartlepool United, battling for a Play-off spot, were next at Belle Vue. Before this game a minute's silence was held in memory of Frank Wilson, a former Rovers Chairman,

Players celebrate a goal with fans at Barnsley.

who had died earlier in the month. The Rovers gave themselves an outside chance of making the Play-offs when goals from Ravenhill (58) and Fortune-West in added time at the end put a dent in Hartlepool's hopes. In midweek two new appointments were made to the backroom staff. Paul Wilson, Youth Development Officer at Scunthorpe United, was appointed as Head of the Rovers Centre of Excellence that would initially run the Under-16s and Under-18 youth teams in the following season. Eventually, more age groups, from Under-8s upwards, would also operate. Then, later in the week, came the announcement that Mickey Lewis, a former Derby County and Oxford United player, was to be first-team coach. The last away game of the season, on the last day of April, was at Bristol City, who also had an outside chance of a Play-off place. But the final result of two goals apiece scuppered the Rovers' hopes and left Bristol's chances hanging on the results of the final games. A terrific, hard-fought game had the Rovers going in at half-time with the lead, courtesy of a goal from Fortune-West after 32 minutes. Then, just past the hour, Brooker equalised and the City threw everything into attack to get the win they needed. Ricky Ravenhill was sent off on 72 minutes after receiving a second yellow card, with the home fans sensing that this was a chance for their team to take the required full points. But Fortune-West put the Rovers back in front on 86 minutes, with Brooker again levelling three minutes later. Four minutes of added time, with at times desperate defending from the Rovers, could not alter the scoreline.

The last match of the season, on 7 May, was at home to Luton Town, runaway champions of League One. Before the match Paul Green was presented with the Supporters' Club Player of the Year award and Tim Ryan received the Disabled Supporters' award. The match started sensationally, with a goal after 30 seconds from Guy, followed a few minutes later by an early booking for Fortune-West after a clash with the Luton captain, Nicholls. It took the Champions some time to get into the game but they went in at the break leading 2–1 after two goals in four minutes. An own-goal early in the second half put the Rovers on level terms but Nicholls restored Luton's lead on 64 minutes. It was short-lived because Guy got an immediate equaliser. A cracking match ended a relatively successful season for the Rovers in front of a near 9,000 crowd. Introduced to the fray early in the second half were two youth-team members, Adam Brown, who had already made an impact in the first team and Craig Nelthorpe at left-back.

The Rovers' final position was 10th, three places and three points off the Play-offs. It can be said, however, that if it had not been for the colossal amount of injuries suffered there would no doubt have been a worthy challenge for a promotion/Play-off place. The average home gate was 6,886, against the break-even figure of 7,000.

After the last match of the season, Mrs Joan Oldale, secretary of the club for over 20 years, retired. Dave Morris took over as secretary, with Mrs Jenny Short coming in as assistant secretary, a position she had held at Scunthorpe United. John Doolan was offered a new one-year contract by the club and Leo Fortune-West accepted a new contract, also for a year but Jon Maloney, Ben Jackson, Guy Ipoua, Jamie Price, Stuart Jones and Nic Priet were released. Tim Ryan won the Players' Player of the Year award, Paul Green was awarded the Young Player of the Year and Adam Brown was the Youth Team Player of the Season.

The close season is a busy time for the management staff and Dave Penney and Mickey Walker were not exempt. Andy Warrington had a double hernia operation in May, having played for some time with it. Ricky Ravenhill and Tim Ryan signed extensions to their contracts until June 2007. Steve Roberts refused a new contract at Wrexham and joined his brother Neil at the Rovers on 1 July after his contract ended. John Doolan refused a new one-year contract as he wanted a longer one and joined Blackpool when his contract expired on 30 June. Mickey Walker had been scouting in Denmark, which led to the arrival of a couple of giant goalkeepers, Jan Budtz, aged 26, standing 6ft 5in, from FK Nordjaelland and Tonny Nielsen, 21 years old and 6ft 7in from Fremad Amager. The really exciting news came when the Rovers forked out a club record fee of £125,000 to obtain striker Paul Heffernan from Bristol City in early June. To add to the backroom staff, Barry Richardson was appointed goalkeeping coach, having served in the same capacity at Nottingham Forest. Ben Saunders, a young forward from Southwell City, a local Nottingham team, was signed on professional forms on a one-year contract, defender Phil McGuire joined the club on a free transfer from Aberdeen and the Rovers paid a new club record fee of £175,000 for midfielder Sean Thornton from Sunderland, the previous record having lasted only a month. This was partly offset when Gregg Blundell moved to Chester City for £105,000. Paul Green and James Coppinger signed two-year extensions to their contracts and full-back Sean McDaid, released by Leeds United, impressed on trial to sign a week-to-week contract, which was later upgraded to a full contract for a year. Richard Offiong, who had been playing abroad, joined the Rovers on a one-year contract, Australian midfielder Adam Hughes was signed on a six-month contract and Uros Predic, a Serbian international midfielder, was signed on loan from FK Hajduk Kula until the end of December.

The club restricted their pre-season friendlies to just five public games: away at Billingham Synthonia (1–0), in which the Rovers played each half with a different line up, at home to Peterborough United and Notts County, losing both of them by the same score (1–2), at home to Grimsby Town, winning easily over a second-string team (4–1) and finally away at Worksop Town (2–1).

Having finished the previous season away at Bristol City with a 2–2 draw, the Rovers started this season away at Bristol City on Saturday 6 August and got a goalless draw after a hard-fought, even game. In midweek they could only draw again, against MK Dons, with Heffernan scoring his first League goal for the club to level the score at 1–1. John Ryan was critical of the attendance figure of 5,232 but there were nearly 200 less for the following Saturday's game at Belle Vue to see Hartlepool United go away with all three points with a single-goal win, scored on the stroke of half-time, simply because the Rovers could not find the net from the chances they had. A visit to Swansea City's new stadium followed a week later. The home team took the lead on 44 minutes after an exciting first half, in which the Rovers played their fair share of good football. The second half continued in the same vein, with both sides having chances but it was the Rovers who eventually came out on top with two goals in the last 18 minutes from Mulligan and Guy to gain an impressive win. The midweek brought a trip to North Wales to play Wrexham in the Carling League Cup first round, which the Rovers won by a late strike from Aussie Adam Hughes in a poor match. They then went to Port Vale on the last Saturday of August but lost their unbeaten away record when the Vale scored on the half-hour and added a second goal three minutes into the second half. Although the home team were reduced to 10 men after 56 minutes when Steve Rowland was sent off for a second booking, the Rovers could not take advantage. On bank holiday Monday they gave an improved display at Belle Vue but lost out to visitors Huddersfield Town, the joint leaders, by the odd goal in three, the Rovers goal coming from a McIndoe penalty just past the hour. Ten minutes later Lewis Guy was sent off after retaliating when fouled. Consequently the team found themselves next to the bottom of the table with five points from six games and only Yeovil Town below them.

The first match in September included a new striker, 19-year-old Jonathan Forte, on a month's loan from Sheffield United, for the match against Blackpool at Belle Vue. Michael McIndoe was missing from the line up. The Rovers could not turn their possession into goals in the first half and suffered the consequences when Blackpool, marshalled by John Doolan, took command in the second half to score the vital goal halfway through and take the points that lifted them away from the bottom of the table. A week later Dave Penney made seven changes for the match at Colchester United but they were a goal down after just 44 seconds. They hit back after five minutes through new boy Forte. On 28 minutes McIndoe, back defending a Halford long throw, deflected the ball into his own net and Foster followed suit two minutes later to put Colchester 3–1 up at half-time. The Rovers regained their composure in the second half and McIndoe converted a penalty after 53 minutes. An end-to-end struggle followed but the Rovers could not add to their score. The Rovers were now bottom of the table and the next match was a local derby at home to second-placed Scunthorpe United. But one could be forgiven for thinking the places should have been reversed, because the Rovers played Scunthorpe off the park in the first half and took a two-goal lead in at the break through Fortune-West and McIndoe. The visitors came out with more intent in the second half and pulled a goal back through Sharp but his former teammate at Sheffield United, Forte, restored the Rovers' two-goal advantage on the hour and they held it to the final whistle. Then, on the Monday, came the announcement that all Rovers fans had been waiting for. The contract to build a new stadium had been signed. The work would commence three weeks later.

On Wednesday 21 September the Rovers met Premier League Manchester City in the second round of the Carling League Cup before over 8,000 spectators at Belle Vue and thousands more watching live on Sky Sports television. Unlike a number of the top clubs in the competition, Stuart Pearce brought a full first team because his aim was to win the Cup and take a place in Europe. The Rovers more than matched the Premier Leaguers and the 90 minutes came up with a goalless scoreline. Five minutes into extra-time Vassell put City in front from a penalty. Ten minutes later, Warrington went down to save a shot but Onuoha collided with him, with the result that the 'keeper broke a leg. Unfortunately for Onuoha and the City, the referee deemed it a sending-off offence and Manchester City were reduced to 10 men. It was later established that the City player was entirely innocent in the incident. Jan Budtz came on for his first-team debut. Three minutes from the end McIndoe brought the scores level from a penalty, which is how the

Saturday 17 December 2005: v Swansea City. Ricky Ravenhill, Michael McIndoe, Neil Roberts and Lewis Guy celebrate a goal.

match ended, meaning penalty-kicks would decide the result. McIndoe took the first kick and for the second time that evening put the ball past England 'keeper James. Vassell stepped up for the City, having scored against Warrington but this time he hit the bar. Coppinger made it 2–0, while Budtz saved Sibierski's effort. Heffernan scored a third and Dunne's shot was saved by Budtz, which therefore transformed him into an instant hero. It also put the Rovers into the next round. Three days later came another local derby at Oakwell, the home of Barnsley FC. The Rovers dominated from the kick-off and went in front after 13 minutes through Green firing in from the edge of the penalty area. Four minutes later Neil Austin of Barnsley put Coppinger over the perimeter wall and on to the concrete terracing, earning

Players line up for a penalty shoot-out against Manchester City in the League Cup.

himself a red card from referee Uriah Rennie. Barnsley tried hard but on 71 minutes they went down to nine men when Tony Kay received his marching orders for a late high tackle on Coppinger. With eight minutes left, former Barnsley player Mulligan scored a second goal and wrapped the points up to take back to Belle Vue. In midweek the Rovers won their third successive League match with a goal scored by Forte in the first half. He saw red three minutes from time when he received a second yellow card, followed by Swindon's Ifill in added time, also for two yellows. The Rovers had hauled themselves off the bottom up to 12th, with 14 points from 11 games.

On 1 October Bradford City visited Belle Vue and against the run of play obtained a goal either side of the break. But 10 minutes into the second half Ravenhill got one back for the Rovers. Two minutes later he went for a bath after receiving a second yellow card following an altercation with Windass, who was also booked. Even with 10 men the Rovers forced the pace and equalised through Fenton following a corner. The following Friday the Rovers journeyed to Bournemouth for an evening game because England were playing in a televised World Cup qualifying match in Poland on the Saturday. Neil Roberts, who was due to play, collapsed about two hours before kick-off with a flu virus that was doing the rounds and was replaced by Fortune-West. Heffernan took just six minutes to get on the scoresheet, a lead that the Rovers held until the 82nd minute when Surman turned the Cherries' second-half dominance into goals. In added time Stock got a winner and ended the Rovers' five-match unbeaten run. However, in the next game it was the Rovers' turn to spoil a record run. The visitors to Belle Vue were leaders Southend United, on the back of a club record run of eight successive wins but goals from Ravenhill and Forte in the last 17 minutes ended that particular record. On the following Tuesday evening the Rovers made 11 changes from Saturday in the League (LDV) Trophy at Barnsley, who made just two. Barnsley took just six minutes to get off the mark through Devaney. Halfway through the half the fourth official had to take over in the middle after the referee suffered a leg injury. On 39 minutes the Rovers equalised through Guy. Then, with 19 minutes left to play, what had been a hard-fought derby game turned into a goal feast when Kay of Barnsley put into his own net. After 79 minutes Offiong made it three for the Rovers and a fourth came from Barnsley full-back Austin diverting a shot from Fortune-West into his own goal just three minutes later. Four minutes from the end Guy made it five before Nardiello pulled one back for Barnsley in added time. The

Barnsley crowd of around 4,000 were stunned and manager Andy Ritchie was beside himself with anger at the abject way in which his side had capitulated. They may have surrendered but the Rovers second XI had made them look second best. On the Saturday, however, the first XI went to Walsall and lost out to a goal scored in the second half. In midweek came another Cup game, at home to Gillingham in the Carling League Cup third round. The Gills were next to bottom of League One but they kept the Rovers at bay until six minutes from time when second half substitute Heffernan headed in a cross and then made the game safe five minutes later with a fine drive. However, the Cup win did not inspire the League form, because the Rovers ended the month with a home defeat to fourth-from-bottom Tranmere Rovers by two clear goals, leaving them in 18th place with 18 points from 16 games. The good news, however, was the laying out of the ground for the new stadium, ready for building to begin.

Because of racing on Town Moor on the Saturday, the FA Cup first round against Blackpool at Belle Vue was moved to Sunday 6 November. The Seasiders had already won in the League at Belle Vue but this time it was totally different. The Rovers simply tore the opposition to shreds. A first-half goal from Heffernan was added to in a three-minute spell early in the second half when McIndoe scored twice from the penalty spot. Heffernan got a fourth after 72 minutes and Blackpool got a consolation goal from a penalty in added time. A return to League business a week later, again on a Sunday, at Oldham Athletic, brought a hard-earned win when McIndoe converted a penalty late in the game. The following Saturday, at home to Bournemouth, the Rovers had Jonathan Forte back on loan for another month. The Rovers started well and were awarded a penalty after 15 minutes but McIndoe's shot was saved by 'keeper Stewart. They eventually got their due reward for dominating the play when Heffernan fired in after 41 minutes. Another penalty on the hour was easily despatched, this time by McIndoe and two minutes later Ravenhill made it 3–0. Bournemouth hit back immediately through Surman and continued their fightback with a goal from Rodrigues on 79 minutes. Five minutes from time Green made the game safe for the Rovers with a fourth goal before their lowest League gate of the season, 4,803, a figure that John Ryan was not happy with and said so. In midweek the Rovers had a date at Cambridge United, from the Conference, in the League (LDV) Trophy second round. This was a competition that John Ryan wanted to win but Dave Penney reiterated that the League was his number-one priority and said he would use his squad to pursue the Cups since they were all experienced first-team players. For the Cambridge game he made eight changes from the previous Saturday. Cambridge were really up for it and went ahead after eight minutes, increasing the lead on 34 minutes when Richardson blocked a shot that hit Fenton and bounced into the net. Calamity then hit Richardson when he suffered a broken leg after 39 minutes and was replaced by Budtz. A minute later Fortune-West pulled a goal back for the Rovers to go in at the break just a goal down. They came out fighting in the second half and Fortune-West levelled the score after 69 minutes but nine minutes later Cambridge got a third, to which the Rovers could not reply. They were out of one Cup. Dino Seremet from Luton Town was brought in on loan as goalkeeping cover for Budtz, while defender Sam Oji also came in on loan from Birmingham City. For the Bristol City game on the last Saturday of the month the Rovers cut their admission charges and were rewarded with an attendance of 7,876, who witnessed a goal from Heffernan after five minutes and one from Coppinger halfway through the second half to give Rovers a 2–0 victory that took them to eighth place, just three points outside the Play-off places.

Premier League Aston Villa, with a host of foreign stars, were the visitors to Belle Vue in the Carling League Cup fourth round on the evening of Tuesday 29 November. Anybody who was anybody wanted to be a part of the show, which was live on Sky Sports Television and Radio 5 Live, with the inimitable Alan Green commentating live. The Rovers, with a scintillating display of pure football, were far too good for their full-strength 'superiors' as the goals from McIndoe, a penalty after 19 minutes, Heffernan, on 53 minutes and a real thunderbolt of a shot from Thornton after 79 minutes showed. The bulk of the 10,590 crowd were delirious with delight and the supporters of Aston Villa were in disbelieving shock at what they had just witnessed as the result reverberated around the football world, causing the club's website to be jammed with messages of congratulations from around the globe, including many from Aston

Wednesday 21 December 2005: v Arsenal. Michael McIndoe signs autographs outside the players' entrance on the Main Stand.

Villa fans. Dave Penney won the League One Manager of the Month award for November after three League wins and two Cup wins.

However, there was no time to dwell on the celebrations because there was another Cup game, an FA Cup second-round tie at Boston United, to play on the Sunday. Two identical free-kicks from 25 yards brought two identical goals into the top corner of the net from Mulligan and earned the Rovers the win and Mulligan the nomination of Player of the Round and an appearance at the FA Cup Final. Ben Futcher got a consolation goal for Boston in the third minute of added time at the end but it was a comfortable win for the Rovers. Two days later they travelled to Gillingham for a League game but lost, rather unluckily, to an 18th-minute goal. They made no mistake at Milton Keynes Dons on the following Saturday when they went ahead with two goals in the first 23 minutes from Fenton and Steve Roberts. The Dons hit back on 73 minutes but five minutes from time Heffernan scored a third for the Rovers. Two minutes later the Dons scored their second, prompting them to throw everything at the Rovers defence but they held out to take the points. The next match was a home game against top-of-the-table Swansea City at Belle Vue in front of just over 7,000 spectators, who were entertained before the start and during half-time by Martin Toal, a leading opera singer. The Swans started badly when Kevin Austin was sent off after 11 minutes for a professional foul and five minutes later went behind to a McIndoe penalty-kick. However, it only took the 10 men of Swansea eight minutes to level the score and despite their numerical disadvantage they had their fair share of the game until five minutes from time when Heffernan rifled in the winning goal.

The Carling League Cup quarter-final at Belle Vue, where the Rovers faced the mighty Arsenal for a place in the semi-final, was watched by 10,006 in the ground and thousands more on Sky television. McIndoe put the Rovers in front on four minutes and continued to have a fair share of the play but Arsenal equalised after 63 minutes through Quincy. Green put the Rovers in front in the 104th minute and their supporters were getting ready to salute their heroes for a famous victory when, with one last throw of the dice in added time at the end, Arsenal drew level through Gilberto, who hooked the ball in from close range as he was falling. Gilberto was first to go in the penalty shootout and scored, McIndoe did the same, Cygan put the ball away but Neil Roberts hit a post. Larsson made it 3–1 but Heffernan had his shot saved by Almunia. Hleb's effort was saved by Budtz but Green's shot was saved by Almunia and a much-relieved Arsenal team celebrated their victory by 3 penalties to 1 as if they had won the Cup. Arsène Wenger, the Arsenal manager, was effusive in his praise of the Rovers' efforts and well-wishers from all points of the globe bombarded the Rovers website and message boards with their praise.

The champagne and adulation of mixing with the top teams was at an end, so it was back to the bread and butter of League football and on Boxing Day the Rovers had to meet Nottingham Forest at the City Ground. They did well in the first half and could have had a couple of goals but, in the last action of the first half, Breckin for Forest headed in from a corner to take them into the break with a one-goal lead. The Forest came out in the second half and took over the game. They were 3–0 up after the first seven minutes and made it four 15 minutes later. The match was over.

The game against Brentford two days later was postponed because of the weather, so it was Rotherham United next at Millmoor on New Year's Eve. A fairly even match evolved and the Rovers should have got something from the game but the referee decided in the 68th minute that Heffernan had dived to win a penalty, much to the crowd's surprise and booked him for the second time in the match. This left the Rovers with 10 men. To round off their ill fortune they lost the match in the last 30 seconds of added time when Williamson converted a cross. The referee later admitted he was wrong to send Heffernan off and apologised to the club but it was scant consolation after losing three points and having a player suspended.

The transfer window opened on 1 January and it was expected that Dave Penney would make some signings because nine players were out with injuries, seven of them with broken bones, including three goalkeepers. The following day, Bank Holiday Monday, against Yeovil Town at Belle Vue, the first match of 2006, they suffered another single-goal defeat, while Jan Budtz broke a bone in his hand during the game. The manager had to bring in another goalkeeper. Alan Blayney was the man chosen and he was signed from Southampton for a £50,000 fee and made his debut on the following Friday evening at Port Vale in the third round of the FA Cup. The Vale had lost their previous three home games and the Rovers were soon on their way to extend that record when Heffernan bulleted a header into their net after 12 minutes and took a well-merited lead into the break. A different Port Vale turned out after half-time and registered two goals as they took command of the game to progress to the next round. Ironically, the draw for the fourth round paired them with Aston Villa at Villa Park. No doubt the Villa would have loved to have met the Rovers! The Rovers' Cup adventures were over for the season, so attention could be concentrated on pushing for a Play-off place. With the next game eight days away, John Ryan sanctioned a few days away in Cyprus for some rest and recuperation. Unfortunately, this decision rebounded on them because two days before the first League game after the Cup exit against Chesterfield came an announcement that the club and Steve Foster had come to a 'mutual agreement' to cancel his contract. It was a shock that stunned the fans because he was the inspiration behind the team on the field and had captained them through from the Conference to League One. No reasons were given but it was understood to be a disciplinary matter. The following day Graeme Lee was signed from Sheffield Wednesday for a £50,000 fee to replace him. Neil Roberts became the new club captain but he was out with a broken toe, so Michael McIndoe led the team out at Belle Vue against Chesterfield, who took away a point. Heffernan scored in added time in the first half and Allison equalised just past the hour. A week later came a visit to Scunthorpe United, for whom Steve Foster made his debut. Ross McCormack, a 19-year-old forward from Rangers, had been signed on loan to the end of the season and made his English League debut in the game. The home team had the better of the first half but it remained goalless at half-time. Four minutes into the second half Goodwin, who had come on as a substitute at the start of the half, headed in a cross to put Scunthorpe in front. The Rovers took the long-ball route for McIndoe to level the score on 63 minutes. This brought the match alive as both sides sought a winning goal. It fell to Lee to snatch it when he met a clearance out of the Scunthorpe defence and hit a tremendous shot from 35 yards into the top of the net in the 89th minute. As added time came up, the match boiled over following a bad challenge by Coppinger. The usual gathering of players in an unseemly mêlée was concluded by the referee sending off James Coppinger, followed by Steve Torpey, who had only been on the pitch for 10 minutes, for laying hands on the Rovers player. Early in the week Jason Price was signed from Hull City for a nominal fee on a contract to the summer of 2008. The game in midweek at Blackpool on a pitch resembling the beach at the resort was brought to life in the 17th minute when the home team scored but the Rovers equalised nine minutes later with a penalty put away by McIndoe. With two minutes to go to half-time the whole complexion of the game changed when Blackpool scored twice in 60 seconds to go in with a 3–1 lead, which they increased nine minutes into the second half. The game was effectively over but McCormack got one back in added time at the end. The Rovers team had a rest on the last Saturday in January because their scheduled game at home to Colchester United was postponed due to Colchester's involvement in the FA Cup. The fall-out from the Cyprus trip

Monday 2 January 2006: v Yeovil Town. Ricky Ravenhill clears a Yeovil corner.

brought Tim Ryan to the end of his association with the Rovers when his contract was terminated by 'mutual consent', again with no reasons given but understood to be a disciplinary matter. The Rovers were in 12th position in the table, 11 points away from the Play-off places. Meanwhile, the construction of the new stadium went on apace, with new roads laid and the skeletal outline of the steelwork for the stands standing stark against the sky.

With constant speculation going on in the media about Dave Penney being in the running for the manager's job every time a club found themselves without a manager, he reiterated that he had had no approaches from anybody and was happy to stay at Belle Vue and try to take the club forward.

The opening game in February, after their enforced break, took the Rovers to relegation-haunted Swindon Town. Jason Price made his debut for the club on the right of midfield in the company of another debutant, Antony Griffith from the youth team. Swindon belied their position and took the game to their visitors with goals coming after 29 and 57 minutes. Heffernan headed in after 65 minutes and the Rovers then began to pressure the home team but time ran out as they lost their second successive away game. In midweek Adriano Rigoglioso was released by the club and David Wheater, an 18-year-old centre-half from Middlesbrough, along with Kevin Horlock, an experienced midfielder from Ipswich Town, were brought in on loan. For the next match, at home to fifth-placed Barnsley, the Rovers found themselves down to the bare bones when illness for Fenton, suspension for Lee and injury to Heffernan had depleted the squad. Dave Mulligan gave up a chance to play for New Zealand so that he could help the Rovers out of their crisis and both Horlock and Wheater made their debuts for the club. Despite all this, they got back to winning ways with two goals from new boy Price, one in each half, to give the Rovers a League 'double' over their rivals. This was the first of a seven-match undefeated run. In midweek Alun Armstrong, a former Middlesbrough and Ipswich Town forward, was signed until the end of the season and a hard-earned victory at Chesterfield by a Price goal was followed by a win at home to Gillingham, with goals from Wheater and a penalty from McCormack. During the following week Jermaine McSporran, happily recovered from his horrendous injury, went on loan to Boston United and Mark Albrighton was loaned out to Chester City. Two draws followed before the end of February, the first at Hartlepool United when a spectacular last-minute strike from 30 yards by McCormack earned them a point and the second, on the last day of the month, a goalless draw at home to Play-off contenders Brentford, despite the Rovers having most of the play. After 11 minutes Nick Fenton was booked for a tackle on Owusu and two minutes later he had to be substituted because of a leg injury, which was subsequently diagnosed as a broken leg. The Rovers were left in ninth position, 10 points behind Brentford in the last Play-off place.

The first match in March was at second-placed Huddersfield Town, where the Rovers came back twice to take a point home. The Town scored first on nine minutes but Price equalised six minutes later. Five minutes from half-time the home team went in front again but Green levelled after 59 minutes. It was a hard-earned point gained after an entertaining game. During the following week, changes were announced on the Board of Directors. Mr Jim Beresford of Beresford's Solicitors and his son-in-law Mr Aaron Rea, joined the Board, with Mr Beresford taking over as vice-chairman from Mr Stuart Highfield, who became managing director. On Wednesday 8 March came an announcement that Michael McIndoe had submitted a written request for a transfer and the club had given him permission to talk to clubs in the Championship. This was followed by the news that Derby County had taken him on loan to the end of the season. The following Saturday Port Vale, two places below the Rovers, were the visitors to Belle Vue but once again the Rovers struggled to capitalise on their majority possession. Fortune-West scored an excellent goal on 59 minutes but with just four minutes of normal time left the Vale levelled. The Rovers' run of seven games undefeated came to an end when Nottingham Forest came to Belle Vue the following Saturday and went away with a 2–1 win. They started the game a point behind the Rovers having played a game more, so these points were priceless to both teams as they tried for those all-important Play-off places. The Rovers never looked like getting a result and were two down after 47 minutes. Although Coppinger put away a penalty after 86 minutes, Forest held out against the Rovers grandstand finish over the five minutes of added time. Another goalless draw in midweek, at home to fifth-placed Colchester United, showed that they missed the presence of the top two goalscorers, Michael McIndoe and Paul Heffernan, at the most crucial stage of the season. While McIndoe was totally out of the equation, Heffernan had missed the last 10 games with a groin problem. He had returned for the Huddersfield game but he was not right. It was decided that, as the possibility of making the Play-offs was now remote, both he and Jason Price, with a double hernia, would have operations in midweek to sort out the problems once and for all and give the players time to get fit for the start of the following season. The last Saturday of March brought a 1–0 win at second-placed Brentford courtesy of a goal from Thornton after 59 minutes, to leave the Rovers eight points behind Barnsley in the last Play-off place, with seven games to play.

Saturday, April Fools' Day, brought Rotherham United to Belle Vue for a real local derby. However, the Millers were in financial trouble and close to going out of business, as well as struggling against relegation. As the Rovers had been down that road in recent times, the Board had authorised a bucket collection on behalf of Rotherham United to be collected outside Belle Vue on the occasion of a home game back in

Saturday 14 January 2006: v Chesterfield. Doncaster players celebrate their goal against Chesterfield. The final result was 1–1.

Saturday 11 February 2006: v Barnsley. David Wheater, Jason Price and Mark Albrighton at a corner against Barnsley.

February against Gillingham. Now, in front of 7,500 fans, they had to forget Rotherham's plight and take the points in pursuit of their own goal. A perfectly observed minute's silence was held before the start in memory of Mark Hickling, a Rovers fan who had collapsed at the ground after the Colchester game and died later in hospital. Included in the Rovers line up was Michael Timlin, a midfielder, brought in on loan from Fulham to fill the left midfield position. The first half of the game was tremendous entertainment, with four goals scored in the first 21 minutes. The Rovers got three of them through Neil Roberts (6), Thornton (10) and Guy (21), with Forte getting one for Rotherham on the quarter hour. The second half was scrappy compared to the first and the score remained at 3–1 to the Rovers. The following week, at Yeovil Town, although the Rovers had their chances, they were well-beaten by three clear goals. Injuries and illness had ravaged the Rovers squad and with David Wheater recalled by Middlesbrough Mark Albrighton was brought back from his loan period at Chester to partner Lee in the centre of defence and Alun Armstrong made his first start in the visit to Bradford City. Two goals in the first half for City left the Rovers a lot to do but they could only manage one goal halfway through the second half from McCormack. After the game, Kevin Horlock returned to Ipswich Town at the end of his loan period. Two days later, on Easter Monday, relegation candidates Walsall came to Belle Vue and were only beaten by a goal direct from a free-kick by Coppinger three minutes before half-time. There were three games left to play but Ricky Ravenhill would not participate because of a four-match ban imposed after being sent off in a reserves game. Antony Griffith came back from a loan spell at Oxford United at the beginning of the week and 'Jocky' McSporran proved his fitness in the reserves with some sparkling displays, so both were included in the team for the following Saturday when the Rovers went to potential champions Southend United, who only needed a win to earn that accolade. The Rovers had other ideas and instead of being the sacrificial victim they became party-poopers, winning with a solitary goal from Coppinger immediately after the break, although they had to weather severe pressure for the rest of the game. The last Saturday in April brought another win, with Coppinger again on the mark after 66 minutes at home to Oldham Athletic. Thus with one game to go they were just two points behind Swansea City in the last Play-off place and Nottingham Forest, outside the mark on goal difference. Everything depended on the last round of games played on 6 May.

Meanwhile, the reserve team were heading for their own share of glory. Catching up on their programme, they found themselves in the position of having to play their last game against Sheffield United B at Worksop to win their Division. United could also win the Division if they took the points but the Rovers, including half a dozen youth-team players and a couple of trialists, went on to win comfortably by scoring three times, through McCormack (2) and Adam Brown, without reply, taking the Eastern Division title. Two days later the same line up turned out at Hillsborough to play the Wednesday Reserves, Central Division Champions, in the Play-off semi-final, coming away with a fantastic 4–1 win with goals from Craig Nelthorpe (2), Adam Brown and Adam Lee, all youth-team players. In the Final, on Wednesday 3 May, to determine the overall Champions of the Central League, they met Carlisle United reserves at Belle Vue and ensured that the club would be able to display some silverware for the season's exertions. Before a crowd of 2,017 they came out on top of Carlisle United, winning the overall title 5–2 in a thrilling Final. Neil Roberts, Ross McCormack with a couple and Paul Green, also with two, scored the goals. Four of the youth team, Adam Brown, Liam Green, Craig Nelthorpe and Robert Pacey, accepted an offer of a one-year professional contract.

Saturday 6 May took the Rovers to Prenton Park, Tranmere. The weather was perfect for playing football and as they waited for the start of the game at 3 o'clock the considerable number of Rovers fans mulled over the chances of their team making the Play-offs. The mathematical equation was easy: a win for the Rovers would be nullified if Swansea City or Nottingham Forest gained as much as a point from their games at Chesterfield and Bradford City respectively. At five minutes past three, news came through that Swansea had gone ahead at Saltergate. Surely our friends at Chesterfield would help us out by going for a win! However, it was not to be. Swansea went on to hammer the Spireites by four clear goals and Forest scored two minutes from time to take a point home from Valley Parade. The Rovers did their job, winning by two goals, scored by Guy on 12 minutes and Neil Roberts half an hour later. These results put Swansea City into the Play-offs, leaving Nottingham Forest and the Rovers trailing two points behind, with the Rovers' final position being eighth on goal difference behind the Forest. So near, yet so far! A rollercoaster of a season had come to a disappointing end, yet at one stage they could not have envisaged getting so close. As someone remarked, every season that Dave Penney was in charge the Rovers finished higher up the scale.

On Monday 8 May the Awards Dinner was held at the Mount Pleasant Hotel on Bawtry Road. John Ryan spoke of making a major assault on the League next season, with Dave Penney being given the wherewithal to bring the necessary new faces in. The awards were then presented to the relevant winners. These were: Youth Player of the Year – Robert Pacey; Youth Players' Player of the Year – Robert Pacey; Young Player of the Year – Sean McDaid; Players' Player of the Year – Sean McDaid; *Doncaster Star* Player of the Year (voted for by the readers) – Steve Roberts. Two days later the retained list was announced, with the following players being released: Leo Fortune-West, Alun Armstrong, Mark Albrighton, Jermaine McSporran, Simon Marples and Richard Offiong. The players made available for transfer were Ricky Ravenhill, Tonny Nielsen and Phil McGuire. On Saturday 13 May a Charity Match between teams representing the Rovers and Sheffield United was played at Belle Vue before a crowd of 1,300 or so fans, who had come to watch some old favourites – Paul Barnes, Barry Miller, Colin Douglas, John Buckley and John Ryan – play on the sacred turf for one more time. Fans were also included in the teams upon payment of a suitable donation. The star attraction, though, was the appearance of Tony Woodcock, former Nottingham Forest, Arsenal and England forward, who had a loan spell with the Rovers in 1976 and now made his first visit in 30 years to once again grace the turf of Belle Vue. In the meantime, the Lakeside Stadium was well on its way to completion.

The playing season might be over but for the manager this is where the new season starts as he begins the task of reorganising the team and bringing in the necessary players to fulfil the club's ambitions of moving up the ladder. On 15 May came the announcement of the signing of Kevin Horlock on a two-year contract, followed two days later by James O'Connor signing for the club in exchange for a fee of £130,000 going to his former club, Bournemouth. That same day came the news that Adam Lockwood, released by Yeovil Town, would also join the Rovers on 1 July after the expiry of his contract at Yeovil. These signings no doubt influenced the club to withdraw the offer of a contract to David Mulligan, after both parties failed to agree new terms. Later in the month a further signing was announced when Gareth Roberts of Tranmere Rovers agreed to sign for the Rovers on 1 July when his contract with Tranmere had expired. There was also a change on the managerial side when Mickey Walker was given a new role as director of football. It was not just the first team that was bringing in new players: the youth team followed suit with their own intake of new players for Paul Wilson and Paul Stancliffe to mould into future Rovers stars. The month of May ended with a further signing, Bruce Dyer from Sheffield United.

Dave Penney's successes with the Rovers earmarked him, for the press at least, as someone who would move into the higher echelons of management eventually. So, having discussed his credentials after the Cup successes in the previous season, he was once more being connected to various vacant management posts. On 1 June John Ryan issued a statement denying that Ipswich Town had approached the club about the availability of manager Dave Penney. He went on to say that while the club would not stand in his way if he was wanted by a club of higher status than the Rovers, it was a matter of fact that he still had two years left on his contract. This statement was issued to scotch the rumours going round that Dave Penney was going to Ipswich Town. During June the Rovers had a £100,000 bid, plus Ricky Ravenhill, for Rotherham United's midfielder Lee Williamson turned down and did not pursue it any further. At the end of the month Neil Roberts was told that he could leave if he found another club. He left and eventually rejoined his first club, Wrexham.

The players reported back for pre-season training in July and spent time at a training camp at Denton Hall at Ilkley in the Yorkshire Dales. The pre-season friendlies that followed were at Retford United (7–1), Worksop Town (2–0), Grimsby Town (2–0), home to Hull City (0–0), home to Real Sociedad from Spain (1–0), at Notts County (2–2) and at home to a Middlesbrough XI (2–0). Jan Budtz broke a finger early in training and did not play any part in the pre-season games. However, a number of trialists were given a run but only Mark McCammon, a big, strong forward, was offered a contract, which he duly signed. Michael McIndoe left the Rovers to join Barnsley for £125,000 and Ricky Ravenhill returned from Chester City after delays by the Cheshire club in completing the transfer. He went back on the transfer list but before the season started he returned to Chester on loan. Jonathan Forte joined the club on a six-month loan period from Sheffield United and James Coppinger signed a new three-year contract. On the 25th of the month, Antony Griffith put pen to paper on a three-year contract but the month was rounded off on the Saturday when a Rovers XI went to Gainsborough to face the Trinity. A goalless draw ensued but the game was marred by the loss of goalkeeper Andy Warrington with ankle ligament trouble that would keep him out of action for three months.

To cover for the injured Andy Warrington and Jan Budtz the club signed a young 'keeper, Ben Smith, on a non-contract basis until the end of August but after impressing in the reserves he was offered and signed a one-year contract. The first League game of the season was at newly promoted Carlisle United on Saturday 5 August. The Rovers were not at their best and lost to a fourth-minute goal by Murray. The following Tuesday evening 6,000 fans turned up at Belle Vue to see the Rovers come from behind to beat Crewe Alexandra by the odd goal in five. Bruce Dyer got the

Rovers' first goal of the season after 19 minutes, with Horlock and Coppinger adding to it in the second half. The unwelcome news, however, was a knee injury to Kevin Horlock, which would eventually put him out for the season. A goalless draw on the Saturday at home to Tranmere Rovers followed. Then on the Monday, after a game at Everton behind closed doors, Italian Michele Di Piedi, formerly with Sheffield Wednesday, impressed enough to be offered a contract up to January, which he duly accepted. A visit to Swansea followed on the Saturday and despite playing reasonably well the Rovers lost out to two late Trundle goals. The first, on 83

Saturday 28 February 2006: v Brentford. Coppinger flies through the air.

minutes, prompted Penney to send on another forward, Dyer, but he was injured and replaced after just four minutes on the pitch. The following Tuesday Rochdale visited Belle Vue in the Carling League Cup and took the lead but were eventually beaten by two goals from McCammon and a cracker by Coppinger scored in the space of 12 minutes early in the second half. The transfer window was still open, thus giving Nick Fenton the chance to join Grimsby Town. On the penultimate day of the transfer window Ricky Ravenhill arrived back at Belle Vue from Chester City because they had no room for any further signings at this stage. This was because of the financial constraints under which all Football League clubs now operated. In the middle of these happenings, the Rovers entertained Bournemouth, under the stewardship of Sean O'Driscoll, at Belle Vue. A goal from Lewis Guy on the hour looked as if it would be worth three points but deep into added time Steve Roberts was adjudged to have handled the ball in the penalty area and Hayter and Bournemouth gratefully accepted the chance to take a point back south and deprive the Rovers of two points. On Tuesday 29 August the reserves played York City reserves at Belle Vue. It was noticed that Mickey Walker was in charge, taking the warm-up before the match and directing operations from the dugout throughout the game. Where was Mickey Lewis, whose remit was the reserve team? He was nowhere in sight. What was going on and what was it all about? The answer came the following day with earth-shattering force. Mickey Lewis had been relieved of his duties forthwith and left the club. But it was the follow-up to that which hit the Rovers supporters when it was announced that, by 'mutual agreement', Dave Penney had left the club and Mickey Walker would take over temporary charge of the team until a successor was appointed. The last day of the month heralded the closing of the transfer window, with Ricky Ravenhill being the last one out of the door, on his way to Grimsby Town to sign a two-year contract.

Mickey Walker's first task as acting manager was to prepare the team for Sunday's televised League match at Port Vale. It was wet and windy at Vale Park but despite losing a goal just before half-time and Lewis Guy having a penalty saved after the break the Rovers, in a terrific second-half display, gained just reward for their efforts with two late goals from substitute Paul Heffernan, one a penalty. Following the game, news filtered through that Charlie Williams, a stalwart centre-half for the Rovers in the fifties, who later found fame as a comedian and television game show host, had died. It goes without saying that speculation about a new manager was rife in the media, with John Ryan helping it along by saying he wanted Kevin Keegan as manager but Kevin did not bite. A Board meeting was held on Wednesday 6 September, to mull over a short list of three applicants, which included Mickey Walker. Two days later an announcement came from the club that Sean O'Driscoll, manager of Bournemouth at the time, was the new manager. Mickey Walker turned down the job as assistant to the new manager to continue in the position of Director of Football. So Richard O'Kelly, O'Driscoll's assistant at Bournemouth, came with him to Doncaster. The next day, Saturday, the

Saturday 11 March 2006: v Port Vale. David Wheater gets up to clear.

game at home to Gillingham was Mickey Walker's last match in charge. A minute's silence was observed before the match started in memory of Charlie Williams. The Rovers lost the game by the odd goal in three after playing against 10 men for an hour, Jackman having been sent off after 32 minutes following a second yellow card. Despite having 95 per cent of the play in the second half, they only managed an own-goal on 75 minutes. Around this time, following a poll by Doncaster Council, the Rovers announced that the road around the new stadium would be entitled 'Alick Jeffrey Way'. Sean O'Driscoll took over on Monday 11 September and had a derby League game on Tuesday at Huddersfield Town, so his only look at his new charges had been a fortnight earlier when he was in charge of Bournemouth for their League match at Belle Vue. He immediately requisitioned midfielder Brian Stock from Preston North End on loan and thrust him straight into the team on the following evening. Stock had been at Bournemouth under O'Driscoll, so he knew his attributes. However, defences dominated and the match ended in a goalless draw. Another derby match followed at the weekend against arch rivals Rotherham United at Millmoor. Only a penalty of 10 points for being in administration was keeping the Millers at the bottom of the table and they had already wiped that out after eight games. Thus their first plus point was gained in a non-stop action match that surprisingly ended without any score. However, before and after the game there was a furore over an article in the Rotherham programme from a London-based Rotherham fan that was derogatory about the fans of Doncaster Rovers. The Rotherham hierarchy was made aware of this and apologised instantly, then later on, having investigated the matter internally, they issued a formal apology, which was accepted. Meanwhile, a lot of e-mails came from Rotherham fans apologising for the gaffe and thanking the Rovers fans and club for assisting them in their financial crisis of recent months. On the Wednesday it was announced that Chief Executive Dave Morris had been appointed to the Board. That evening the Rovers had an important game, a Carling Cup second-round tie against Championship side Derby County at Belle Vue. However, Rovers would be without Graeme Lee and James Coppinger, both suffering injury during training that morning. A terrific display by the Rovers, who rammed in three goals inside the hour through Forte twice and Stock, rocked County but they fought back well and scored three in the last 18 minutes to force extra-time. Extra-time produced no further score, although the Rovers dominated, especially after Lupoli had been dismissed in the 94th minute. So to penalties! How would the Rovers fare this time? It was not a problem – they rammed in all eight penalties taken. The young Welsh international, Nyatanga, had missed with Derby's eighth penalty, so the Rovers went through by 8–7. A follow-up to the Derby game was a loan deal that brought a young central-defender, Theo Streete, to the Rovers from the Derbyshire club. The following Saturday brought another scoreless game against Blackpool at Belle Vue, making it three in a row in the League. Yet the following Tuesday they put three goals past Bradford City at home after going two goals down in the first 23 minutes, the first one after only 40 seconds from Windass. A goal just before half-time and shortly after the break by Green was crowned by a terrific goal from Coppinger on 53 minutes to put them 3–2 in front. The Rovers dominated the second half and had a goal by Green ruled out by the referee, the only one to see a push by somebody on somebody else. On 82 minutes the referee influenced the game again when he ruled that Lee had halted Windass's progress illegally. Lee was cautioned for the second time in the match and sent off. From the resulting free-kick Bradford equalised and what was a great match to watch ended in another stalemate for the Rovers but at least it had been entertaining and goals had been scored. Somehow a win had to be garnered from somewhere. It certainly was not coming on the last day of the month at Scunthorpe, where a poor display by the Rovers let Scunny take the three points with two second-half goals from Sharp and Keogh. The Rovers had 12 points from 12 games and were in 19th place in the table.

In the first week of October the floodlights went up at the new stadium. However, the next game was at Belle Vue against Oldham Athletic on Friday 6 October, due to England's European Championship qualifier against Macedonia being shown live on television on Saturday. Injuries were a bugbear for the manager, with 10 players out and with three goalkeepers injured he brought in John Filan from Wigan Athletic on a month's loan. Lee headed the Rovers in front but Porter levelled in added time in the first half. While it was a better performance from the Rovers, it did not suit some supporters, who were beginning to have a go at the manager, particularly after the Scunthorpe match. In midweek Craig Nelthorpe was allowed to go to Kidderminster Harriers on a month's loan to experience first-team football. Kevin Horlock had come back in a reserve game but suffered some reaction on his knee injury, so he was operated on, effectively finishing his playing time at the Rovers. A visit to Cheltenham Town on the Saturday provided a good win for the Rovers by two clear goals, scored by Guy in added time in the first half and Forte late in the game, giving Sean O'Driscoll his first League win since taking over. Then in midweek it was back to Huddersfield Town in the League Trophy, now renamed the Johnstone's Paint Trophy. A goal from Jason Price after 26 minutes was equalised by Booth on 61 minutes but three minutes from normal time Guy gave the Rovers that winning feeling again as they ran out comfortable winners by the odd goal in three. The following Saturday Chesterfield visited Belle Vue for the last time and had the better of the play. But after 24 minutes Forte, for the Rovers, chased a ball through the middle, even though Roche, the Spireites 'keeper, was clearly going to get there first. His clearance, however, hit the oncoming Forte, looped into the air and the Rovers man calmly slotted in for the only goal of the game. There followed another midweek game in another Cup, the Carling League Cup third round, at Wycombe Wanderers. John Filan failed a late fitness test on a leg injury sustained against Chesterfield so Ben Smith made his debut in the first team, his deputy on the bench being coach Barry Richardson, because the other three 'keepers were injured. The Rovers went in front on 65 minutes through Forte but six minutes later Oakes equalised. Oakes then received a straight red card on 74 minutes for a foul tackle on Stock. With the chances the Rovers had, they should have won in the 90 minutes. Extra-time came and the Rovers took the lead again through an own-goal but four minutes from the end of extra-time Wycombe equalised through Easter. The Rovers had already won one tie on penalties, so what would they do this time? Paul Green scored with the first kick for the Rovers while Easter's effort for Wycombe was saved by Smith. However, the Rovers only scored once, through Heffernan, from their next four penalties and Wycombe scored three in succession to take the plaudits and the place in the next round. The last Saturday of the month was a trip to Ashton Gate to play third-placed Bristol City. John Filan failed a fitness test on his injured knee, so Ben Smith continued in goal but James O'Connor came through his test on a groin injury. However, the Rovers found Brazilian goalkeeper Adriano Basso in such fine form that he kept them at bay single-handedly throughout the second half, allowing his team to take the points by a single goal scored in the first half. His reward was the Man of the Match award. The following Monday John Dickens, a physiotherapist from Sheffield Wednesday, joined the backroom staff. He had previously worked with Sean O'Driscoll and was highly regarded in the football world, so he was a valuable addition to the medical side at the club. The last day of October, Tuesday, had the Rovers making another long trip for a Cup tie to Hartlepool United in the second round of the Johnstone's Paint Trophy. A comfortable 3–1 win was gained, with strikes from Heffernan, twice in a minute just after half-time and Price late in the game.

During the first week of November Wigan Athletic recalled John Filan after one of their 'keepers went down with a virus, leaving the Rovers with Ben Smith as their sole fit 'keeper. The good news for the club was the enrolment of two new directors, Mr Terry Bramall and Mr Dick Watson, the major shareholders of Keepmoat PLC, a Doncaster-based construction company. The first Saturday brought bottom-of-the-League Leyton Orient to Belle Vue, where they picked up the point they came for, following a goalless draw and left after stifling the Rovers and the game as a

Saturday 1 April 2006: v Rotherham United. Rovers players observe a minute's silence for fan Mark Hickling.

spectacle. A minute's silence was observed before the game in respect of Albert Broadbent, a former player with the club, who had died earlier that week. But the fans were getting restless, booing the team off at the break and full-time. Graeme Lee sustained an ankle injury, which a scan showed as ligament damage. In midweek the youth team played an FA Youth Cup tie against Rochdale youth at Belle Vue and had their share of luck, running out winners by two clear goals. Both sides had chances to score but it was still goalless after 79 minutes when the Rovers were awarded a free-kick about 40 yards out. Matt Noble, the captain, took the kick and placed it into the Rochdale penalty area. The visiting 'keeper, Lloyd Rigby, who had performed well all evening, came out to catch it but he misjudged it so badly that it sailed over his outstretched hands and into the net. This seemed to knock the stuffing out of a very spirited side and they succumbed to a second goal in the last minute from Waide Fairhurst. More good news was that Andy Warrington was back training. The second Saturday was the day of the first round of the FA Cup. It was also Remembrance Day. A minute's silence was perfectly observed before the game at Brentford, which the Rovers went on to win by a goal from Guy just after the half hour. The score should have been 2–0 but a 69th-minute 'goal' by Mark McCammon had gone in and out through a hole in the net. The referee would have none of it, so Mark was unable to claim his bonus for scoring. In midweek Andy Warrington played in the reserves at Rotherham United and Jan Budtz started training. The club also signed Mark Wilson, back in England after a stint in America, on a short-term contract to the end of the year. In the next match at Millwall the Rovers twice took the lead through Forte, with a terrific strike on 16 minutes and Price, just after the break but Millwall belied their 22nd position and fought back, with a goal just before half-time and then after 59 minutes to take a point from a 2–2 draw in an exciting, fast-paced match, played in an excellent spirit. Then, on Tuesday 21 November, it was announced that the new Lakeside Stadium would be known henceforth as the 'Keepmoat' Stadium, the Keepmoat Company having won the naming rights. The following evening at good old-fashioned Belle Vue, the youth team faced Hartlepool United in an FA Youth Cup second-round tie. Another hard-fought game ended in a 1–1 draw after extra-time. Little did the spectators know that they would see history made, club history at the very least and in the dying days of the old stadium. Hartlepool took the first penalty and Higgins, in the Rovers goal, saved. The scoring then went (Hartlepool first) 0–0, 1–0, 2–1, 3–2, 3–3, then both sides scored continuously until the score reached 11–11. Hartlepool's next penalty was saved and Fairhurst scored to make the score 11–12 to the Rovers and they were through, after a total of 28 penalties had been taken, with 17 of them being converted in succession. So far this season Rovers teams had won twice and lost once in penalty shootouts. The next day, the last day for loan moves, the manager brought in another experienced goalkeeper, Neil Sullivan, on loan from Leeds United. On the Rovers' part, Antony Griffith moved on loan to Dave Penney's Darlington and Andy Warrington went to Bury to get some first-team games under his belt. Craig Nelthorpe had already gone to Gateshead earlier in the week and Brian Stock extended his loan for a third month. The last Saturday of the month brought Brighton & Hove Albion to Belle Vue. A scrappy game was won by the Rovers, with a single goal scored after 25 minutes by McCammon heading in at the far post from Forte's cross. On the Tuesday following, another cup tie was played at Belle Vue, a third-round game in the Johnstone's Paint Trophy against Accrington Stanley, the clubs meeting for the first time in 44 years. Mark Wilson was able to take a place on the bench when his international clearance from the US came through that afternoon. The game itself was a battle, which the Rovers won by two clear goals from Heffernan and Thornton in the first half but at the expense of Sean McDaid suffering a medial ligament injury in a tackle that went unpunished by the referee. He would be out of action for a lengthy period. Steve Roberts was also 'hors de combat' after a neurologist recommended two weeks rest for him to recover from the head injuries he had received in recent games. However, defender Theo Streete agreed a third month's stay on loan. On the evening of the last day of the month a 'Farewell to Belle Vue' banquet was held at the Dome, attended by around 600 guests, among whom there were many former players of the club.

The Rovers first team, after hearing on the morning of 2 December that they had drawn Darlington at home in the semi-final of the Northern section of the Johnstone's Paint Trophy, visited Field Mill in the afternoon to play Mansfield Town in the third round of the FA Cup. Ben Smith returned in goal because Leeds United did not want Neil Sullivan Cup tied, although Brian Stock had been allowed to play by Preston. The Rovers struggled to get to grips with the Stags, a team in the lower half of League Two and went a goal down after 22 minutes when Mansfield scored from a penalty. Try as they might, the Rovers could not score until the 91st minute when Stock hit a 15-yarder that zipped past the 'keeper for the equaliser and a replay at Belle Vue. On Tuesday a visit to bottom-placed Brentford for a League game brought three points from a scintillating display by the Rovers, who caned the home team to the tune of four clear goals from Price in the first half, Forte, O'Connor and Heffernan in the second. That same evening, at Belle Vue, the youth team played Derby County in the third round of the FA Youth Cup. A gritty display by the Rovers youngsters saw them come from behind to end the 90 minutes at 2–2. Extra-time, however, proved to be a step too far as Derby ran out winners by 4–2. On the following Saturday the first team went to Northampton Town and came away with a comfortable two-goal win from Heffernan (75) and Guy (86), who both scored seven minutes after going on as substitutes. In midweek Mansfield Town made their last visit to Belle Vue for the FA Cup replay, the last evening match under the Belle Vue floodlights. The heavy pitch, following a lot of rain, took its toll and Heffernan replaced Price just before the half hour. Goals from McCammon after 22 minutes and Heffernan after 50 minutes gave the Rovers a comfortable victory on a pitch that resembled a ploughed field at the end of the game. Further incessant rain over the following days caused the match against Yeovil Town at Belle Vue, scheduled for Saturday 16, to be called off after an early inspection by the referee on the day. The team now had a whole week to rest after their recent exertions playing two games a week. Two days before the Nottingham Forest game Leeds United recalled Neil Sullivan from his loan period.

Saturday 23 December 2006 would see the end of the Belle Vue era after 84 years as the mecca for football in Doncaster. The last

Saturday 29 April 2006: v Oldham Athletic. The directors' box.

The successful Pontins Holidays League Play-off Final winning team.

competitive Doncaster Rovers match at Belle Vue was against top-of-the-table Nottingham Forest. Fans started rolling up early for this historic day and when they were allowed into the ground they were entertained by the singer Redd, followed by Martin Toal, an operatic singer of international reknown, who ended his contribution with a moving rendition of *Abide with Me*. The players of both teams came on to the pitch through a cacophony of noise from 8,923 spectators and smoke as fireworks exploded in the sky.

The Rovers line up for this last match consisted of Ben Smith in goal; Theo Streete, Adam Lockwood, Graeme Lee, Gareth Roberts; James Coppinger, Paul Green, Brian Stock, Jonathan Forte; Mark McCammon and Paul Heffernan. An entertaining first half ended goalless but the second half belonged to the Rovers, with Streete scoring his first-ever League goal after 60 minutes when a shot-cum-cross from the right touchline deceived Paul Smith in the Forest goal, who allowed it to go over him into the net. This proved to be the winning goal, the LAST GOAL to be scored at Belle Vue. Martin Toal entertained at half-time and full-time, rounding the entertainment off with a song, *Goodbye Belle Vue* sung to the tune of *We are sailing* which the crowd joined in with gusto. The day was rounded off with a firework display as tears were shed by old and young alike.

On Thursday afternoon, 28 December, a testimonial event was held for Brian Makepeace, a former player and captain of the Rovers from the 1950s. A team of former Rovers players under the title of Rovers Legends, represented by: Mark Samways, Colin Douglas, Ian Snodin, Jim Dobbin, Mark Rankine, Paul Raven, John Stiles, Daryl Pugh, Billy Russell, John Buckley, Lee Turnbull, Steve Gaughan, Vince Brockie, Lee Warren and Scott Maxfield, alongside guest stars Cyrille Regis and Richard O'Kelly, took on four separate teams of fans over periods of about 25 minutes for each team. The fans had all paid £50 a head to play on the sacred turf and oppose the players they had cheered on over the years. Around 500 spectators turned up to see the event, which was enjoyed by all concerned, raising about £6,000 for Brian. The doors were now locked for the very last time as the club moved lock, stock and barrel to the new stadium in time for the New Year's Day match against Huddersfield Town. Before that, though, there were two away games to play, the first at Valley Parade on Boxing Day. A goal from Heffernan after 13 minutes in a splendid game gave the Rovers three points but four days later their 12-match unbeaten run in all competitions came to an end at Blackpool. All the goals, three to Blackpool and one to the Rovers, came in the last 13 minutes, with Heffernan getting a consolation goal two minutes into added time. So at the end of the year the Rovers stood ninth in the League with 39 points from 25 games, three points behind the sixth-placed club, Swansea City.

New Year's Day 2007 and Huddersfield Town were the first visitors to the Keepmoat Stadium, with 14,470 fans also coming along to christen the new stadium. The Town were soundly beaten by three clear goals from McCammon on eight minutes, the first goal at the stadium, Heffernan two minutes after the break and Forte after 51 minutes. Seven minutes later the game erupted when a terrible challenge by Adnan Ahmed on McCammon led to his expulsion from the game. However, in the ensuing mêlée of players there were other incidents that caused the referee and his linesman to hold a two-minute discussion before despatching Pawel Abbott of Huddersfield to the dressing room. Then, 10 minutes from time, Gareth Roberts of the Rovers was sent off for a two-footed tackle on Hardy. The Keepmoat Stadium had definitely been christened! Two days later Brian Stock, who had returned to Preston after the Forest game, was signed for a fee of £150,000. The following Saturday Bolton Wanderers took to the Keepmoat pitch and outplayed and outclassed the Rovers in the FA Cup third round, played before 14,297 fans. They went in at the break leading by three goals from Davies andranik and Tal and added another from Andranik four minutes into the second half. Bolton did not stop there, they wanted more but at last the Rovers got a grip on the game and stemmed the tide. The next day at the 'Rovers Return' at Belle Vue an auction was held of items ranging from floodlights to turnstiles to corner flags, all mementoes of Belle Vue Stadium, which added £50,000 to the club's coffers. The manager moved on the Monday to bring in a left-back on loan because Sean McDaid was injured and Gareth Roberts was suspended, so Peter Gilbert came in from Sheffield Wednesday and made his debut the following day against Darlington in the Johnstone's Paint Trophy Northern Area semi-final at the Keepmoat. Dave Penney's team were halfway in League Two and gave the Rovers a good game but were eventually defeated by goals from Heffernan after 54 minutes and Price a minute from time. An away game was next at Gillingham, with late goals from Price and Stock taking the points back to Doncaster. In midweek Andy Warrington moved to Bury on a permanent transfer, ending an eight-year association with the Rovers. Another 'keeper, Jan Budtz, played for the reserves after being out for several months with a groin injury. Jonathan Forte's loan spell was at an end but Sheffield United agreed to extend his loan to the end of the season. The next two games were contrasting 'derby' games at home. First came table-toppers Scunthorpe United for their first visit to the Keepmoat and they enjoyed it so much they were two goals up in the first 23 minutes through Keogh and Talbot but the Rovers battled back in the second half, scoring twice in two minutes through Lee and Price just before the hour in front of an attendance of nearly 12,500. The following week Rotherham United, who were next to the bottom in the table, also scored first on their debut at the Keepmoat when Partridge rifled into the bottom corner from 25 yards after 10 minutes but Heffernan levelled in the next minute. In a good, exciting local derby it was the Rovers who extended their lead immediately after the break when Lee headed in following a corner and then Heffernan made it three for the Rovers on 58 minutes. The best goal of the game came after 70 minutes when Woods, for Rotherham, smashed in a shot from out on the right into the far top corner of goal. A crowd of just over 12,000 went home happy after some excellent entertainment. In between these two games Alan Blayney left the club by 'mutual consent' and Jan Budtz, just back to fitness, moved to Wolverhampton Wanderers on an emergency loan. From having four goalkeepers at the beginning of the month the Rovers were down to just one, Ben Smith. The last game of the month was at Gresty Road, in the first leg of the Northern Area Final of the Johnstone's Paint Trophy against Crewe Alexandra. Almost a quarter of the 4,631 fans in the stadium came from Doncaster and they saw their team take the lead through a Heffernan penalty on 28 minutes. Stock increased that lead on 40 minutes and the Rovers went in at the break having controlled the game thus far. In the second half Crewe at last got going and six minutes in pulled a goal back through Moss. Lowe equalised just past the hour in what was now an even contest. Heffernan put the Rovers back in front on 74 minutes but Varney squared things up four minutes from the end of normal time. It was all to play for at the Keepmoat in the second leg. Meanwhile, Bruce Dyer was loaned out to Bradford City and Robert Pacey went to Gateshead on loan to get some first-team football. The Rovers finished January in eighth place with 46 points from 29 games, just one point behind Swansea City in the last Play-off place.

During the week a gas explosion ripped through the Main Stand at Belle Vue causing injury to two men who were up to no good, one of them finishing up in hospital. Sean O'Driscoll was named the League One Manager of the Month for January, thus silencing the critics from his early days at the club. However, the curse of the monthly award struck, because in the opening match of February against Carlisle United at the Keepmoat Stadium Coppinger scored in the third minute to give the Rovers a good start but Carlisle hit back in the second half with two goals to take the points from a pulsating match that entertained the 9,000 crowd. Then, a week later, the Rovers lost, unluckily, to a sixth-minute goal at Tranmere Rovers, a good effort considering that a number of players had flu symptoms a couple of days before the match. A roll-call on the day before Monday's second leg of the Johnstone's Paint Trophy Northern Area Final showed just 11 senior players fully fit to play. A request for a postponement was turned down and the game went ahead. Making up the required 15 players for the game meant some of them were not 100 per cent fit. Twelve and a half thousand fans were in attendance, plus Sky Sports cameras televising the match live. Before the match former goalkeeper Andy Warrington was presented with a special award by Managing Director Stuart Highfield in recognition of his service to the club. The Rovers started well but Crewe scored first, completely against the run of play, on 31 minutes through Varney. This inspired them to add another four minutes later from Lowe and go in at the interval with a two-goal lead, 5–3 on aggregate. The Rovers stormed to the attack in the second half and netted through Heffernan on 63 minutes. With Crewe continually forced to defend and doing it well, a defining moment came 10 minutes from the end when the Rovers were awarded a penalty. Heffernan scored but the referee ordered a retake. 'No problem' said Heffernan and coolly put it into the roof of the net. The Rovers crowd, who had backed them vociferously to this point, upped the decibel level and urged one last effort for a winner before the lottery of penalties came. In the 89th minute it came, courtesy of Price at the second attempt, having been ably set up by Coppinger. Sean O'Driscoll managed to last out to the final whistle before finally succumbing to the flu virus and going home to rest. The training ground at Cantley Park was closed for two days in a bid to get rid of the virus. Gareth Roberts came off against Crewe with a pulled hamstring and with Sean McDaid also injured the manager brought in, on loan, experienced veteran Alan Wright from Sheffield United for the next League match at home to Swansea City. The Rovers trailed 2–1 at half-time in this match, Akinfenwa having opened the scoring in the 19th minute. Price levelled the score just past the half hour but two minutes from the break Swansea were awarded a penalty, which Trundle duly put away. Heffernan equalised for the Rovers early in the second half but nobody could find a winner. On the Monday Paul Heffernan signed an extension to his contract to take it to the summer of 2010. The club also brought in a young defender, Sam Hird from Leeds United, on loan until the end of the season and goalkeeper Neil Sullivan, also from Leeds United, on loan until late April. Sullivan went straight into the team for the League match at Crewe Alexandra the following day. Another terrific game between these two teams, the third in a month, was shaded this time by Crewe, who came out on top by two goals to one, the winning goal arriving in added time at the end after Heffernan had levelled with a penalty just before the hour. The following Saturday Port Vale visited the Keepmoat and went away empty-handed after Price gave the Rovers their first League win of the month with a 49th-minute goal but it was at a price because Heffernan suffered torn ankle ligaments. In midweek Yeovil Town trekked up to Doncaster and went away with a point after a goalless draw before an 8,000 attendance. The Rovers were ninth in the table, two points shy of the Play-offs.

Sean O'Driscoll, Richard O'Kelly, James O'Connor and Brian Stock returned to their old club on Saturday 3 March but it was not a happy return as they suffered defeat by a couple of goals, a minute before and a minute after the break. On the Monday Harry Worley, a young centre-half, was signed on loan from Chelsea to augment the defensive cover for an assault on the Play-off places. However, goalkeeper Ben Smith had a cartilage operation that kept him out for over a month. The following evening the team gained a first-ever win at the City Ground, Nottingham, with a terrific 35-yard strike from Stock to complete their first-ever 'double' over Nottingham Forest. For Mark McCammon it was the end of his season when he dislocated his shoulder in a fall during the first half. The next game was on a Sunday at Oldham Athletic, where the Rovers were severely trounced by four clear goals. The scoreline was not a reflection of the game but of Oldham's ability to take what chances they had. Already short of two forwards in Heffernan and McCammon, Price suffered an ankle injury in the game. On the Friday before the match against Cheltenham Town at home, the Rovers signed Danny Cadamarteri on a month's loan from Leicester City. He took his place alongside Forte but the Rovers lost out to a goal in each half after Cheltenham had done a good job containing the Rovers. The crowd, below 7,000 for the first time at the Keepmoat, booed their players off at half-time and at full-time as the team, with their third defeat in the last four League matches, were fast dropping behind in the promotion chase. The following Wednesday a visit to Saltergate to play relegation-threatened Chesterfield in a match brought forward from 31 March, the Johnstone's Paint Trophy weekend, ended in a 1–1 draw, a result that was not much good to either side. Stock put the Rovers in front with a drive from 25 yards but a hotly disputed penalty to

First game at Keepmoat stadium v Huddersfield – Mark McCammon and James Coppinger celebrate the first ever goal at the stadium.

Chesterfield five minutes before the interval was scored by Hall. The transfer deadline for loans passed with only Jan Budtz's loan being extended at Wolverhampton Wanderers. On the Saturday, however, they lost their fourth home game in the last seven League matches to second-placed Bristol City by a goal scored after 88 minutes by McCombe, which was a big disappointment for the 7,945 spectators. The Rovers' position was 10th, with 55 points from 40 games, one game more than everyone else.

Sunday 1 April 2007 duly arrived and around 20,000 Rovers fans travelled to Cardiff's Millennium Stadium to see their favourites in a national Cup Final for the first time ever. Their opponents were Bristol Rovers from League Two. The Doncaster lads got straight into their stride and took only 55 seconds to register the first goal when Heffernan robbed Phillips, the Bristol 'keeper, of the ball and set up Forte to place into an empty net. On five minutes they went two up when a long clearance from Sullivan was picked up by Heffernan and rifled into the far bottom corner. It took Bristol another quarter of an hour to get into the game but they still went in two goals down at the interval. Bristol were awarded a penalty in their first attack of the second half after 49 minutes, with Walker doing the necessary. On the hour Price suffered a ruptured Achilles tendon injury and Thornton replaced him. Bristol were on top until around 10 minutes from time when at last the Rovers got a grip on the game. Extra-time was even until the 109th minute when the Doncaster captain, Lee, met a corner-kick with a header that bulleted into the roof of the net. Bristol stormed back but to no avail as Lee marshalled his defence and then went on to lift the trophy for Doncaster Rovers. The Rovers team was: Neil Sullivan; James O'Connor, Adam Lockwood, Graeme Lee, Sean McDaid; James Coppinger, Paul Green, Brian Stock (Mark Wilson 101), Jonathan Forte (Lewis Guy 88); Jason Price (Sean Thornton 60), Paul Heffernan. Substitutes not used: Gareth Roberts, Bruce Dyer.

The following Saturday was a return to League business at Brighton & Hove Albion. With another game coming up on Easter Monday the manager rested some players and others were injured, so six changes in all were made. A comfortable win for the Rovers came via goals from Lee after 27 minutes and Cadamarteri two minutes into the second half. Two days later Millwall came, saw and conquered after a good game in which the Rovers had gone in front through Coppinger on 13 minutes. It proved an unlucky number because two second-half goals gave Millwall the points and put them three points in front of the Rovers in the table. The Rovers were now 11th and 11 points adrift of the Play-offs with four games to play. The next Saturday was a visit to Leyton Orient where a 1–1 draw resulted, Lockwood scored in the second half to equalise a first-half strike for the Orient. A home game against already-relegated Brentford a week later brought a comfortable three-goal win through Lockwood (45), Wilson (66) and a penalty from Guy after 74 minutes. Osborne of Brentford was sent off after 61 minutes for kicking out at Forte.

Johnstone's Paint Trophy Final 2007.

On Sunday 22 April the Rovers squad paraded the Johnstone's Paint Trophy through the town on an open-top bus before being received at the Mansion House by Mayor Martin Winter for a civic reception. The last Saturday of April was earmarked for a visit to Yeovil Town, who needed a win to cement their place in the Play-offs. They achieved it but were perhaps a shade fortunate because the Rovers were possibly the better team overall. However, Yeovil got the goal that mattered after 73 minutes and that was all that counted. The Rovers had to bring Jan Budtz back from his loan spell at Wolverhampton Wanderers because Neil Sullivan had come to the end of his loan period and Ben Smith was still recovering from his cartilage operation.

The last League game on Saturday 5 May was against Northampton Town at the Keepmoat Stadium. The referee and one of his assistants for this game were father and son, Clive and Michael Oliver. Considering that both teams were in mid-table, it was a surprisingly combative match watched by 7,500 fans. Injuries had ravaged the Rovers team and out of six recognised strikers only Dyer, after a fitness test, was fit to play. The Rovers took the lead twice but on each occasion were hauled back. Nelthorpe got his first League goal for the club with a terrific shot on 12 minutes but Crowe got an equaliser in added time at the end of the first half. Gareth Roberts put the home club in front after 59 minutes but five minutes later Hughes levelled things for the second time. The end of the season showed the Rovers in 11th place with 63 points from their 46 League games but also with the added bonus of a major trophy in the Boardroom.

While some may say that the successful Cup run in the League Trophy affected the Rovers' chances of promotion, it is more likely that it was the volume of injuries that affected the club most of all. Despite having a big squad plus loan signings, it was still a difficult task to play 60 League and Cup games in the season, covering 40 Saturdays, with the number of players available at any given time because of injuries.

On the evening of Tuesday 8 May a special presentation dinner was held at the first *Star & Green 'Un* Football Awards at Sheffield's Park Hotel. Football VIPs, specially invited guests, players and officials from Sheffield United, Sheffield Wednesday, Barnsley, Doncaster Rovers, Rotherham United and Chesterfield were present. Sean O'Driscoll and John Ryan collected the Team of the Year award, Paul Heffernan won the 'Golden Boot' award for his 21 goals in the season and Graeme Lee won the Doncaster Rovers Player of the Year award voted for by readers of the *Star and Green 'Un*.

In the club's own awards Graeme Lee was voted the Supporters' Club Player of the Season, Paul Heffernan was Players' Player of the Season and Ben Smith was Young Player of the Season. A mini-clearout of players came, with Adam Brown, Liam Green, Rob Pacey, Jan Budtz, Jon-Paul Pittman and Sean Thornton released. Matt Noble was signed from the youth team on a one-year contract, while Craig Nelthorpe and Mark McCammon also accepted one year deals.

2007-08
The Fulfilment of a Dream

The philosophy of manager Sean O'Driscoll was to have more quality in the squad instead of quantity, although as was found in the previous season an excessive amount of injuries needed covering. But the loan rules are more liberal these days and would come into play when required. The club had come a long way since dropping into the Conference nine years previously. The ultimate aim was Championship football and John Ryan expressed the view late in the close season that, with the quality signings made, this was the year it was going to happen.

The first signing at the end of May was James Hayter from the manager's former club Bournemouth, for a new club record fee of £200,000. In July Neil Sullivan and Sam Hird were signed after their contracts at Leeds United expired on 30 June. Martin Woods, a left-sided midfielder, was acquired from Rotherham United, also on a free transfer. Midfielder Richie Wellens moved from Oldham Athletic to the Rovers after his contract with the Latics had expired and centre-half Gordon Greer joined the club from Kilmarnock after impressing in the pre-season friendlies. With Graeme Lee and Steve Roberts injured and out for the early part of the season, a central-defender would be needed.

The first pre-season friendly was against a local team, Retford United, at Retford, where a record crowd saw the Rovers' new players for the first time and the team come away with a 3–1 win. Other games were at Worksop Town (4–1), at York City (4–3) and at home to Wolverhampton Wanderers (1–0), followed by a 1–1 draw at home to Hull City and a defeat at home to a strong Manchester City side under former England Manager Sven Goran Eriksson (1–3). A representative Manchester United XI, with Sir Bobby Charlton kicking-off, officially opened the Keepmoat Stadium and won by two clear goals in front of 13,080 fans. But injury problems still bedevilled the club. Graeme Lee was out with a neck injury, Jason Price with a ruptured Achilles' tendon, Kevin Horlock with a shoulder injury and Brian Stock had had a hernia operation, so none of them would be fit until after the League season had got under way.

Making their League debut for the club against Millwall on Saturday 11 August at the Keepmoat Stadium were Gordon Greer, Richie Wellens, Martin Woods and James Hayter. A goalless draw resulted but unfortunately some of the Millwall fans caused trouble at the North Stand end. The police eventually sorted things out and a number of the troublemakers were later prosecuted. Three days later, the first round of the Carling League Cup at home to Lincoln City from League Two ended with a comprehensive win for the Rovers by four goals to one. Hayter in the first half and Wellens in the second half scored their first goals for the club and Heffernan and McCammon got the others. Sean O'Driscoll welcomed the result but reiterated that the club's main ambition was to win promotion to the Championship. To cover the defensive positions, he went to Manchester City and took 21-year-old Matt Mills on loan. The next two League games were lost by the same score of two goals to one, away at Hartlepool United, where Hayter scored for the Rovers and at home to Bournemouth, the Rovers goal coming from Greer. James Coppinger tore an ankle ligament in the Bournemouth game and

Jason Price at Leeds United.

Mills came on as a substitute for Gareth Roberts on his debut and then made the starting line up in the midweek game at Plymouth Argyle in the Carling League Cup. After the Rovers' display on the night the gulf between the Championship and League One was a chasm as Plymouth proved to be far superior and won comfortably by two goals, although one could argue that the Rovers were poor.

On Saturday, the first day of September, came a long trip to Swansea City, who were in the top half while the Rovers were in the bottom four. Brian Stock came in for his first game of the season and Gordon Greer returned

Jason Price celebrates a goal against Southend in the Play-off semi-final.

in a five-man back line. Swansea took the lead just before half-time but then had Ferrie Bodde sent off just past the hour for a head butt on Stock. The Rovers took full advantage with two well-taken goals from Wellens for their first League victory of the season. This result lifted them up eight places to 13th and set them up for the midweek game at home to Bradford City in the Johnstone's Paint Trophy first round. The Rovers rattled in five goals, with only one against. McCammon with two and Guy scored in the first half, Woods and an own-goal in the second half, with Bradford getting a goal between the Rovers goals in the second half. The Rovers had made six changes in the starting line up from the Swansea game as the manager utilised the resources at his disposal. The next League game was on the Friday evening at Northampton Town because England were on the television the next day playing Israel in a European Championship qualifying game. The Cobblers gained their first win of the season, beating the Rovers by two second-half goals. Man of the Match Mark Bunn, Northampton's goalkeeper, deservedly won the award because of an outstanding display to keep the Rovers out. The following week it was Sunday when Rovers played Crewe Alexandra at the Keepmoat because of the St Leger meeting on the previous day. Their first League win at home was comfortably gained by a goal from Heffernan in the first half and an own goal by Woodards in the second half. The next match was at Southend United, relegated the previous season from the Championship and already battling for the Play-off places. The home team scored first but a two-goal blast from a Gareth Roberts free-kick and Guy put the Rovers in front at the interval. Southend hit back hard in the second half, scoring twice, the second one a penalty, to run out winners by 3–2 but the Rovers were unlucky to lose at the end. A win at home to lowly Cheltenham Town on the last Saturday of September through goals in each half from Guy and Mills left the Rovers in 10th place.

The first game in October was a midweek visit from bottom club Walsall. In a real game of two halves the Rovers could have had a cricket score in the first half but had to settle for two goals from Mills and Guy. In between the Rovers' two goals, Walsall got one from a free-kick completely against the run of play. But the second half was a different story as Walsall came out with all guns blazing. Halfway through the half they scored twice in four minutes, the second one a penalty. The Rovers were also awarded a penalty at the beginning of added time but Coppinger scuffed it wide. A minute later Guy received his marching orders, apparently for something he said to the referee and the Rovers' hopes of salvaging a point were lost. The following Saturday they went to Luton Town and came away with a point from a 1–1 draw, with Hayter scoring halfway into the first half and the home team early in the second. A game in the Johnstone's Paint Trophy against Oldham Athletic had been scheduled for the following Tuesday at the Keepmoat but because Oldham had three players on international duty it was postponed until the 23rd. So the next game played was on Sunday 14 October at home to Huddersfield Town in front of the Sky Sports cameras, with the Rovers winning comfortably by two goals, from Stock in the first half and Wilson in the second. Once again the Rovers showed the armchair audience the quality of their football. The following Wednesday, the 17th, chairman John Ryan issued a statement announcing Terry Bramall and Dick Watson as equal controlling shareholders with him. The City Ground was the venue the following week against third-placed Nottingham Forest. It was a fiercely contested battle, from which the Rovers got a point from a goalless draw. In midweek Oldham Athletic came to the Keepmoat Stadium in the Johnstone's Paint Trophy second round with a strong team but were well beaten by three clear goals from Price, Green and Woods in the second half. The last game of October was on a Sunday and brought League leaders Leyton Orient to the Keepmoat. The first half was a non-event but the second half was a cracker. Jason Price replaced Sean McDaid after the interval and had only been on the pitch seven minutes when he fired the Rovers in front. Two goals then put the Orient in front but Price levelled things up a couple of minutes later. A brilliant overhead kick by Hayter put the Rovers in front again and Wellens made sure of the points two minutes from time. At the end of October the Rovers had moved up the table to 11th place.

The Rovers spent the first two weeks in November on the road, having four away games in succession. The first was at Swindon Town on Saturday 3 November and goals from Stock and Guy, one in each half, brought another three points from a win by the odd goal in three. This was followed three days later by a trip to Gillingham, where a Hayter penalty midway through the second half salvaged a point. The following Saturday it was FA Cup first round day and a short journey over the Pennines to play Oldham Athletic. The Rovers were two goals down after 49 minutes but battled back to parity, with goals from Hayter after 63 and 86 minutes. The last away game in the quartet, on 13 November, was a Northern Area Johnstone's Paint Trophy quarter-final at Grimsby Town. The Rovers made seven changes from the Oldham game but they did not infringe the new rule because their replacements were all first-team men. Grimsby took an early lead but Guy equalised halfway through the first half. Two minutes before the interval a back-header by Mills to Smith was carried by the strong wind over the 'keeper and into the net to give the home team the lead. It took the Rovers until 11 minutes from time to equalise with a penalty from Heffernan. With the scores level after 90 minutes the match moved straight to penalties. Green had the first penalty saved but Wilson, Heffernan, Wellens and Greer scored for the Rovers. Grimsby scored with their first four penalties and with one penalty to take would win the match if it was scored. Smith saved the kick from Bolland but to the Rovers' consternation and Grimsby's delight the referee ordered a retake for encroachment. This time Bolland made no mistake and Grimsby Town progressed to the Northern Area semi-final. Meanwhile, on Wednesday 7 November the youth team began their FA Youth Cup campaign in the first round at home to Rochdale youth. A comfortable win by 3–1 was memorable for a splendid hat-trick by Jordan Lodge. The first team continued their unbeaten run to seven games with a goalless draw at home against Tranmere Rovers, who went down to 10 men after 47 minutes when Carl Tremarco was red-carded for a rash challenge on Wellens. Matt Mills suffered cartilage damage and returned to his parent club, Manchester City, for an operation. The following Tuesday, the 20th, the Youth team went to Port Vale in the second round of the FA Youth Cup but the Vale youngsters proved to be just that bit stronger and edged a result 2–1. Also in midweek, Gareth Roberts had an operation for a double hernia. On the Saturday it was the first team's turn to visit Burslem. This time it was the Rovers who were the stronger, although they had to wait for the second half to prove it. Next-to-the-bottom Vale had a good first half but the second half belonged to the Rovers. The Valiants scored an early goal and held the lead until the 58th minute when Guy netted. Two more goals followed, from Hayter and Wellens, to wrap the game up at 3–1. However, the celebrations were tempered by the fact that Heffernan had received a bad ankle injury. The Rovers exited November by losing at home to Oldham Athletic in the FA Cup first round replay at the Keepmoat Stadium. McCammon put the Rovers in the lead on 26 minutes but on the stroke of half-time Oldham equalised and four minutes into the second half they went in front. Despite persistent pressure on the Oldham defence, especially after Neal Trotman had been sent off on 84 minutes following two bookings, the Latics held out to claim their place in the next round. The Rovers, however, were now out of all the Cups and would have a rest on that Saturday before concentrating on the League. The Rovers were in sixth place in the League table at the end of November after an unbeaten run of seven League games.

Tuesday 4 December brought a home game against Brighton & Hove Albion, which ended in another goalless draw. The two teams were level in every aspect of their record and were only separated for sixth and seventh places by the fact that the Rovers had scored one goal more than Brighton. Both teams cancelled each other out on the pitch as well so that there were few scoring chances. The following Saturday they met Oldham Athletic for the fourth time in six weeks but this time in the League at Boundary Park. A penalty by Hayter in the last minute of normal time rescued a point for the Rovers. The next game was on a Sunday against the Rovers' perennial bogey team, Yeovil Town, at the Keepmoat Stadium. As usual, the Glovers went away with the three points from a 2–1 victory. A rather fortuitous goal for the visitors came in the first half when Way's shot, covered by Sullivan, hit Steve Roberts's foot and cannoned away from the 'keeper and into the net. Twelve minutes from time Stewart made it 2–0 but in the 90th minute of normal time he was sent off after a couple of bookings. In a last desperate effort to get something from the game the Rovers got a consolation goal when Skiverton put into his own goal. Thus the Rovers unbeaten League run ended in the 11th game. The last Saturday before Christmas, the 22nd, took the Rovers to Crewe Alexandra. In a match that was so one-sided it was a wonder the score was not doubled, the Rovers played some scintillating football against a team that gradually buckled under the strain, resulting in Gary Roberts of Crewe being sent off on 77 minutes after two bookings. Price scored twice five minutes either side of the interval but it was not until the last minute of normal time that Green added a third and two minutes into added time Guy put the final touch to the scoreline. Boxing Day, a Wednesday, brought Northampton Town to the Keepmoat and provided the Rovers with three more points following a win by two clear goals, both scored inside the first half hour by McCammon and Lockwood. The last match of December and of the year 2007 came on Saturday the 29th at home to Southend United, who were two places and one point below the Rovers and it resulted in another win by three goals to one. Lockwood injured his shoulder in the first minute and was off the field for several minutes receiving treatment. He returned to the pitch in time to take his place for a corner to the Rovers and was in the right place to head in for the first goal after seven minutes. Southend equalised some 10 minutes later but Green put the Rovers in front on the half hour and a volley from Gareth Roberts following a corner three minutes before half-time gave the Rovers a third goal. This win put the Rovers into fourth place in the table at the end of the year.

The New Year began with a visit to Walsall on New Year's Day. Walsall were just a point behind the Rovers as a result of an unbeaten run of 14 games. In added time at the end of the first half Price put the Rovers in front but the home team responded in the second half and equalised on 73 minutes to get a 1–1 draw. The Rovers had a free weekend after this game because their scheduled opponents, Bristol Rovers, were still involved in the FA Cup. So the next match was a home game against second-placed Carlisle United a week later. Substitute Hayter provided the difference between the teams when he scored the only goal of the game seven minutes from time after a cracking game of football as it should be played. In midweek, Matt Mills returned to the club from Manchester City, on loan to the end of the season. The contest at Leeds United on the next Saturday then took centre stage, a game everyone had been looking forward to, with over 3,000 Rovers fans taking the attendance to 31,402, the second-highest attendance in the Division. The Rovers showed no nervousness about going out in front of the partisan crowd and playing their brand of football. After 21 minutes a free-kick to the Rovers just outside the Leeds penalty area was rifled into the net by Stock for the only goal of a good, hard game. Leeds fought hard to get back on level terms but the Rovers matched them all the way. The following Friday, however, the Rovers came down to earth with a big thump when runaway leaders Swansea City came to the Keepmoat in front of a season's best crowd of 10,358. A 4–0 drubbing certainly avenged their defeat at

Fans celebrate at the end of the game against Southend when going to Wembley.

the Liberty Stadium but their task was made easier when the Rovers went down to 10 men after Steve Roberts was sent off for a professional foul after 58 minutes. However, the Rovers were already two goals down when that happened and two more goals late in the game put a shine on it for the Swans. The Rovers were still in fourth place as they went into the next game at home to Hartlepool United four days later and immediately got back to winning ways. A goal in each half from Wellens and Lockwood gave the Rovers the victory that took them into second place, the automatic promotion position, but 10 points behind the leaders Swansea City. James Hayter had a hernia operation during the week and on the last day of the January transfer window two players were brought to the club to bolster the club's push for promotion. Gareth Taylor was signed from Tranmere Rovers and Stuart Elliott from Hull City joined on loan until the end of the season.

The first three games in February, away at Millwall, at home to Bristol Rovers and away at Bournemouth, were won without conceding a goal, making it four clean sheets in succession. The first match at the New Den saw the Rovers totally dominate the game and blast three goals into the Millwall net courtesy of Price just before half-time, Coppinger with a thunderous drive from 25 yards after 77 minutes and Green in added time at the end. A week later Bristol Rovers visited the Keepmoat Stadium for the first time and went away protesting about the two penalties awarded against them in the second half. Stock scored the first after 64 minutes and substitute Heffernan put the second one away deep into added time at the end. At Bournemouth three days later two goals from Price secured the points. The eagerly awaited return game against Leeds United was due on the 16th in front of a sell-out attendance but a heavy overnight frost on the uncovered pitch left it frozen and unplayable for the 12 noon kick-off time set by the police. Recriminations were soon flying around but the club have no responsibility for the maintenance of the pitch, which rests with the stadium authorities. It was revealed by the club that Lewis Guy was suffering from glandular fever and had been sent away on a fortnight's warm weather break. The last game in February was at fellow promotion candidates fourth-placed Carlisle United. A hard fought, excellent game of football was decided five minutes from half-time when Graham lost his marker and met a cross at the near post to slot in for the only goal. This loss dropped the Rovers down a place to third but only on goal difference to Nottingham Forest. Carlisle were one point behind but the battle for the coveted second place and automatic promotion would rest with these three clubs.

Dick Watson, Paul Mayfield, John Ryan, Len South and Trevor Milton pay tribute to Billy Bremner before the game against Leeds at Elland Road.

Two games a week was the programme for the Rovers in the first two weeks in March: Saturday at Tranmere Rovers, Tuesday at Bristol Rovers, Saturday at home to Port Vale and Tuesday at home to Gillingham. All four games were won but the value of having a big enough squad was proved when injuries once again began to take their toll. For the game at Tranmere James O'Connor was missing having had a hernia operation, Matt Mills taking over at right-back. Tranmere were in the last Play-off place after an unbeaten run of nine games and were four points behind the Rovers, who took the lead in the second minute with a tremendous strike from Coppinger into the top corner from just outside the penalty area. This set up a tremendous battle, with the Rovers under the cosh for periods of the game but a tremendous defensive display kept a clean sheet and the three points to go back to second place. The downside was that Price received an ankle injury. At the Memorial Stadium in Bristol, Paul Heffernan came in for Price and immediately made his mark when Coppinger set him up to volley home from just inside the penalty area after two minutes. This precipitated a battle that got rather scrappy and heated at times in the second half but again the Rovers kept a clean sheet. This time Steve Roberts received a foot injury, which necessitated Green going to right-back for the game against the bottom club, Port Vale and Mark Wilson taking his place in midfield. Two goals from Heffernan and McCammon in the first 18 minutes set the Rovers on their way but a defensive slip let Vale pull one back just past the half hour. That was the end of the scoring, giving the Rovers another three points. An unchanged team achieved the same result against Gillingham, when goals from Coppinger after four minutes and a penalty from Heffernan two minutes into the second half were enough to take the points, despite a fightback by the Gills, who scored on 56 minutes. However, Mark Wilson suffered a groin injury that kept him out for the rest of the season. The Rovers had now narrowed the gap to Swansea City, who seemed to have hit a dip in form, to six points, so visions of becoming Champions were beginning to formulate. Two more away games followed and put such thoughts to bed. A visit to the Withdean Stadium at Brighton produced an even game, with a controversial penalty being the deciding factor. Stock hit the bar early in the game but other chances for both sides were few. On 56 minutes Stock was adjudged to have brought down Forster in the penalty area and was booked for his protests. The decision looked harsh from the sidelines but it stood. Forster took the kick, which Sullivan saved, only for the Brighton player to net from the follow-up. The following Friday, Good Friday, brought a visit to Yeovil Town for an afternoon kick-off. A blustery wind and occasional rain made it hard going but Yeovil were soon on the goal trail when Skiverton headed in after 22 minutes. Nine minutes later they went two goals up when Sullivan came out of his area to field a long ball out of the Yeovil defence. Owusu chased it down as Sullivan controlled the ball, tried to dribble round the Yeovil player then lost the ball to Owusu, who had the simple task of hitting an empty net from 25 yards. While the Rovers were not out of the game, they only found the net on 73 minutes when Heffernan rifled in. In the final 15 minutes the Yeovil defence were under tremendous pressure but held out to take the three points that lifted them further away from the relegation zone. Easter Monday brought Oldham Athletic to the Keepmoat Stadium for the fifth meeting between the two sides in the season. The Rovers, who were third after the Easter Saturday games, three points behind Carlisle United but six in front of Nottingham Forest, badly needed points to keep in touch with

Carlisle but they could only manage one from a 1–1 draw while Carlisle went five points in front. Heffernan put the Rovers in front after 37 minutes but Oldham fought back and levelled seven minutes into the second half. The Rovers could not make the breakthough as the snow came down to provide a winter setting. This was 24 March and it was supposed to be spring! The following Friday evening came a crunch game at home to Nottingham Forest. The Rovers, by playing some good football, had the majority of play but could only muster a single goal from a terrific free-kick after 74 minutes by Gareth Roberts a couple of yards outside the penalty area to the right of goal. His left-footer hit the inside of the near post and bounced in, giving the Rovers the goal that divided the teams at the end of the game. As Carlisle only drew on the following day the Rovers were back to three points adrift of them. Forest had dropped below Southend United into fifth place, nine points behind the Rovers.

Tuesday 1 April and Leeds United were in town before a full house at the Keepmoat Stadium. An unchanged Rovers team turned out against a team struggling to get into the Play-off places. The Rovers once again dominated the game with their football but despite their majority of possession they still lost the game to a goal out of the blue after 20 minutes when Alan Sheehan rifled in a free-kick from 25 yards. The Leeds defence was pounded in the second half but held firm, with 'keeper Casper Ankergren in fine form. Adam Lockwood suffered a badly cut foot injury early in the game and would be out for some time. So for the next match at Huddersfield Town Steve Roberts came in for the injured captain and Brian Stock took over the captain's armband. The Rovers got a bad start when they went behind to a goal from Williams after six minutes and were definitely second best in the first half. The two strikers, Price and Heffernan, were replaced five minutes from half-time by Gareth Taylor and Mark McCammon. The move paid off seven minutes into the second half when Taylor shot in after good work by Green but, with the Rovers threatening to take over the game, they were pulled up short on 59 minutes when Mills was adjudged to have brought down Brandon as he ran clear on goal. Mills was sent off and Holdsworth put the Town back in front from a free-kick just outside the area. With their backs to the wall, the Rovers defence saw off the Town's attempt to make their numerical advantage count and then, six minutes from time, Coppinger fed Green, who went on to hit a terrific drive into the home net and give the Rovers a point. The Rovers were still in third place but were five points behind Carlisle United and only four points in front of Nottingham Forest. Another Friday evening game on the 11th brought Swindon Town to the Keepmoat. The manager had to make a number of changes, one of which brought in Sam Hird for his first League start of the season in place of the suspended Mills. The Rovers did enough to win the game with goals from McDaid five minutes before the break and a penalty converted by Stock halfway through the second half, after McCammon had been brought down and Aljofree sent off for the offence. The following day, Carlisle United lost at Leeds United but Nottingham Forest won at Tranmere Rovers. So Swansea City were top with 86 points from 43 games, Carlisle United second with 79, Rovers third with 76, Forest fourth with 73, Southend United fifth with 72, all from 43 games, Leeds United sixth with 67 from 42 games. Swansea City were sure of promotion to the Championship and Carlisle United and the Rovers were now certain of a Play-off place. On the following Saturday the Rovers visited Leyton Orient, whose hopes of a Play-off place had vanished after five successive losses. The Orient did not let their recent record keep them from giving the Rovers a game and they took the lead after 45 minutes when Wayne Gray headed in a cross. McCammon equalised for the Rovers on the hour and a competitive game ended all square at a goal apiece. Swansea City lost at home to Yeovil Town but were still crowned Champions because Carlisle United had lost at home to Southend United. Nottingham Forest won at home to Luton Town and Leeds United took the points at Millwall, so the League positions remained the same. The penultimate game for the Rovers was at home to Luton Town, who were in bottom place and already relegated after a very troubled season in which they had been deducted 10 points for going into administration. Sam Hird came in for Steve Roberts, injured in the Orient game. Although Luton made a game of it there was never any doubt about the Rovers being in charge and goals by Mills in the first half and McCammon late in the game gave them the three points. The Rovers were now in second place, one point in front of

Carlisle United, who had lost at Millwall and dropped to fourth place on goal difference, while Nottingham Forest took the third position after winning at Hartlepool United. Southend United lost at Tranmere Rovers but stayed in fifth place, with Leeds United in sixth place after winning at Yeovil Town on Friday evening. With one game to go, the top six teams were now known. Swansea City were champions, so it was a question of what order would the other five clubs finish in at 4.45pm on Saturday 3 May. One would be automatically promoted and the other four would contest the Play-offs.

Fans celebrate a win at the Play-off semi-final.

On Sunday 27 April Richie Wellens was named in the PFA League One Team of the Year at their annual dinner. The following evening he collected another piece of silverware when he was voted by the *Star & Green 'Un* readers as Doncaster Rovers Player of the Year. Sean O'Driscoll was voted Manager of the Year and John Ryan was awarded a Special Award to reflect the role he had played in the rise of the Rovers in the past 10 years. The next day Richie Wellens was presented with the Supporters' Club Player of the Season award.

The day of reckoning arrived and the Rovers knew what their task was. They were in second place, one point in front of Nottingham Forest, their only real opposition because of their overwhelming goal difference over Carlisle United. A draw was no good: only a win would see them promoted to the Championship automatically. The Rovers played Cheltenham Town at Cheltenham and Forest played Yeovil Town at home. The Rovers' opponents had their own battle to win, because that was all that would save them from relegation to League Two. News soon came through that the Forest were leading 2–1 after 20 minutes, while the Rovers game was goalless but that changed after 24 minutes when Cheltenham took the lead through Gillespie. News then came through that Forest had scored again and were 3–1 up as the Rovers battled to get on equal terms but they went in at the interval still a goal down. Although they fought hard in the second half, they found goalkeeper Shane Higgs in brilliant form. The Rovers totally dominated the second half and drew level on 76 minutes when Green latched on to a flick on by Price and lashed his shot into the net. Still they poured forward but foundered on the obdurate defending of the home team and the magnificence of their 'keeper. A rare foray by the home team led to a corner, which was played back to Keogh. He crossed into a crowded six-yard box, where Connor got the touch to push it past Sullivan into the net and put Cheltenham in front, completely against the run of play and with just five minutes left to play. But the Cheltenham players and their fans did not care how the goal had come, because if they held on they were saved from relegation. The ground was rocking with the intense excitement of the home crowd, while the Rovers fans, over 1,500 of them, watched in disbelief. The Rovers tried hard to put things right in the remaining time but Higgs foiled them yet again. Time ran out for them and while the home crowd celebrated staying in League One the Rovers learnt that Forest had won and would take the automatic route to promotion, while the Rovers would have to contend with the Play-offs from third place. Carlisle United drew at home to Bournemouth and equalled Rovers' points total but had an inferior goal difference so were fourth. Leeds United beat Gillingham at Elland Road and leapfrogged Southend United, who could only draw at home to Port Vale, into fifth place by virtue of a vastly superior goal difference. These positions meant that the Rovers would play Southend United and Carlisle United would take on Leeds United over two legs.

The body-blow of letting automatic promotion slip through their fingers hit the players so hard that they held a meeting among themselves and resolved to rectify matters. The first match was at Roots Hall on Friday evening, 9 May, in front of the Sky Sports cameras. A good, hard-fought game ensued but it ended as it had begun, goalless. However, a good result was spoiled when Heffernan flicked his head into Mulgrew's face and received his marching orders just two minutes from the end of normal time. This meant he would receive a three-match ban and be out of the second leg and the Final if they got there. So it was all to play for a week later at the Keepmoat Stadium, again shown live on Sky Sports. This time the watching audience would be treated to a right royal goal feast and some good football to go with it. The winners already knew that they would play Leeds United at Wembley after they had beaten Carlisle United on aggregate. The Rovers started well and were awarded a penalty after 10 minutes when Price was brought down. Stock put it away and the Rovers were up and running. Price made it two on 20 minutes and Coppinger added a third in the 39th minute after cutting inside from the right and shooting hard and low into the net from the edge of the penalty area. Four minutes into the second half Coppinger made it 4–0 when he ghosted past three defenders before rifling in from 20 yards. Ten minutes from time Coppinger completed his hat-trick with the best goal of the night. He took a free-kick on the right of goal just outside the angle of the penalty area and played a 1–2 with Green before curling the ball into the far top corner of the net to set the seal on a great win that took the club to Wembley. Bailey scored for Southend two minutes from the end of normal time and although they had shipped five goals against a rampant Rovers team they had played a full part in the game by never giving up, while their travelling supporters in the 13,000 crowd never stopped singing.

Wembley, on Sunday 25 May, brought the first-ever Yorkshire Play-off Final in front of an attendance of 75,132, the biggest live crowd that a Rovers team had ever played in front of. There were also millions watching live on Sky Sports. The stadium was magnificent, the pitch in great condition, it was a fantastic crowd and a fabulous occasion. All the Rovers fans wanted was a win to take their team back to the second tier of English football after a 50-year absence. Five years earlier Leeds United were in the Premier League and UEFA Cup, while Doncaster Rovers were in the Conference, a gap of three Divisions; now they were in the same Division and playing each other at Wembley for the right to play in the second tier next season. John Ryan had a dream 10 years ago when he took over the club he had supported all his life. He wanted to get them back to where he thought they belonged. At Wembley he would see that dream come true.

The Rovers line up for the biggest game in the Club's history and of the players lives was: Neil Sullivan; James O'Connor, Matt Mills, Sam Hird, Gareth Roberts; James Coppinger (Lewis Guy 86), Paul Green, Brian Stock, Richie Wellens (Mark McCammon 72); Jason Price (Adam Lockwood 80), James Hayter. Substitutes not used were Gareth Taylor and Ben Smith.

The Rovers went for it from the word go and could well have been in front in the first 20 minutes as they carved open the Leeds defence time after time with some brilliant football. However, heroics from the Leeds goalkeeper, Casper Ankergren, with four fine saves from Coppinger and Hayter, saved Leeds. Gradually the West Yorkshire team

Wembley celebrations.

Doncaster Rovers, 2007.

came into it and even play followed to the break. The turning point of the game came two minutes into the second half. Stock swung a corner into the penalty area for an unmarked Hayter to bullet a header past an astonished goalkeeper. The Rovers continued to play their brand of football but were gradually pushed on to the defensive as Leeds set out to redress the balance. They spurned the few chances they had but a terrific display from the Rovers defence in the last quarter of the game meant that Hayter's goal would take them all the way to the Championship Division. It was time to celebrate for the Rovers as their fans took over Wembley. The following day, Bank Holiday Monday, the players and officials did an open-top bus tour of the town before receiving a civic reception at the Mansion House.

In May 1998 Doncaster Rovers fans were staring into the abyss as the club slid into terminal decline. The fairy godfather, or rather leprechauns, in the shape of Westferry, bought Richardson out and gave John Ryan the chance to take control of the football side. Ian Snodin was given the task of resurrecting the team on the field of play, winning the Conference League Cup at the end of the first season to announce to the people that they were back in business. Steve Wignall carried that on by winning the Sheffield Senior Cup before off-the-field problems at the club caused his departure. Dave Penney took on the mantle of messiah and took the club back into the Football League and through to the third tier. Sean O'Driscoll has carried the success story further by winning the Football League Trophy, the first major trophy win for the club and taking them to the second tier of English football. Of course, the players were the ones who did it on the field, all 198 of them in the 10 seasons of success. But the man who has driven the quest for success has been John Ryan, who has overseen the renaissance of this famous old club by putting his money where his mouth is. The fans have been behind John Ryan and the various managers and players watching history being made before their very eyes. With a new stadium now a reality, there are those of many years standing who still have to pinch themselves to make sure they are not dreaming. From non-League Conference, the fifth tier, to the second tier of English football in six seasons is an unparalleled record in modern times. Doncaster Rovers have made the record books again, this time for the right reasons.